AVCE
Business Law

E MacIntyre LLB, Cert Ed

Lecturer in Law

New College, Nottingham
and
Nottingham Law School,
Nottingham Trent University

Cartoons by Amy Angus

First Edition

Porchester Publishing
www.porchesterpublishing.com
2001

A CIP catalogue record for this book is available from the British Library

First Edition 2001

ISBN 0–9540047–0–1

Published by

    Porchester Publishing Ltd,
    54 Sandford Road,
    Mapperley,
    Nottingham, NG3 6AJ
    England

    0115 962 6614

Typeset by

    Andre Francis, Nottingham, England

Printed in Great Britain by

    Redwood Books, Trowbridge, Wiltshire

Preface

In 1995 Pitman Publishing published my first book, 'Advanced GNVQ Business and the Law'. The book was highly successful and for some time a second edition had become overdue. However, for several years changes to the GNVQ specifications were proposed, and it was decided that a second edition should wait until the new specifications became finalised. The changes have now been made and have been more radical than many supposed. A new qualification, the Advanced Vocational Certificate in Education, has replaced the Advanced GNVQ. Although the new qualification is definitely recognisable as a development of the Advanced GNVQ, two major changes are apparent as regards the Edexcel Business Law unit. First, the subject has become examinable. Second, the content of the unit is very different. These changes have been so fundamental that a new book, rather than merely a new edition, became appropriate. This is that new book. However, to a large extent the style of the first book has been maintained, and in many ways this is the long proposed second edition of the original book.

This book has one aim - to ensure that students taking the Business Law unit of the Edexcel AVCE qualification are as well prepared for the exam as it is possible to be. I have discussed the new specification at some length with an Edexcel principal examiner for this Unit, and in the light of these discussions have tried to reflect what appears to be needed for exam success. In particular, I have included 'Essential Points' at the end of each chapter. These Essential Points are the matters which the students need to know and understand. It is not necessary that students should know and quote cases or sections of statutes.

It might be thought that if students need only to know the Essential Points then there is no need for the substance of each chapter which sets out cases, statutes and examples. This, I feel, would not be correct. Students need not only to know the Essential Points but also to understand them and to be able to apply them in the externally assessed exam. The main text of this book sets out the law in a logical form, and the many cases and examples illustrate how the law is applied. Students who understand these matters, and who know the Essential Points, should be very well prepared for the exam.

'Advanced GNVQ Business and the Law' made extensive use of various types of questions, which I called Student Activity Questions, Further Activity Questions or Tasks. This book adopts the same approach. However, the Further Activity Questions have to some extent been replaced by End of Chapter Questions. The book is designed for use in the classroom. I have found that most students enjoy working through the text under the guidance of their lecturer. A section of text is read, then it is explained and then the students solve the Student Activity Questions which follow. These questions are designed to check that a basic understanding has been grasped. The End of Chapter Questions, like the Further Activity Questions, are designed to let the students go further and to apply the law. Both the Tasks and the End of Chapter Questions can be used for revision or homework.

This book has a Website, which can be accessed on www.porchesterpublishing.com. This Website features an Introductory chapter, which deals with background matters in some depth. (Sources of law, statutory interpretation, judicial precedent, European Community law, the Human Rights Act 1998, the distinction between civil and criminal law, the distinction between common law and equity and the adversarial nature of an English trial.) There is no absolute necessity for the students to understand this background material, but an understanding of it will definitely enhance an understanding of the matters covered in the book itself. The answers to the Student Activity can also be found on the Website. It is envisaged that the Website will have a further role in that major changes to the law will be posted upon it. On request, suggested answers to the Further Activity Questions and End of Chapter Questions will be sent to lecturers, either by post or by EMail attachment.

I would like to thank Amy Angus for her excellent cartoons and also to thank Hire Association Europe for permission to use their standard form contract.

I sincerely hope that students and lecturers will enjoy using this book. The law is often perceived as a dry and uninteresting subject. Nothing could be further from the truth. The law is interesting and highly relevant to everyday life. At any level, a study of the law can give the scope for creative interpretation and deduction. I very much hope that this book will allow readers to discover for themselves that this is true.

Contents

> Definition of a contract. Offer. Invitation to treat. Acceptance. Postal rule. Certainty of agreement. Termination of offers. Intention to create legal relations. Consideration. Formalities. Minors.

> Express terms. Terms implied by the courts. Terms implied by statute. Sale of Goods Act 1979. Supply of Goods (Implied Terms) Act 1973. Supply of Goods, and Services Act 1982. Conditions, warranties and innominate terms. Exclusion clauses. Unfair Contract Terms Act 1977. Unfair Terms in Consumer Contracts Regulations 1999

> Difference between terms and representations. Actionable misrepresentation. Silence as a misrepresentation. Fraudulent, negligent and wholly innocent misrepresentation. Losing the right to rescind. Mistake. Common mistake. Unilateral mistake. Mistake as to what is being signed. Duress and undue influence. Illegal contracts.

> Discharge by performance. Discharge by agreement. Discharge by frustration. Discharge by acceptance of breach. Remedies for breach of contract. Refusal to perform the contract. Damages. Remoteness of damage. Agreed damages. Specific performance. Injunction. Time limits on remedies.

> Passing of ownership and risk. Insolvency of the buyer or seller. Passing of ownership of specific goods. Risk, mistake and frustration. Passing of ownership of unascertained goods. Passing of specified quantity of identified bulk. Duties of the buyer and seller. Delivery of the goods. Remedies of the buyer and seller. Acceptance by the buyer. Real remedies of the unpaid seller. Reservation of ownership by the seller.

> Sources of law. Statutory interpretation. Judicial precedent. European Community
> law. The Human Rights Act 1998. Civil and criminal law distinguished. Common
> law and equity. The adversarial system of trial.

Table of cases

Table of statutes

1 Making a contract

Definition of a contract

A contract is a legally binding agreement. In order for a contract to be created one of the parties must make an offer to the other party and the other party must accept this offer. Furthermore, the circumstances in which the offer and acceptance were made must indicate that the parties intended to enter into a legal relationship. A final requirement, which distinguishes contracts from gifts, is that the two contracting parties must both give some benefit (known as consideration) to the other. There are then four requirements of a contract. There must be an offer, an acceptance of that offer, an intention to create legal relations and consideration given by both parties. In this chapter we consider these four requirements, which are shown in Figure 1.1.

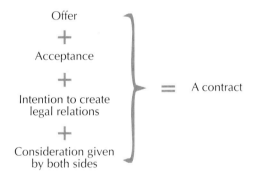

Figure 1.1

Once a contract has been made both sides will be bound to honour its terms or take the legal consequences. A party who does not stick to what was agreed in a contract is said to have breached the contract. Whenever one of the parties breaches a contract legal remedies will be available to the other party.

Offer

A person who makes an offer is known as an offeror. A person to whom an offer is made is known as an offeree. An offer is made when an offeror proposes a set of terms to an offeree, with the intention that if the proposed terms are accepted they will create a binding contract between the two parties. By accepting the terms proposed, the offeree would also agree to become legally bound by them. This acceptance would therefore form a contract. As a contract is a legally binding agreement, neither an offer nor an acceptance should be made without a willingness to accept the legal consequences.

Neither the offer nor the acceptance need to be made in writing, or even in words. For example, when goods are auctioned a contract is formed even though both the offer and the acceptance were made by conduct. Each bidder makes an offer to buy the particular Lot being auctioned by making a gesture which the auctioneer recognises as a bid. The auctioneer accepts the highest bid by banging the gavel on the table. At that moment the contract is created, even though both the offer and acceptance were made without the use of words.

Invitations to treat

It is important to make a distinction between an offer and an invitation to treat. An invitation to treat is not an offer, it is only an invitation to make an offer.

An offer should not be made by a person who is not fully prepared to take the legal consequences of its being accepted. For example, I should not offer to sell you my car for £100 unless I am fully prepared to go through with the deal. Because if you accept my offer, I will either have to go through with the contract which will have been created or take the legal consequences. But a response to an invitation to treat cannot result in a binding contract. It is quite safe for me to ask you how much you would give me for my car. You might name a price (thereby making an offer) but I would have no obligation to agree to the deal.

A court decides whether or not one of the parties has made an offer by looking at what it considers that both of the parties intended. All the circumstances of the case will be considered in reaching this decision.

Advertisements can amount either to offers or to invitations to treat. If an advertisement is an offer then a person who accepts the offer makes a contract with the person who advertised. If an advertisement is only an invitation to treat then it cannot be accepted in such a way that a contract is thereby formed.

In the following two cases the court had to decide whether or not an advertisement was merely an invitation to treat or whether it was in fact an offer.

Partridge v Crittenden [1968]

The defendant had advertised bramblefinches in a magazine at £1.25 each. A customer sent the defendant £1.25 and a bramblefinch was sent to him. The defendant was charged with offering for sale a wild live bird, contrary to the Protection of Birds Act 1954.

Held *The defendant was not guilty because his advertisement was an invitation to treat, not an offer. As the advertisement was not an offer, the defendant had not 'offered for sale' a wild bird. (The defendant had committed a different crime, selling a wild bird. However, he had not been charged with this offence.)*

At first sight it seems as if the defendant in *Partridge v Crittenden* did make an offer. However, the court reasoned that this could not be the case. If the advertisement had been an offer, then the defendant would have had to supply a bird to everyone who wrote in accepting the offer. The defendant had only a limited supply of birds and so could not have intended that any number of customers would be supplied with one. Therefore his advertisement was an invitation to treat not an offer.

Although the majority of advertisements will amount to no more than invitations to treat, some advertisements do amount to offers. The following case shows that if all advertisements were only invitations to treat then this would lead to unfairness.

Carlill v The Carbolic Smoke Ball Co [1893]

The defendants manufactured smoke balls. They claimed that the use of these smoke balls cured many illnesses and made it impossible to catch flu. A large advertising campaign stated that if anyone used a smoke ball correctly but still caught flu they would be paid £100 reward. One advertisement stated that the defendants had deposited £1,000 in a Regent Street bank to show that they meant what they said. The claimant, Mrs Carlill, was persuaded by this advertisement to buy a smoke ball. Despite using the smoke ball properly, she still caught flu. When Mrs Carlill claimed the £100 reward the defendants refused to pay, arguing that their advertisement was not an offer.

Held *The advertisement was an offer. The claimant had accepted this offer by using the smoke ball in the correct way and catching flu. She was therefore entitled to the £100 reward.*

In *Carlill v The Carbolic Smoke Ball Co* the offer was made to the whole world. Offers are more usually made to just one person or to a limited number of people. Only a person to whom an offer was made, an offeree, can accept an offer. For example, an offeror might offer to sell a car very cheaply to one particular person, a friend. Only the person to whom the offer was made, the offeree, could accept the offer.

Offer of a unilateral contract

The vast majority of contracts are bilateral (two-sided) because both parties make a promise to the other. Let us assume, for example, that Martin phones John and asks whether or not he wants to buy a consignment of goods. John accepts the offer. This is a bilateral contract because both of the parties have made a promise to the other. Martin has promised to deliver and give ownership of the goods at the price agreed. John has promised to pay the price and take delivery of the goods. A bilateral contract such as this is comprised of an exchange of promises. When one of the parties makes an offer of a unilateral contract, as happened in *Carlill v The Carbolic Smoke Ball Co*, only one promise is made. The party making the offer promises that if the offeree performs some specified act then the offeror promises to do something in return. The offeree makes no promises. The offeree either performs the specified act, thereby creating a contract, or does not. For example, in *Carlill v The Carbolic Smoke Ball Co* the Smoke Ball Co promised that if Mrs Carlill, or anyone else, properly used a smoke ball but still caught flu, they would be entitled to the £100 reward. Mrs Carlill did not promise to use a smoke ball and catch flu. Furthermore, she could not have accepted the offer by promising to do these things. The only way in which she could accept the offer was by conduct, that is to say by doing the acts requested.

Student Activity Questions 1.1

1) What is the definition of an offer?

2) What is an invitation to treat?

3) How are the offer and acceptance made when goods are auctioned?

4) If the Court of Appeal had decided that the advertisement in *Carlill v The Carbolic Smoke Ball Co* had been only an invitation to treat, would Mrs Carlill have been entitled to the £100 reward?

Further Activity Questions 1.1

1) Which of the following would amount to an offer and which would amount to an invitation to treat? Which of the offers would be of a unilateral contract?

   a) A supermarket advertises in a newspaper that any customer who spends £10 on vegetables in one visit will be entitled to a free bottle of wine.

   b) A supermarket advertises in the local press, 'Crazy prices! All tins of baked beans 5p a tin for the month of December.'

    c)   A farmer says to his neighbour, 'You can have my old combine harvester for £3,000. If you want it, let me know when we see each other at the market tomorrow.'

    d)   An accountant tells his clerk, 'If you qualify as an accountant within 5 years I will give you a £1,000 bonus.'

2)   What undesirable consequences would be likely to follow if all newspaper advertisements were held to be offers for sale?

3)   Why should advertisements which offer rewards be held to be offers? What undesirable consequences would follow if these advertisements were held to be only invitations to treat?

Goods in Shops

Customers who buy goods in shops make contracts to buy those goods. In the following case the court had to analyse exactly when the offer and acceptance were made when goods were purchased in a self-service shop.

Pharmaceutical Society (GB) v Boots [1953]

The Pharmacy and Poisons Act 1933 made it a criminal offence to sell listed drugs without a pharmacist being present. The defendants displayed listed drugs on a supermarket shelf in an area of their supermarket where no pharmacist was present. However, a pharmacist was present near the till. It therefore had to be decided where the drugs were sold, that is to say where the contract to sell the drugs was made. If the contract was made in the area of the supermarket where the drugs were displayed then the defendants would have been guilty of the offence. But if the contract was made at the till then the defendants would not have been guilty. The prosecution argued that the displayed drugs amounted to an offer and that this offer was accepted when customers put the drugs into their baskets.

Held *The defendants were not guilty. The display of goods on supermarket shelves amounts only to an invitation to treat. A customer makes an offer to buy the goods displayed by selecting the goods and taking them to the till. The cashier can accept this offer by ringing up the price. However, the cashier has no obligation to accept the offer and can refuse to sell. So the defendants were not guilty of the offence because any contract to sell the listed drugs was made at the till and would therefore have been made in the presence of a pharmacist.*

A display of goods in a shop window does not amount to an offer to sell the goods displayed. The display is only an invitation to treat.

Fisher v Bell [1961]

The defendant was charged with offering for sale an offensive weapon, contrary to the Restriction of Offensive Weapons Act 1959. He had displayed a flick knife in his shop window and a ticket behind the knife had said, 'Ejector knife - 4 shillings'.

Held *The defendant was not guilty. The display of the knife amounted only to an invitation to treat and not to an offer to sell. The defendant had not therefore offered for sale the offensive weapon.*

Lord Parker:

> '....the display of an article with a price on it in a shop window is merely an invitation to treat. It is in no sense an offer for sale the acceptance of which constitutes a contract. That is clearly the general law of the country.'

Student Activity Questions 1.2

Jenny visits a shop where she sees a television for sale at £44. Jenny thinks that this a great bargain and tells a shop assistant that she will buy the television. The assistant refuses to sell at this price, saying that the price tag was a mistake and should have said that the price was £440. What is the legal position?

Further Activity Questions 1.2

1) A shopkeeper advertises in a local newspaper, giving indications of the prices of the goods in the shop. What undesirable consequences would follow if all such advertisements were regarded as offers to sell?

2) A customer in a supermarket sees a packet of meat upon which the following label has been stuck, 'Special offer. Reduced from £3.20 to £1.60. Must sell by today's sell-by date.' Has the supermarket made an offer or an invitation to treat?

3) Identify the offer and acceptance when goods are sold in a shop which does not operate a self-service system.

4) Could a display of goods in a self-service shop ever amount to an offer to sell?

Acceptance

As we have already seen, a contract comes into existence as soon as an offer is validly accepted. However, the acceptance of an offer is regarded as complete only when it is received by the offeror, as the following case shows.

Entores Ltd v Miles Far East Corporation [1955]

The claimants, who were in London, telexed an offer to buy goods to the defendants, who were in Holland. The defendants telexed acceptance of the offer back to the claimants. A dispute later arose and the defendants were sued on the contract in an English court. The defendants argued that the contract was made in Holland, not England, and that the English courts therefore did not have the jurisdiction to hear the case. This defence was based on the argument that the acceptance was effective as soon as it was typed out in Holland.

Held *The acceptance only became effective once it was received. Therefore the contract was made in England, where the acceptance was received, and so the English courts had jurisdiction to hear the case.*

An acceptance cannot be made by doing and saying nothing, even if the offeror specifies that the acceptance should be made in this way. For example, in *Felthouse v Bindley [1862]* the claimant wanted to buy a horse from his nephew for £30.75. The claimant was fairly sure that his nephew would want to sell at this price. He therefore wrote a letter saying that if he heard no reply he would take it that the horse was sold at this price. The nephew wanted to sell at £30.75 and so he did not reply. When a dispute later arose, the court held that there had been no acceptance and so there was no contract.

Although *Felthouse v Bindley* established that a person cannot accept an offer by doing and saying nothing, some businesses try to sell goods by sending them to people who have not requested them. They then follow this up with a letter demanding the return of the goods or payment for them.

Section 2 of the Unsolicited Goods and Services Acts 1971 makes it a criminal offence to demand payment for unsolicited goods. (Goods which have been sent to a person who is not in business and who has not asked for the goods.) The Act also provides that if unsolicited goods are sent, the recipient may keep them and regard them as an unconditional gift after six months have passed. (If the recipient gives written notice, stating the place from where the goods can be collected, they become an unconditional gift after 30 days have passed.)

As the fact of acceptance means that a contract has been concluded, a court may decide that once a person does an act which makes payment for goods or services inevitable that act must be an acceptance (if no earlier act was acceptance). For example, in *Thornton v Shoe Lane Parking Ltd [1971]* Lord Denning held that once a customer had driven into a multiple storey car park, and had passed the point where it would not be possible to get back out without taking a ticket and paying, the contract had been concluded. Driving past the point of no return was acceptance. The car park, being open and available for use, was the offer.

The Postal Rule

Whenever an acceptance is made by either letter or telegram the possible effect of the postal rule has to be considered. If the rule applies then the acceptance is effective when the letter or telegram is posted, not when it is received. The rule originated in the following case.

Adams v Linsell [1818]

On 2 September 1818 the defendants posted an offer to sell some wool to the claimant. The offer asked for a reply by return of post. The letter containing the offer was misdirected because it was not properly addressed. It therefore arrived on 5 September, whereas if it had not been misdirected it would have arrived on 3 September. The claimant posted a letter of acceptance by return of post. This letter arrived on 9 September. If the first letter had not been misdirected a reply by return of post would have reached the defendants by 7 September. On 7 September the defendants sold the wool to someone else because they had not received a reply to their offer. The claimant sued for breach of contract.

Held *The defendants were in breach of contract. The claimant's acceptance was effective on 5 September, as soon as it was posted.*

The following points should be noticed.

❐ The rule only applies where it could reasonably be expected that the acceptance would be made by post.

❐ The rule can apply even if the letter of acceptance is lost in the post.

❐   The rule will not apply if the offeror makes it plain that the acceptance will be effective only when it is received.

In *Holwell Securities v Hughes [1974]* the defendant offered to sell his house to the claimants and said that he wanted an acceptance 'by notice in writing'. The claimants posted a letter of acceptance which was never delivered. The court held that the postal rule did not apply because the offer, by asking for 'notice in writing', had expressly stated that an acceptance had to reach the offeror. The court said that the postal rule would not apply where all the circumstances of the case indicated that the parties did not intend there to be a binding contract until an acceptance was actually received. Furthermore, the court stated that the rule would never apply where its application would produce *'manifest inconvenience and absurdity.'*

Acceptance of the offer of a unilateral contract

We have seen that, the postal rule apart, an acceptance of a bilateral contract is effective when it is received rather than when it is sent. But acceptance of an offer of a unilateral contract is effective as soon as the act requested is fully performed. This is the case even if the offeror does not yet know that the act has been performed. This can be demonstrated by considering the decision in *Carlill v The Carbolic Smoke Ball Co.* Mrs Carlill could not have accepted the offer by promising that she would buy a smoke ball and then catch flu. She accepted by actually doing these things. Furthermore, her acceptance was complete as soon as she had done the acts requested, even though the company did not yet know that she had done them.

Student Activity Question 1.3

In what two circumstances can an acceptance be effective before it is received by the offeror?

Further Activity Questions 1.3

1)   Marie, in the normal way, fills her car with petrol at a self-service petrol station. She pays for the petrol and drives off. A contract has been concluded. Identify the offer and the acceptance.

2)   Analyse the offer and acceptance position when a customer buys a can of soft drink from a vending machine. Would it make a difference that the machine did or did not have a coin refund?

3)   For what main reasons is it important to know exactly when a contract has been concluded?

Counter Offer

A counter offer rejects an offer and replaces it with a different offer. Having rejected the original offer, an offeree who responded with a counter offer can no longer accept the original offer.

Hyde v Wrench [1840]

The defendant offered to sell his farm to the claimant for £1,000. The claimant offered £950 for the farm. The defendant wrote to the claimant declining the counter offer of £950. The claimant immediately wrote back saying that he accepted the original offer to sell the farm for £1,000. The defendant refused to sell the farm at this price.

Held *There was no contract. The defendant's original offer had been revoked by the claimant's counter offer. The original offer had therefore ceased to exist and could not later be accepted.*

The decision in this case makes good sense. If a business offers an asset for sale at a certain price and receives a counter offer, then the counter offer is a refusal of the offer to sell. The business wishing to sell might therefore reasonably enough sell the asset to someone else. If the original offeree could then accept the original offer and make the business liable for breach of contract this would be very harsh.

Auctions and tenders

As we have seen, a Lot at an auction is sold when the auctioneer's gavel hits the table. Before such an acceptance is made, a bid can be withdrawn. When a person makes a new bid, all previous bids lapse. As soon as the gavel hits the table a contract is formed and the highest bidder has bought the Lot which is up for sale. A bid can be withdrawn before the gavel falls, but not after the gavel has hit the table.

If an auction is advertised as being 'without reserve' this means that the auctioneer makes a definite promise that if the auction of any particular Lot is commenced, that Lot will be sold to the highest genuine bidder. This is the case no matter how low the highest genuine bid might be. Furthermore, the person who put the goods into the auction, the owner of the goods, cannot make a genuine bid. These principles are demonstrated by *Warlow v Harrison [1859]* in which the defendant advertised an auction, stating that a certain horse would be sold 'without reserve'. The claimant made the highest bid for the horse, but the auctioneer did not sell to him. Instead the auctioneer took a higher bid from the horse's owner. The auctioneer was held to be in breach of contract. He had made a unilateral offer to sell to the highest genuine bidder. This offer had been accepted by the claimant when he made the highest genuine bid for the horse.

The fact of advertising that an auction will take place 'without reserve' does not amount to a promise that the auction will actually take place, or that any goods will actually be included in the auction. For example, in *Harris v Nickerson [1873]* an auctioneer placed advertisements in London newspapers, stating that office furniture was to be sold by auction, without reserve, in Bury St. Edmunds. The furniture in question was not included in the auction. A dealer, who had travelled to the auction from London sued the auctioneer. The auctioneer had committed no breach of contract as the advertisement was just an invitation to treat.

It must be remembered that most auctions do allow reserves. At such auctions the auctioneer will take bids in the normal way but refuse to sell if the highest bid does not exceed the reserve.

Tenders

Goods can be either bought or sold by tender. This is perhaps best explained by considering an example. Let us assume that a business will need a very large quantity of a particular type of paper. The business might place an advertisement asking for tenders to supply the paper needed. This advertisement could either be an offer or an invitation to treat, depending upon the words it used. If the advertisement merely asked for tenders to supply the paper, without anywhere including a statement that the lowest tender would definitely be accepted, then the advertisement would be just an invitation to treat. Those who responded by putting in tenders to supply the paper would be making offers. The business which asked for tenders could choose to accept one of these offers but would have no obligation to do so. It might accept the lowest offer, or any other offer, or just not accept any of the offers. However, if the advertisement stated that the tenderer who submitted the lowest price would definitely be awarded the contract to supply the paper, then the advertisement would amount to an offer of a unilateral contract. This offer could be accepted by submitting the lowest price.

A person who submits a standing offer agrees to supply such goods as the invitor might require from time to time. Such a standing offer remains in force for an agreed period or until it is revoked. Every time an order is placed this is an acceptance of the standing offer and so each acceptance leads to a new contract being formed. However, unless some consideration was given in return for its being kept open, a standing offer offer can be revoked at any time. If a standing offer is revoked then orders which have already been made will be contracts and must be honoured. But future orders, even those which are made within the time limit originally stipulated, will not lead to the creation of a contract.

'Referential tenders' refer to other tenders. In *Harvela Investments Ltd v Royal Trust Co of Canada Ltd [1986]*, the House of Lords held that referential tenders can have no effect because to give them effect would destroy the whole idea behind fixed competitive tendering. The facts of the case were that two people had been invited to put in tenders to buy a parcel of shares and it was promised that the highest bid would get the shares. One tender offered to pay $2,175,000. This tender was successful because the other tender, which had agreed to pay $101,000 more than any other tender, was held to be invalid.

Certainty

Even if an offer is accepted, a contract will be created only if the reasonable person could state with certainty exactly what it is that has been agreed.

The courts use the device of the reasonable person because this gives an objective view of what the parties intended. If the court looked at what the parties actually intended these subjective views might well be of little benefit. (One of the parties would claim that the agreement was definite enough to be a contract, the other party would claim that it was not.)

In the following case the House of Lords had to decide whether or not a written agreement was sufficiently certain to amount to a contract.

Scamell v Ouston [1941]

A firm of furnishers agreed to take a van from the defendants. It was agreed that the price should be £288 and that £100 should be allowed against an old van which was traded in. The agreement then said, 'this order is given on the understanding that the balance of the purchase price can be had on hire purchase terms over a period of two years.' The parties began to disagree. Later, the defendants refused to supply the van, arguing that there had never been an agreement which was certain enough to amount to a contract.

Held *There was no contract. The agreement was not certain enough to amount to a contract because the reasonable person would not have known exactly what had been agreed.*

A contract may contain a *price variation clause*, which allows the price to be adjusted to take account of matters such as a rise in the cost of raw materials. Such a term will not make the contract void for uncertainty. The clause does not allow the terms of the contract to be changed later, it allows the performance of the contract which is required to be varied later.

Meaningless terms

It is not unusual for a written business contract to contain one or more meaningless terms. Such terms can be ignored and will not therefore invalidate the contract. For example, in *Nicolene Ltd v Simmonds [1953]* the defendants agreed to sell 3,000 tons of reinforced steel bars to the claimants. It was agreed that 'the usual conditions of acceptance apply'. There were no usual conditions of acceptance and the defendants therefore claimed that there was no enforceable contract. However, the Court of Appeal held that if the words were meaningless they could be ignored, leaving behind an enforceable contract.

Lord Denning argued that if a party to a contract could escape from it on account of having discovered a meaningless term, anyone who did not want to be bound by a contract could be found looking through it for a meaningless term which would provide an escape from liability.

When the parties have previously dealt with each other their previous dealings might well indicate what has been agreed. For example, if in *Nicolene Ltd v Simmonds* the two parties had made similar contracts on several previous occasions it might well have been certain what the usual conditions of acceptance were. The decision in *Scamell v Ouston* might also have been different if there had been previous dealings between the parties. If the furnishers had previously taken vans from the defendants on hire purchase terms, the words 'the balance of the purchase price can be had on hire purchase terms over a period of two years' might have been sufficiently certain to mean that there would have been a binding contract.

Student Activity Questions 1.4

1) Alan writes to Brian offering to sell his car for £5,000. Brian writes back offering £4,800. Alan refuses to accept this. Brian then states that he will pay the £5,000 which was originally asked, but Alan now refuses to sell. Must Alan sell the car to Brian for £5,000?

2) Several old houses are auctioned in London. The auction was advertised as being 'without reserve'. The highest bid for one of the houses is an absurdly low £100. Must the auctioneer accept the bid?

3) a) X Co Ltd placed the following advertisement in a newspaper, 'Tenders invited for the supply of 100 tons of phurnacite coal.' Only one supplier of coal, Brogden, replied to the advertisement. Brogden's tender was rather expensive. Does X Co Ltd have to take the coal from Brogden at the price contained in Brogden's tender?

   b) Would the answer be different if the advertisement had also said that the lowest tender would definitely get the contract?

Further Activity Questions 1.4

1) At a Dutch auction the auctioneer begins by inviting bids at a very high price and then steadily reduces the price until a bid is made. As soon as a bid is made there is no further bidding and the Lot is regarded as sold. Analyse this in terms of offer and acceptance.

2) What undesirable consequences would follow if an advertisement that an auction would be held 'without reserve' amounted to a definite promise that the auction would actually take place and that all Lots advertised would be auctioned and sold to the highest genuine bidder?

... continued

> 3) Anjana agrees to sell her car to Barry. Both Anjana and Barry are keen to make the deal but they cannot agree about the price. Would the agreement be certain enough to amount to a contract if the price was agreed to be:
>
> a) A price which Charlene would later set.
>
> b) The price which a similar car fetches at an auction which is to take place on the following day.
>
> c) A price which the parties would later agree.

Termination of offers

As soon as an offer is accepted a contract is created. However, an offer which has been made might cease to exist in various ways, and once an offer has ceased to exist it can no longer be accepted.

Revocation

If an offer is revoked it is called off by the offeror. Once an offer has been revoked it can no longer be accepted. A revocation is effective when it is received rather than when it is sent. We have already seen that acceptance of an offer is also effective when received. Therefore cases involving revocation often amount to asking which of the parties managed to communicate with the other first. Was the acceptance communicated before the revocation was communicated? If so, there will be a contract. Or was the revocation communicated before the acceptance was communicated? If so, there will be no contract. The following case provides an example of this type of dispute and also demonstrates that revocation can be communicated by an unauthorised third party.

Dickinson v Dodds [1876]

On Wednesday 10 June the defendant wrote a letter to the claimant offering to sell his house. The letter stated that the offer would be kept open until 9 am on Friday 12 June. On Thursday the defendant sold the house to a third party, Allen. Yet another person, Berry, found out about this and told the claimant. At 7 am on Friday 12 June the claimant accepted the defendant's offer. The defendant told the claimant that he was too late to accept. The claimant sued for breach of contract.

Held *There was no contract because the offer to sell had been revoked by Berry when he told the claimant that the house had been sold to Allen. Therefore the offer no longer existed when the claimant attempted to accept it.*

The postal rule, which we examined earlier, has always been confined to acceptance of offers and has never applied to revocations. Revocations are always effective when received, whether sent by letter or not.

An offer of a unilateral contract can be revoked before the offeree has begun to accept it. If the offer was made to the whole world by means of an advertisement it can be revoked in two ways. First, by direct communication with an offeree. Second, by another advertisement likely to reach the same audience as the advertisement which made the original offer. However, it is not possible to revoke the offer of a unilateral contract once the offeree has begun to perform the act which was requested as acceptance.

In *Errington v Errington & Woods [1952]*, for example, a man bought a house for £750, taking out a mortgage of £500. He promised his daughter-in-law that if she paid all of the mortgage instalments she could have the house when the mortgage was paid off. This unilateral offer could not be revoked once the daughter-in-law started to pay the mortgage instalments as they became due.

Refusal

If an offeree refuses an offer then, as far as that offeree is concerned, the offer is terminated and cannot later be accepted. We saw earlier, when we considered *Hyde v Wrench,* that a counter offer is regarded as a refusal of the original offer and therefore ends it. Difficulties may arise in distinguishing a counter offer from a request for more information about the offer. As a request for more information does not imply a rejection of the offer, it does not terminate it. For example, in *Stevenson, Jacques & Co v McLean [1880]* the defendant offered to sell a quantity of iron at £2 a ton. The offeree asked if he could have credit. The defendant did not reply, but instead sold the iron to a third party. Then the offeree accepted the offer to sell at £2 a ton. The defendant was in breach of contract because the offeree had only made a request for more information. Unlike a counter offer, this request did not revoke the original offer.

Lapse of time

If a time limit is put on an offer then the offer will end when the time limit expires. However, even where there is a time limit the offeror can revoke the offer before the expiry time (unless some consideration was given for keeping the offer open). We saw an example of this in *Dickinson v Dodds.* When no time limit is placed upon an offer it will remain open for a reasonable time. The amount of time which is reasonable will depend upon all the circumstances of the case. If, for example, a business made two offers, one to sell a boatload of ripe fruit and the other to sell the company car, the offers would not remain open for the same length of time.

Subject to contract

Houses and land are often said to be sold 'subject to contract'. It has become established that this means that no contract has yet been concluded. This principle is not confined to contracts for the sale of land and houses. If goods are sold 'subject to contract' then a court would be likely to infer that no definite contract had yet been concluded.

Condition not fulfilled

An offeror might expressly or impliedly state that an offer is to remain open only until a certain condition is fulfilled. For example, when an offer to buy goods is made it is implied that the offer will lapse if the goods are damaged before acceptance.

Alternatively, it might be agreed that a contract will only become operative if a condition is fulfilled. If A and B make a contract and agree that C will fix the price this agreement is sufficiently certain to amount to a contract. However, if C refuses to fix a price then the agreement will be avoided.

Battle of the forms

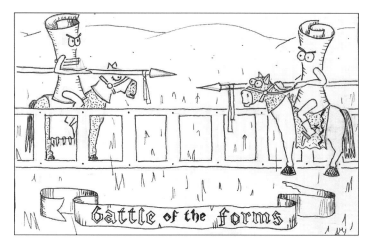

We shall see in Chapter 2 that many businesses use their standard terms and conditions when buying or selling goods. This can cause difficulties when both the buyer and the seller of goods insist that a contract is made upon their own particular standard terms. If the parties refuse to agree whose terms are to apply then there will be no contract. If the parties do agree, so that a contract is formed and the goods are sold and delivered, a court might need to discover which set of terms was agreed to. This would be done by applying the ordinary principles of offer and acceptance, as the following case demonstrates.

Butler Machine Tool Co Ltd v Ex-Cell-O Corporation Ltd [1979]

On 23 May the claimants offered to sell a machine to the defendants. This offer was made on the claimants' standard terms and conditions, which said that they were to prevail over any terms and conditions contained in the buyer's order. On 27 May the defendants ordered a machine. This order said that it was made on the defendants' terms and conditions. The claimants' terms and conditions contained a price variation clause whereas the defendants' terms and conditions did not. The defendants' terms and conditions contained a tear-off slip at the bottom of the order. This said, 'We accept your order on the Terms and Conditions stated thereon.' On 5 June the claimants signed this slip and returned it to the defendants. They also added that the order 'is being entered in accordance with our revised quotation of 23 May'. After the machine had been delivered the claimants argued that their terms and conditions prevailed and that they were entitled to an additional £2,892 under their price variation clause.

Held *The claimants were not entitled to the extra money. The price variation clause did not apply as the contract was made on the defendants' terms and conditions. On 23 May the claimants made an offer. On 27 May the defendants made a counter offer. On 5 June the claimants accepted this counter offer when they signed the acknowledgement slip and returned it to the defendants.*

Student Activity Questions 1.5

1) Jim offers to sell 100 cases of wine to George and gives George one week to make his mind up. Within the week, George receives a phone call from Jim saying that the offer is called off. George says that the offer cannot be called off before the time limit is up, and that he is accepting the offer. Is there a contract?

2) Alan has agreed to sell his house to Jim, 'subject to contract'. Can Alan change his mind and sell to someone else?

3) In *Carlill v The Carbolic Smoke Ball Co* could the company have revoked its offer once Mrs Carlill had bought and used a smoke ball but before she had caught flu?

Intention to create legal relations

The acceptance of an offer will only create a contract if the offeror and offeree appeared to intend to create a legally binding agreement. It is therefore said that it is a requirement of a contract that there must be an intention to create legal relations. This requirement can be demonstrated by considering an example. Let us assume that one motor dealer says to another, 'I've got to sell that Ford Ka you were interested in. If you want it, you can have it for £5,500,' and that the other motor dealer replies, 'Thanks a lot. I'll definitely take it.' If this conversation took place in a business context, for example if the dealers were speaking on the phone during office hours, then there would be a contract. All of the circumstances would indicate that by making the offer and the acceptance the parties did intend to enter into a legally binding agreement. But if the offer and acceptance were made jokingly, for example in a pub as part of a long-standing joke between the parties, then there would be no contract. The circumstances would indicate that the parties did not intend to enter into a legal relationship.

In deciding whether or not there was an intention to create legal relations the court takes an objective view of the parties' intentions. The court does not ask what the parties actually intended, but looks at what they appeared to the reasonable person to intend.

Agreements made in a business or commercial context

If an agreement is made in a business or a commercial context there is a presumption that the parties did intend to make a contract. As this is only a presumption, it is not a cast-iron rule but only a starting point. It will therefore be up to the party who is claiming that there was no intention to create legal relations to introduce evidence to rebut the presumption (to show that it was not correct). It might be possible to do this, but if the presumption is not rebutted then there will be a contract.

In *Esso Petroleum Ltd v Commissioners of Customs and Excise [1976],* Esso advertised that they would give a World Cup coin to any motorist who bought at least four gallons of petrol at an Esso garage. (The coins showed the images of one of the England players taking part in the 1970 World Cup.) For tax reasons it became necessary to know whether or not the coins were supplied under a contract. The House of Lords held that there was an intention to create legal relations and so there was a contract to supply the coins.

In *Esso Petroleum Ltd v Commissioners of Customs and Excise,* the advertisement made a definite promise which motorists were entitled to believe would be kept. Many claims made in advertisements, such as that a particular type of beer refreshes the parts that other beers cannot reach, are regarded as mere 'sales puffs'. These sales puffs do not make any definite binding promise and are not intended to be taken seriously. They are either obviously untrue or incapable of being proved true or false. So even though sales puffs are made in a commercial context, the reasonable person would not think that they were intended to be legally binding.

It is quite possible to make an agreement, even a business agreement, on the basis that it will have no legal effect at all. But if a contract is made, it is not possible for a term of the contract to prevent the parties from suing upon the contract. (Arbitration, which is considered in Chapter 9 is the one exception to this rule.)

Agreements made in a social or domestic context

Social agreements are made between friends. Domestic agreements are made between the members of a family. When either a social or a domestic agreement is made the courts begin with the presumption that the parties do not intend to make a contract. A party who claims that such an agreement is a contract will need to introduce evidence to show that this is what both parties appeared to intend.

Student Activity Questions 1.6

In *Carlill v The Carbolic Smoke Ball Co*, which is set out on page 3, the defendants argued that their advertisement was not intended to create legal relations. The Court of Appeal disagreed. Why do you think that the court decided that there was an intention to create legal relations?

Consideration

A contract is a bargain under which both parties must give some benefit, known as consideration, to the other. The consideration of one party is given in return for the consideration of the other. For example, let us assume that I visit a garage and agree to buy a new car for £9,999. A contract has been made. My consideration is the promise to pay the £9,999 to the garage. The garage's consideration is its promise to pass ownership of the car to me. In bilateral contracts, such as the one used in this example, the consideration of both parties consists of a promise to do something. The one promise is given in return for the other. In unilateral contracts the consideration of only one of the parties consists of a promise to do something. The consideration of the other party consists of actually performing the act requested by the promisor. For example, if I offered a £100 reward to anyone who found my lost dog, and you found the dog, a unilateral contract would have been created. My consideration would have been the promise to pay the reward. Your consideration would have been the act of finding the dog.

If only one of the parties gives some consideration then a contract will not be created. Instead, any agreement will be a gift. So if a garage offered to give me a car for nothing, and I accepted this offer, there would be no contract. The garage would have provided some consideration to me, by promising to give me the car. But I would have provided no consideration to the garage. Therefore there would be no contract.

Later in this chapter we shall see that the promise of a gift is not enforceable unless the promise was made by a deed. When an agreement is made by a deed it is enforceable as a specialty contract even if no consideration was received by one of the parties.

Consideration can be defined as a benefit given by one party or a loss suffered by the other. Usually consideration is both a benefit to one party and a loss to the other. For example, if I buy a car from a garage, the garage's promise to give me ownership of the car is a benefit to me and a loss to the garage. Conversely, my promise to pay the money is a benefit to the garage and a loss to me.

Past consideration

It is not possible to give as consideration a promise to do some act which has already been done. Past consideration is no consideration. This seems sensible enough, because to promise to do something which has already been done is to promise nothing at all.

For example, in *Re McArdle [1951]* the claimant lived in a house which she did not own, and spent a considerable amount of money on having the house repaired. After the claimant had done this, the owners of the house signed an agreement to pay the claimant £488 in consideration of her having had the repairs done. The owners did not have to pay. When the promise to pay was made the claimant had already had the repairs done.

Despite the rule that past consideration is no consideration, a past act can be good consideration if two conditions are satisfied. First, the other party must have requested that the act be performed. Second, both parties must all the time have contemplated that payment would be made. The following case provides an example.

Lampleigh v Brathwaite [1615]

The defendant had killed another man and needed to get a pardon from the King. He asked the claimant to get him a pardon. The claimant managed, at considerable personal expense, to obtain the necessary pardon. Upon hearing that the pardon had been granted, the defendant agreed to pay the claimant £100 for what he had done. Later the defendant grew less grateful and refused to pay. The claimant sued for breach of contract.

Held *The defendant had to pay the £100. Both of the conditions were satisfied. First, the defendant had asked the claimant to get the pardon. Second, both parties had contemplated that the claimant would be paid for his services.*

Comment *This case demonstrates the principle that a past act can amount to good consideration if the two conditions are satisfied. The amount of money payable would now be governed by section 15(1) of the Supply of Goods and Services Act 1982. Section 15(1) implies a term that where the price of a service supplied under a contract is not fixed by the parties it is implied that a reasonable price will be paid.*

Sufficiency and adequacy

A well-known principle of the law of contract holds that consideration must be sufficient but does not need to be adequate. At first sight this can seem puzzling, as in everyday language the words 'sufficient' and 'adequate' have a very similar meaning. However, in the context of the law of contract the two words have quite different meanings.

By saying that consideration must be sufficient it is meant that consideration must be of some recognisable value, however small.

By saying that consideration does not need to be adequate it is meant that consideration does not have to be of the same value as the other party's consideration.

An example demonstrates what is meant. If I agree to buy a new television from a shop for its ordinary selling price of £299.99 then my consideration, like that of the shop, is sufficient and adequate. My consideration is sufficient because it is has some recognisable value. It is adequate because my promise to pay the money is worth much the same as the shop's promise to give me ownership of the television. If the shop and I had agreed that I could have the television for £1, then my consideration would have been sufficient but would not have been adequate. That is to say, my promise to pay £1 would have been worth something, but would not have been worth as much as I was getting in return. However, a contract would still have been formed, because consideration does not need to be adequate. If the shop had agreed to give me the television for nothing then no contract would have been formed. I would not have given any consideration to the shop in return for the promise to give me ownership of the television.

The performance of a trivial act can amount to good consideration as long as it confers an economic benefit on the other party. For example, in *Chappell & Co v Nestle Ltd [1959]* the defendants advertised that they would 'give away' records to members of the public who sent in 7.5p and three chocolate bar wrappers. For copyright reasons i became necessary to know whether or not the sending in of the wrappers was part of the customers' consideration. The House of Lords held that it was. Customers who sent in 7.5p without the wrappers would not have received a record. The principle in this case is important. As consideration does not need to be adequate, a trivial act could be given as consideration in any contract as long as it conferred an economic benefit on the other party.

Privity of contract

The doctrine of privity of contract holds that only a person who made a contract (and therefore gave some consideration) can sue on the contract. The doctrine has been modified recently by the Contracts (Rights of Third Parties) Act 1999. However, it is still of considerable importance and is considered in more detail in Chapter 6.

Student Activity Questions 1.7

Consideration must be sufficient but need not be adequate. Analyse the consideration of the parties in the following examples, and decide whether the agreements could amount to contracts.

a) An accountant promised a bonus to his clerk because last summer the clerk passed his exams. The clerk accepts.

b) A customer, having queued up all night to be the first person into the New Year sale, buys a new three piece suite for £1.

c) A soap manufacturer offers to give a free box of soap powder to customers who send in proof of having purchased two similar boxes. A customer sends the proof.

d) An employer promises a £500 bonus to a salesman if the salesman increases his monthly sales by 15%. The salesman does increase his monthly sales by 15%.

Further Activity Questions 1.7

1) In *Midland Bank Trust Co Ltd v Green [1981]* a farmer sold his farm for £500 even though the farm was valued at over £40,000. Do you think that this was a good contract?

2) A householder rings Jim, an emergency plumber, and asks him to come around immediately to repair a burst pipe. Jim completes the job before making any mention of the price. Has a valid contract been formed? If so, how much money must the householder pay for the work?

Performing an existing duty

Sometimes one of the parties to a contract claims to have given as consideration a promise to perform an existing duty. Whether or not such a promise amounts to good consideration depends upon how the duty arose in the first place. Three different situations need to be considered. First, it is not good consideration to promise to perform a duty which arose under the general law of the land. For example, it is not good consideration to give a promise to stop committing thefts. Second, it can be good consideration, for two separate contracts, to give a promise to do the same thing to two different people. For example, a person who is sponsored to run a marathon gives the same consideration, running the marathon, to all the sponsors. Third, it cannot be good consideration, for two separate contracts, to give the same promise to the same person twice (unless the second giving of the promise can be seen as an additional benefit to the person to whom it was given).

Settling out of court

A dispute is settled out of court when a person agrees not to pursue a legal action in return for the payment of a sum of money. By way of example, let us assume that X has been injured in an accident and has a claim against Y. It is possible that if X and Y cannot agree on the correct amount of compensation the dispute will go to court. It is much more likely that X will take an amount of money offered by Y, and in return will promise never to bring any legal claim against Y in respect of the accident. If such an agreement was made, the dispute would have been settled out of court. (X and Y would generally make such an agreement through their solicitors.) Once made, such an agreement would be binding upon both of the parties because it is a contract. The consideration of Y would consist of paying the sum of money agreed. The consideration of X would consist of promising not to sue. Most legal disputes are settled out of court. It is obviously good public policy that once a dispute has been finally settled it cannot be reopened.

Part payment of a debt

If one person owes a sum of money to another, the debt can be extinguished in two ways. First, obviously enough, the debt is extinguished if the debtor pays the sum owing in full. Second, the debt is extinguished if the debtor and creditor agree that the creditor will take anything other than money instead of the amount owing. For example, if X owes Y £10,000 the debt can be extinguished either by X paying the full £10,000, or by X and Y agreeing that Y should take X's car in full settlement of the debt. If X and Y do agree that Y should take the car in full settlement of the debt, the court would not be concerned with how much the car was actually worth. As we have seen, the courts are not concerned with the adequacy of consideration. So no matter what X's car might be worth, the full debt would be extinguished.

Difficulties arise where the parties agree that the creditor should take a sum of money which is less than the amount owing, in full settlement of the debt. Let us assume, for example, that X owes Y £10,000 and that Y agrees that if X pays £9,000 the debt will be extinguished and Y will never ask for the rest of the money. *Pinnel's Case [1602]* held that a lesser sum of money cannot be consideration for a greater sum owed. Y would therefore be able to sue X for the balance of £1,000, despite the promise not do this. The promise which Y gave does not create a contract because no consideration was received in return for it. The promise made by X, to pay £9,000 in full settlement of the debt, could not be consideration to extinguish the whole debt of £10,000 because a lesser sum cannot be consideration for a greater sum owed. The decision in *Pinnel's Case* was directly approved by the House of Lords in *Foakes v Beer [1884]*.

Despite the decision in *Foakes v Beer*, the rule that a lesser sum of money cannot be consideration for a greater sum owed has always been subject to some exceptions. First, if the creditor agrees to take anything else instead of, or as well as, a lesser sum of money then the debt is extinguished. Second, if the creditor asks for a lesser sum to be paid before the debt is actually due then the debtor's paying the lesser sum early can amount to good consideration. Third, if the creditor requests that a lesser sum be paid in a different place, perhaps a different country, then the debtor's agreeing to this could amount to good consideration. Fourth, if there is a dispute as to the amount owed and the parties settle out of court the debt is extinguished. A fifth possible exception, known as promissory estoppel, is more dubious.

The theory of promissory estoppel holds that a lesser sum of money can be consideration for a greater sum owed if the three following conditions are satisfied. First, the claimant must have intended to enter into legal relations, by promising not to insist on his strict legal rights. Second, the claimant must have known that the defendant would act upon this promise. Third, the defendant must actually have acted upon the promise. As the theory of promissory estoppel has not been properly tested in the courts, there is some doubt as to whether or not it is correct.

Student Activity Questions 1.8

Which of the following promises, made by a partner in a firm of builders, could amount to good consideration?

a) A promise to sell the firm's van (worth about £6,000) for £150.

b) A promise not to sue for breach of contract, in return for a payment of £500.

c) A promise to pay all the firm's employees £100 each if they agree to work next Saturday.

Formalities

In general, contracts can be created without the need for any special formalities. The types of contracts which can be made only if certain formalities are observed are as follows.

Contracts which must be made by a deed

A conveyance of a legal estate in land must be made by a deed. Also, a lease of land of over 3 years duration must be made by a deed or no legal estate will be created.

Earlier in this chapter we saw that gifts are not contracts and that the promise of a gift is not enforceable as a contract. However, if a gift is made by a deed it is enforceable as a contract, the making of the deed providing the required consideration.

Deeds must be made in writing and must be signed by the maker of the deed in the presence of a witness. The witness must sign the deed to indicate having witnessed the signature of the maker of the deed. The deed must also indicate that it is intended to be a deed. This can be done if the deed states that it is signed as a deed by the maker in the presence of the witness. For example, 'this document is signed as a deed by Jane Smith in the presence of Mary McGuire.'

In Chapter 4 we shall see that the Limitation Act 1980 provides that the right to sue on a simple contract is lost after 6 years have passed from the time when the right to sue arose. When a contract is made by a deed this time limit is increased to 12 years after the right to sue arose.

Contracts which must be in writing

Contracts to sell or dispose of an interest in land must be made in writing. The written contract must incorporate all the terms of the contract in one document, or in both contracts where contracts are exchanged, and must be signed by both of the parties. If these formalities are not complied with the contract will be void and therefore of no effect. There is however one exception. A lease of land for a period of 3 years or less will be valid if made orally, as long as the lease takes effect immediately.

Regulated consumer credit agreements cannot be enforced unless they were made in writing and unless the other requirements of the Consumer Credit Act 1974 have been complied with. An agreement is a regulated consumer credit agreement if an individual (who can be in business, but cannot be a company) is provided with credit of £30,000 or less.

Contracts which must be evidenced in writing

Contracts of guarantee must be evidenced in writing, and signed by the person giving the guarantee, or they will be unenforceable. When a contract of guarantee is made one person agrees to undertake secondary liability to settle the debts or liabilities of another person. Although the contract under which the guarantee is given needs to be evidenced in writing, the contract which created the debt which is being guaranteed does not. An example might make this more clear.

Let us assume that Firm X agrees to buy a new van from a garage for £10,000 and that Y guarantees to pay the price if Firm X should fail to do so. The contract under which Firm X buys the van does not need to be in writing or evidenced in writing. However, the contract under which Y guarantees to pay the price if Firm X fails to do so does need to be evidenced in writing.

A contract which is evidenced in writing does not need to be a written contract as such. However, there must be some written evidence that the contract has been made. This written evidence, which might for example be in a letter or a note, must be signed by the person giving the guarantee and must contain all the material terms of the contract of guarantee.

Minors

A person who is capable of making contracts is said to have capacity to make contracts. Adults have full contractual capacity, but special rules apply to minors (persons who are under the age of 18). Contracts made by minors might be either valid, voidable or void, depending upon the type of contract made.

Valid contracts

Section 3 of the Sale of Goods Act 1979 provides that minors must pay a reasonable price for necessary goods sold and delivered to them. They must also pay a reasonable price for necessary services supplied. Therefore contracts to supply minors with either necessary goods or necessary services are valid contracts. It is worth noticing that the amount which minors must pay is a reasonable price, which might not always be the same as the price agreed in the contract.

A minor can also validly make a contract of employment, as long as the contract is overall beneficial to the minor.

Voidable contacts

Contracts which impose a continuing liability on a minor are voidable by the minor. This means that the contracts are valid, except that the minor has the option to avoid the contract. (The way in which a voidable contract can be avoided is considered in Chapter 3.) A minor who is to avoid these types of voidable contracts must do so either before reaching the age of 18 or within a reasonable time of having reached the age of 18. The main types of contracts voidable by a minor are contracts of partnership, contracts to buy shares and contracts to take a lease of property.

Void contracts

Minors are not bound by contracts to buy unnecessary goods or services. A minor who makes such a contract may be entitled to regain any money paid under the contract, but only if the minor has not received any benefit under the contract. Nor are minors bound by contracts to borrow money. For this reason it would be most unusual for a bank or other commercial lender to lend money to a minor unless repayment of the loan was guaranteed by an adult. Agreements by the minor to repay the loan will be of no effect if they were made before the minor had reached the age of 18. Agreements to repay which were made after the minor had reached the age of 18 will compel the minor to repay the loan.

Student Activity Questions 1.9

1) What formalities, if any, would be needed as regards the following contracts?

    a) A contract to buy a car for £2,000.

    b) A contract under which X agrees to pay a debt owed by Y to Z, if Y should fail to pay.

    c) A contract to convey a legal estate in land.

2) A minor makes the following contracts. Will they be valid, voidable or void?

    a) A contract to buy a personal stereo.

    b) A contract to buy a much needed pair of shoes.

    c) A contract to take a lease of a house.

    d) A contract of employment.

    e) A contract of partnership.

Essential points

Offer

- A contract is a legally binding agreement.

- A contract is formed when an offer is accepted.

- An offer is made when one person proposes a set of terms to another, with the intention that both will be bound if the offer is accepted.

- An invitation to treat is not an offer, but an invitation to negotiate or an invitation to make an offer.

- Generally, there is no requirement that contracts should be made in writing. Most contracts are not.

Acceptance

- As soon as an acceptance of an offer is received, a contract is created.

- It is not possible to accept an offer by doing nothing and saying nothing.

- When the postal rule applies, an acceptance sent by letter or telegram is effective when it is posted.

- The postal rule will only apply where an acceptance by letter or telegram was requested or would reasonably have been expected.

- An offer of a unilateral contract can be accepted only by performing the act requested.

- A counter offer is not an acceptance and revokes the original offer.

- A request for more information about an offer does not revoke the offer.

Certainty

- A contract will be created only if the reasonable person could state with certainty exactly what it is that has been agreed.

- A meaningless term in a contract can be ignored.

Termination of offers

- An offer which has been revoked cannot be accepted.

- Revocation of an offer is effective when it is received. (The postal rule never applies to revocations.)

- A person who refuses an offer cannot later accept it. (A counter offer is regarded as a refusal.)

- If an offer is stated as being open for a certain length of time it will be open for that time, unless it is revoked.

- If no time limit is put on an offer it will remain open for a reasonable time.

- An agreement made 'subject to contract' will not amount to a contract.

Intention to create legal relations

- A contract will only be created if the parties appeared to intend to create a legal relationship.

- Where an agreement is made in a business or a commercial context it is presumed that the parties did intend to create a contract. (However, the circumstances might show that they did not intend this.)

Consideration

- A contract will be created only if the parties give some consideration to each other.

- Consideration consists of a right given to one party, or a loss or detriment suffered by another.

- A contract is a bargain. The consideration of one party is given in exchange for the consideration of the other.

- A past act cannot be given as consideration. (Unless the other party requested that the act be performed and both parties all along contemplated that payment would be made for it.)

- Consideration must be of some value. However, one party's consideration does not need to have the same value as the consideration of the other party which is taken in return.

- It seems likely that a lesser sum of money cannot be given as consideration for a greater sum owed, even if both parties agree that it should be.

Formalities

- Most contracts do not need to be made in writing.

- A very few types of contracts do require formalities. Depending upon the type of contract they might need to be made by a deed, made in writing or be evidenced in writing.

Minors

- Minors (persons under 18) are bound by contracts to buy necessary goods or services.

- Minors must pay a reasonable price for necessary goods or services which they have contracted to buy.

- If minors make contracts to buy goods or services which were not necessary, the contract will be void.

- Loans made to minors cannot be enforced against the minor (unless the minor agrees to repay after he or she has reached the age of 18).

End of chapter questions

Question 1

On 10 July Ace Ltd posted an offer to sell a consignment of 1,000 widgets to Brian, a retailer. The offer said that the price was £10,000 and that the offer would remain open until 31 July. On 12 July Brian telephoned Ace Ltd and asked whether he would be allowed 3 months credit. Ace Ltd's manager replied that payment would have to made in cash, upon delivery. On 29 July Ace Ltd sold the consignment of widgets to a third party, Charles. On 30 July Brian posted a letter accepting Ace Ltd's offer. This letter arrived on 1 August. Upon opening the letter, Ace Ltd's manager telephoned Brain and told him that the consignment of widgets had been sold and that further similar widgets were not available. Advise the parties as to whether or not a contract has been created.

Question 2

Acme Supastore advertised its 'price promise' heavily in the Nottown Evening News. This promise stated that Acme was the cheapest retailer in the city of Nottown and that it would guarantee that this was true. The advertisement stated, 'We are so confident that we are the cheapest in the area that we guarantee that you cannot buy a television anywhere in Nottown cheaper than from us. We also guarantee that if you buy any television from us and give us notice in writing that you have could have bought it cheaper at any other retailer within five miles of our Supastore on the same day we will refund the whole of the purchase price. Offer to remain open for the month of December. Any claim to be received in writing within 5 days of purchase.' Belinda saw the advertisement and was persuaded by it to buy a television from Acme Supastore for £299. The contract was made on Monday 3 December. On Saturday 8 December Belinda found that a neighbouring shop was selling an identical model of television for £289 and had been selling at this price for the past six months. Belinda immediately telephoned Acme Supastore to say that she was claiming her money back. She also posted a letter claiming her money back. The letter arrived on Monday 10 December. Acme Supastore are refusing to refund any of the purchase price. Advise Belinda as to whether or not any contract has been made.

Question 3

A large department store advertised its January sale on a local radio station and in a local newspaper. The advertisement said that the first customer to enter the store when it opened on 2 January would be able to buy a new video recorder for just £1. The advertisement showed the model of video recorder which could be bought. Joanne decides to try to be the first in the department store so that she can buy the video. She camps outside the shop at midday on 1 January, relieved to see that nobody else is yet queuing. At 7 am on 2 January the manager of the department store tells Joanne that the offer has been called off. Joanne refuses to accept this. At 8 am the manager shows Joanne an advertisement in the morning edition of the local newspaper. This advertisement says that the offer has been called off. Again Joanne refuses to leave. When the department store opens, at 9 am, Joanne enters the shop and tells the manager that she is the first customer and that she is buying the video recorder for £1. The manager refuses to accept the money and says that the video recorder is only available at its usual price of £299.99. Advise Joanne as to whether or not a contract has been created.

Question 4

Brogden v Metropolitan Railway Co [1877] concerned a dispute between a coal merchant and a railway company. The House of Lords had to decide whether a contract existed and if so, what the terms of the contract were. The facts of the case can be set out as the following four statements.

a) After the railway company had taken coal from Brogden for many years, the company sent Brogden a written agreement which set out the position as regards future supplies of coal.

b) Brogden altered the written agreement, then signed it and sent it back to the company.

c) The company filed the agreement in a drawer, leaving it there for two years.

d) Brogden delivered coal, which the company had ordered, in accordance with the altered agreement.

Each of the four statements above amounts to one of the following: an offer, an invitation to treat, a revocation, a counter offer, a contract, or nothing at all. Decide which of these matters each of the statements amounts to. (In reaching your decision you should apply at least three of the cases which we have considered in this chapter.)

Task 1

A friend of yours, Rory, works as a self-employed painter and decorator. Rory has heard that materials can often be bought more cheaply at auction or by tender than from wholesalers. Rory has asked you to write a brief report, indicating the following matters

a) The way in which a contract is made by the process of offer and acceptance.

b) How an offer differs from an invitation to treat.

c) How the offer and acceptance are made when goods are bought at auction.

d) How the offer and acceptance are made when goods are bought by tender.

e) The extent to which offers can be withdrawn after they have been made.

f) What is meant by an intention to create legal relations.

g) What is meant by consideration.

h) Whether all contracts can be made without the need for writing.

2 The terms of the contract

The terms of a contract define the obligations which the parties to the contract have undertaken. We begin this chapter by examining the ways in which terms can arise, and see that a contract may contain both express and implied terms. We then consider the different types of terms, seeing that sometimes breach of a term gives the injured party the right to terminate the contract. Breach of any term always gives a right to sue for damages.

Exclusion clauses are terms which attempt to exclude liability for breach of contract or for breach of a tortious duty of care. We conclude this chapter by considering the special rules which apply to exclusion clauses.

Nature of terms

A contract is made up of terms. All of the promises which the contract contains, whether they were made expressly or impliedly, will be terms. If any of these promises are not kept, one or more terms of the contract will have been breached. The injured party will then always have a remedy for breach of contract.

Terms can find their way into contracts in one of two ways; they can be expressed or implied. Express terms are actually expressed by the parties in words. Implied terms are implied either by the court (on the grounds of the presumed intention of the parties) or by a statute.

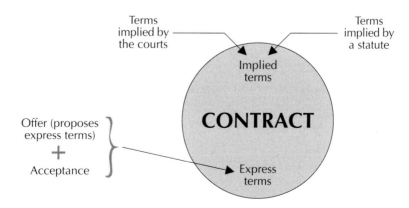

Figure 2.1 The ways in which terms arise

Express terms

A contract is formed when an offer is accepted. The offeror proposes a set of terms. If the offer is accepted by the offeree these proposed terms become legally binding as the terms of the contract. Oral contracts usually contain very few express terms. Written contracts, especially business contracts, usually contain far more. For example, if you look at the specimen contract which is set out on pages 282–283, you will see that it contains 78 express terms. When these express terms are incorporated into a contract of hire, both of the parties agree to be bound by them.

Terms implied by the courts

The courts have the power to imply terms into contracts. Despite having this power, the judges have always made it plain that they are not prepared to make a contract for the parties. The courts will only imply a term on the basis that it was so obviously intended to be a part of the contract that the parties felt no need to mention it.

The Moorcock [1889]

A jetty owner made a contract which allowed a ship owner to moor his ship at the jetty. Both parties knew that the ship would be grounded at low tide. When the ship did touch the ground it was damaged because there was a ridge of rock beneath the mud. The ship owner asked the court to imply a term that the jetty owner had taken reasonable care to ensure that the jetty was a safe place to unload a ship.

Held *The term was implied by the court. The jetty owner had breached the term and was therefore in breach of contract.*

Customary terms

Terms may be implied by the courts on the grounds that they are customary in a particular trade, customary in a particular locality or customary between the parties.

Many trades have customs, and these customs will be implied into contracts made within the context of those trades. In the bakery trade, for example, a dozen used to mean thirteen, and a baker who sold twenty dozen loaves would be deemed to have sold 260, not 240.

In a similar way, customs of a particular locality will be implied into contracts made in that locality.

Hutton v Warren [1836]

A Lincolnshire tenant farmer was given notice to quit the farm. He asked for an implied term that he should be paid an allowance for seeds and labour.

Held *The term was implied because it was an agricultural custom in Lincolnshire.*

A term can become customary between the parties to the contract if they regularly make contracts which include such a term.

In *Kendall v Lillico [1969]* the parties had often dealt with each other. Whenever an oral contract was made, the same 'sold note' containing a large number of terms was always sent the following day. It was held that the terms in the 'sold note' had become customary between the parties and were therefore incorporated into an oral contract which was made.

Terms implied as a matter of law

The courts imply terms into particular types of contracts as a matter of law. These terms are not implied because the parties must have intended them to be a part of the contract. They are implied because, as a matter of law, such terms are always implied into the type of contract in question. For example, in *Liverpool City Council v Irwin [1977]* the House of Lords implied a term that the landlord of a block of flats would keep the flats in reasonable repair and reasonably usable. This term was implied because such a term would be implied generally into contracts between landlord and tenant.

Limits of terms implied by the courts

Care must be taken when looking for terms implied by the courts, as the courts do not imply them freely.

Lord Pearson said in *Trollope v NWRHB [1973]*,

> 'The court does not make a contract for the parties. The court will not even improve the contract which the parties have made for themselves, however desirable the improvement might be.......An unexpressed term can be implied if and only if the court finds the parties must have intended that term to form part of their contract...it is not enough for the court to find that such a term would have been adopted by the parties as reasonable men if it had been suggested to them.....it must have been a term which went without saying, a term necessary to give business efficacy to the contract.'

Exclusion of implied terms

Later in this chapter we shall see that the terms implied by statutes can never be excluded in consumer cases and can only be excluded in non-consumer cases where this is reasonable. But terms implied by the court, being implied on the basis that they are obviously what the parties intended, can always be excluded by an express term.

If, for instance, the lease in *Hutton v Warren* had expressly stated that the tenant farmer would not get an allowance for seeds and labour then he would not have received such an allowance.

Student Activity Question 2.1

In *Liverpool City Council v Irwin* the lease contained express terms, such as that the tenant should pay the rent, and implied terms, such as that the landlord would keep the flats in reasonable repair and reasonably usable. Who put the express terms into the contract, and who put in the implied terms?

Further Activity Questions 2.1

1) Do you know of any trades or professions which have customs? If not, perhaps your friends or relatives work in such areas. Try and get examples of at least four such customs.

2) If a business hired a cement mixer for a week at a price of £70, would it be implied that the business would pay British pounds rather than Irish pounds (which are worth slightly less)? Can you think of other terms which would be implied?

Terms implied by statute

Terms are implied into contracts by three statutes: the Sale of Goods Act 1979, the Supply of Goods (Implied Terms) Act 1973 and the Supply of Goods and Services Act 1982. The terms which these statutes imply are inserted into certain types of contracts without the parties needing to agree to them. Indeed, as we shall see, in consumer contracts the terms can be implied even if the parties expressly agree that they should not be.

The Sale of Goods Act 1979

The Sale of Goods Act 1893 was the first statute to imply terms into contracts. The 1893 Act has been replaced by the Sale of Goods Act 1979. The implied terms contained in the SGA 1979 are virtually identical to those contained in the original 1893 Act. The terms implied by the other two statutes, the SGITA 1973 and the SGSA 1982, are also very closely modelled on the terms implied by the Sale of Goods Acts 1893 and 1979. Almost all of the case law on statutory implied terms is concerned with terms implied by the Sale of Goods Acts. We therefore consider the terms implied by the Sale of Goods Act 1979 before we consider the terms implied by the SGITA 1973 and the SGSA 1982.

Scope of the Sale of Goods Act 1979

The SGA 1979 applies only to contracts of sale of goods. Such contracts are defined by Section 2 (1) of the Act:

> *'A contract of sale of goods is a contract by which the seller transfers or agrees to transfer the property in goods to the buyer for a money consideration, called the price.'*

Reading section 2(1), we can see that a sale occurs when a buyer pays money in return for ownership of goods. It does not matter whether the buyer pays cash, by cheque or by credit card. But a free gift, where the buyer pays no money, cannot be a sale. Nor is it a sale where goods are bartered (exchanged) for other goods.

Note also that the seller must transfer the property in goods (ownership of the goods) to the buyer. This requirement rules out contracts to hire or to lease, where possession of the goods is transferred but ownership is not.

If the contract agrees that the property in the goods should be transferred at some future date, or when some condition has been satisfied, then this is an agreement to sell goods rather than a sale of goods. Agreements to sell goods are governed by the SGA 1979 and become sales of goods when the time elapses or the condition is fulfilled. For example, a merchant might agree to sell 100 tons of wheat of a certain type, to be delivered on 1 August next year. This is an agreement to sell goods and is governed by the SGA 1979. On 1 August next year the agreement becomes a sale of goods.

Meaning of goods

Section 61(1) of the SGA 1979 defines goods as 'all personal chattels other than things in action'.

A personal chattel is a physical thing which can be touched and moved, for example a car, a cup or a computer. Land and houses cannot be moved and are real property rather than personal chattels.

A thing in action is a right which can only be enforced by suing (taking out an action). A guarantee, for example, is a thing in action. A guarantee may be written on a piece of paper but the paper is not the property. The property is the right which the guarantee gives and, ultimately, that right can only be enforced by suing the person who gave it.

Student Activity Questions 2.2

Which of the following contracts would be governed by the Sale of Goods Act 1979?

a)   £5 for a haircut.

b)   A patent on a new invention for £12,000.

c)   A car bought for £3,000, which was paid by cheque.

d)   A trolley of groceries, purchased with a credit card.

e)   A 'free chicken' to customers who spend £20 in a supermarket.

f)   A house bought for £70,000.

g)   Ten tons of potatoes, which have not yet been grown. The potatoes are to be delivered next June and the price is fixed at £1,000.

h)   The copyright in a song for a percentage of the royalties.

i)   A pen for £7.

j)   A bicycle in exchange for a personal stereo.

k)   A landscape painting, commissioned for £200.

l)   A ticket to the cinema for £4.

m)   A television, hire-purchased over three years, at £20 a month.

n)   A share in a company sold for £10.

The terms implied by the SGA 1979

Sections 12–15 of the SGA 1979 contain five major implied terms, known as conditions. These terms do not need to be mentioned by the buyer or the seller, as the Act will automatically imply them into contracts of sale of goods. The five conditions implied by the SGA 1979 are as follows.

Section 12(1) implies a condition that the seller has the right to sell the goods.

Section 13(1) implies a condition that the goods will correspond with any description by which they were sold.

Section 14(2) implies a condition that the goods are of satisfactory quality.

Section 14(3) implies a condition that the goods are fit for the buyer's purpose.

Section 15(2) implies a condition that where goods are sold by sample the bulk will correspond with the sample.

The terms implied by sections 14(2) and 14(3) are implied only into sales of goods which are made in the course of a business. The other terms are implied into all contracts of sale of goods.

These implied terms are vitally important, and each one must be examined closely.

The right to sell (Section 12(1))

Section 12(1) of the SGA 1979 provides that unless the circumstances show a different intention:

> '*There is an implied [condition] on the part of the seller that in the case of a sale he has a right to sell the goods, and in the case of an agreement to sell he will have such a right at the time when the property is to pass.*'

This term, like the others, is a condition. We shall examine the effect of a breach of condition towards the end of this chapter. At this stage it is enough to say that if a condition is breached the injured party can generally treat the contract as terminated and also claim damages. If a seller breaches a condition and the buyer chooses to therefore treat the contract as terminated, the buyer will get all of the purchase price back.

Rowland v Divall [1923]

A thief stole a car from its owner and sold the car to the defendant. The claimant, a motor dealer, bought the car from the defendant for £334. The claimant did the car up and sold it to a customer for £400. On discovering that the car was stolen, the police took it from the customer and returned it to its original owner. The customer complained to the claimant who returned his £400. The claimant asked the defendant for the return of the £334 he had paid. The defendant refused to pay, saying that he had no idea that the car was stolen.

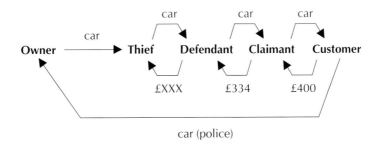

Figure 2.2 The transactions in Rowland v Divall

Held *The claimant got all of his money back. Section 12(1) provides that the seller must have the right to sell, and when the defendant sold the car to the claimant he did not have* this right because he did not own the car. The thief never owned the car. He therefore could not pass ownership to the defendant, who could not pass ownership to the claimant, etc. None of the parties except the original owner ever had the right to sell the car.

Atkin LJ:

> 'It seems to me that in this case there has been a total failure of consideration, that is to say that the buyer has not got any part of that for which he paid the purchase price. He paid the money in order that he might get the property, and he has not got it.'

Where there is a chain of innocent sellers the loser will generally be the person who bought from the thief, as in *Rowland v Divall*. Of course this person could successfully sue the thief, but in practical terms this would probably be a waste of money as it is most unlikely that the thief could be found and would have the money to pay when the case reached court.

However, if any of the the the sellers in the chain has become insolvent then the person who bought from that seller will be the one with no practical remedy.

For example, let's assume that a thief has stolen a car from its owner and then sold the car to A, who sold it to B, who sold it to C, who sold it to D. As can be seen from the diagram, A will be the loser.

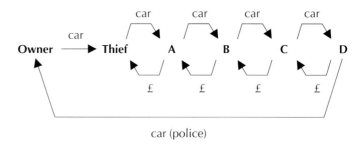

car (police)

Figure 2.3 Who is the loser?

But now let us further assume that B has become insolvent. D can recover from C, but C cannot recover from B. Nor can C leapfrog B and sue A – there is no contract between the two of them.

Section 12(2) implies a warranty that no person will interfere with the buyer's right to enjoy quiet possession of the goods. This term would be important if the seller owned the goods sold and had the right to sell them, but the buyer was later prevented from using the goods because a third party had acquired a property right, such as a patent, in the goods. The term will not be implied if the seller reveals before the sale that the buyer will not enjoy quiet possession of the goods. A warranty is a less important term than a condition. If a warranty is breached the injured party can claim damages for breach of contract, but cannot treat the contract as terminated.

Student Activity Questions 2.3

1) Read SGA 1979 section 12(1) on page 37. Does it provide that the seller must have the right to sell the goods or does it provide that the seller must think that he has the right to sell the goods?

2) A grain merchant agrees to sell 1,000 tons of grain to a buyer, delivery to be made next November. The merchant intends to buy the grain from a Canadian exporter, but as yet this contract has not been made and so the grain merchant does not yet own the grain. Does this mean that the merchant breaches section 12(1)?

Further Activity Questions 2.3

1) A thief steals a consignment of batteries and, after the batteries have passed through a succession of buyers, a shopkeeper buys them in good faith. The shopkeeper sells the batteries to a customer who uses them until their power is exhausted.

   a) Did the customer ever have ownership of the batteries?

   b) Ought the customer be able to claim the whole purchase price back from the shop?

2) In *Niblett v Confectioners Materials [1921]*, 3,000 tins of condensed milk were sold. The milk was labelled 'Nissly Brand.' Nestle Ltd warned the buyers of the milk that the word 'Nissly' was too similar to the Nestle trademark, and that if they attempted to sell the milk they would be prevented from doing so by an injunction. The buyers accepted that this was the legal position, and rejected the milk under section 12(1). The court held that the buyer won. Read section 12(1) and write down why the seller breached it even though he did own the milk when he sold it.

Correspondence with description (Section 13(1))

Section 13 of the SGA 1979 provides that:

> *'Where there is a contract for the sale of goods by description, there is an implied condition that the goods will correspond with the description.'*

A seller has no obligation to describe the goods sold. Furthermore, the fact that the seller has made a description does not necessarily mean that the goods were sold by that description.

If the goods sold are specific goods, then they will have been identified and agreed upon at the time of the contract. The seller must deliver those specific goods, and no others, or be in breach of contract. If the goods sold are unascertained goods they will not have been identified and agreed upon at the time of the contract. For example, If I agree to buy a particular second-hand bicycle from a shop this is a sale of specific goods. If the shop orders 30 new bicycles of a particular type from a manufacturer, without identifying the specific bicycles to be delivered, this is a sale of unascertained goods. The manufacturer can deliver any 30 bicycles which correspond with the description.

When unascertained goods are sold, any descriptive words used in the contract will cause the goods to be sold by description.

Arcos v Ronaasen [1933]

The seller contracted to sell a quantity of wooden staves which were to be used for making cement barrels. The goods were unascertained. The staves had been described as 'half an inch thick.' 90% of the staves were between half an inch and five eighths of an inch, but 10% were over five eighths of an inch. The buyer rejected all of the staves, even though they were perfectly fit for making cement barrels.

***Held** Section 13(1) was breached because the staves did not correspond with the description by which they were sold. The buyer could therefore treat the contract as terminated and was entitled to all of his money back.*

Where specific goods are sold, the sale will only be by description where the description was an important term of the contract on which the buyer relied. For example, in *Harlingdon & Leinster Enterprises Ltd v Christopher Hull Fine Art Ltd [1991]* the Court of Appeal held that two paintings had not been sold by description. The paintings had been described as being by a German expressionist called Munter. The buyer was an expert in German expressionist painting, but the seller was not. In fact, the paintings were fakes and were worth only one per cent of the price which the buyer paid. Section 13(1) provided no help to the buyer. The paintings were not sold *by* description because the description was not an important term of the contract on which the buyer relied.

Having decided that a sale was made by description, we then need to examine how closely the description must be adhered to. A rule expressed in Latin, *de minimis lex non curat* (the law is not concerned with trifles) has always been a general principle of the common law. The effect of the rule here is that if the failure to match the description was very trivial the seller will not breach section 13(1). However, the following case shows that where goods are sold by description in a commercial context the description must be very closely adhered to.

Re Moore and Co and Landauer and Co [1921]

A consignment of 3,100 tins of peaches was sold. The goods were to be shipped from Australia to a buyer in London. The buyer rejected the consignment on the grounds that whereas the peaches had been described as packed 30 tins to a case, about half of the tins were packed 24 to a case instead of 30. The correct number of tins were delivered.

Held *The buyer could reject all of the tins. Section 13(1) had been breached because the goods did not correspond with the description by which they had been sold.*

Section 13(2) provides that goods can be sold by both sample and description. If they are, they must correspond with both the description and the sample. Section 13(3) provides that goods can still be sold by description even if, being exposed for sale or hire, they are selected by the buyer. So the fact that a buyer chooses goods, perhaps in a supermarket for example, will not prevent the goods from having been sold by description.

Student Activity Question 2.4

Before a contract is made, the seller describes the goods to be sold. Is the sale always made by description, so that section 13(1) will require correspondence with the description?

Further Activity Questions 2.4

In *Arcos v Ronaasen* Lord Atkin said:

> *'It was contended that in all commercial contracts.....there must always be some margin.....I cannot agree. If the written contract specifies conditions of weight, measurement and the like, these conditions must be complied with. A ton does not mean about a ton, or a yard about a yard. Still less when you descend to minute measurements does 1/2 inch mean about 1/2 inch. If the seller wants a margin he must and in my experience does stipulate for it. Of course by recognised trade usage particular figures may be given a different meaning, as in a baker's dozen....If a condition is not performed the buyer has a right to reject....No doubt, in business, men often find it unnecessary or inexpedient to insist on their strict legal rights. In a normal market if they get something substantially like the specified goods they may take them with or without grumbling and claim for an allowance. But in a falling market I find that buyers are often as eager to insist on their legal rights as courts of law are ready to maintain them.'*

1) If Lord Atkin had taken the view that a margin of 1% was acceptable, so that a metric tonne of coal could be 10 kilos light, what problems would arise? Would a line still have to be drawn somewhere? What if a coal retailer delivered a tonne of coal which was 11 kilos light?

... continued

2) Do you think the price of the staves had increased or decreased between the time of the making of the contract and the buyer finding that they did not match the description? How do you think the buyer would have acted if the price of staves had increased dramatically, so that it would have cost him double to buy similar staves elsewhere?

3) If the goods do alter in price between the time of making the contract and the time of delivery, would this have any bearing on the court's decision as to whether section 13(1) had been breached?

Section 14: Quality and fitness in business sales

Section 14(2) of the SGA 1979 implies a term that goods sold in the course of a business are of satisfactory quality.

Section 14(3) of the SGA 1979 implies a term that goods sold in the course of a business are reasonably fit for the buyer's purpose.

Business Sales

The terms as to satisfactory quality and fitness for purpose are implied only where goods are sold in the course of a business. Neither section will apply where goods are sold by a private seller. The following case considered the circumstances in which goods are sold in the course of a business.

Stevenson v Rogers [1999]

The defendant had been in business as a fisherman for 20 years. He sold an old fishing boat when he wanted to buy a new one. The boat sold, which was not of satisfactory quality, was not being used as part of the stock in trade of the business at the time of sale. The defendant argued that no term as to satisfactory quality should be implied as the boat was not sold in the course of a business.

Held *The boat was sold in the course of the defendant's business. For the purposes of section 14 of the SGA 1979, the words 'in the course of a business' should be taken at face value. Section 14 applies to any sale made in the course of a business, even if what is sold is not the stock in trade which the business exists in order to sell. Even a one-off sale by the business is a sale in the course of a business. But purely private sales which are made outside the limits of the business would not be made in the course of a business.*

Satisfactory quality (Section 14(2))

Section 14(2) of the SGA 1979 provides that:

> *'Where the seller sells goods in the course of a business, there is an implied term that the goods supplied under the contract are of satisfactory quality.'*

This requirement that the goods supplied under the contract be of satisfactory quality is relatively recent. The Sale of Goods Act 1979 was amended in 1994. Before the amendment the 1979 Act implied a term that goods sold in the course of a business were of merchantable quality. However, the meaning of merchantable quality had become unclear, and so the requirement was changed to one of satisfactory quality. Section 14(2A) of the SGA 1979 now provides the following definition of satisfactory quality.

> *'Goods are of satisfactory quality if they meet the standard that a reasonable person would regard as satisfactory, taking account of any description of the goods, the price (if relevant) and all the other relevant circumstances.'*

We should note three things about this definition. First, the standard required is objective, being that which a reasonable person would regard as satisfactory. Second, any description of the goods may be taken into account. (There is no requirement here that the goods are sold by description, as there was in the case of section 13(1).) Third, any other relevant circumstances, which may include the price, can be taken into account. It is also worth noticing that it is not only the goods sold which must be of satisfactory quality. Section 14(2) requires that 'the goods supplied under the contract' must be of satisfactory quality and this would include any packaging.

Section 14(2B) lists five factors which can be taken into account in assessing the quality of the goods.

> *'For the purposes of this Act, the quality of goods includes their state and condition and the following (among others) are in appropriate cases aspects of the quality of the goods:*
>
> *(a) fitness for all the purposes for which goods of the kind in question are commonly supplied,*
>
> *(b) appearance and finish,*
>
> *(c) freedom from minor defects,*
>
> *(d) safety, and*
>
> *(e) durability.'*

It is important not to get carried away with section 14(2B). The five matters listed are not absolute requirements of quality. They are *aspects of quality in appropriate cases*. For example, if a car which has been written-off in an accident is sold for scrap, the car will be of satisfactory quality even though it might be unfit to be driven, badly battered and completely unsafe. Taking into account the description, the price and all the other relevant circumstances, the reasonable person would regard such a car as being of satisfactory quality.

The liability imposed on the seller by section 14(2) is strict and does not depend upon the seller having been at fault. Shops which sell defective goods will breach section 14(2) even if the goods were sold in packaging which prevented the defect from being discovered.

Section 14(2C) indicates that the term as to satisfactory quality will not be implied in two circumstances. First, it will not apply as regards defects which were specifically pointed out to the buyer before the contract is made. Second, where the buyer examines the goods before buying them, it will not apply as regards defects which the examination ought to have revealed.

If a defect is *specifically pointed out* to the buyer, then that particular defect cannot make the goods unsatisfactory. This is the case even if the defect proves to be more serious than the buyer imagined.

Bartlett v Sidney Marcus Ltd [1965]

A dealer sold a second-hand car and pointed out to the buyer that the car had a defective clutch. The buyer negotiated a reduced price to take account of the defect. Repairing the clutch cost far more than the buyer had anticipated, and he claimed to reject the car under section 14(2).

Held *The defect had been pointed out to the buyer and so it did not cause section 14(2) to have been breached.*

A buyer has no obligation to examine goods before buying them. However, *if the buyer examines the goods*, the goods cannot be rendered unsatisfactory on account of defects which the examination ought to have revealed. However, even the most glaringly obvious defects will make the goods unsatisfactory if the buyer chooses not to examine the goods.

Student Activity Questions 2.5

1) Are the following sales made in the course of a business?

   a) A motor dealer sells a new car to Brian, a postman.

   b) Brian the postman sells his old car to a shop keeper.

   c) A motor dealer orders 15 new cars from a car manufacturer.

   d) A shop keeper buys a new till from a sales representative and sells the shop's old till to a customer.

... continued

2) Apples which have become slightly rotten are sold by a farmer. Would section 14(2) have been breached if:

a) The apples were sold to a shopkeeper who did not examine them and who paid the usual wholesale price for (wholesome) apples of this kind?

b) The apples were sold to a shopkeeper who did examine them carefully, but did not notice that they were rotten, and who paid the usual wholesale price for (wholesome) apples of this kind?

c) The apples were sold to a shopkeeper who did not examine them. The state of the apples was pointed out to the shopkeeper, who paid the usual wholesale price for (wholesome) apples of this type.

d) The apples were sold to a cider maker for a quarter of their usual wholesale price, being described as 'cider apples'? The cider maker did not examine the apples and it was not pointed out to him that they were slightly rotten, as cider apples often are.

Further Activity Questions 2.5

1) Samantha buys a new CD player from a shop. The shopkeeper agrees to reduce the price by 10 per cent because he says that some of the CD players were knocked about a bit during transit. Samantha does not examine the CD player before buying it. When Samantha gets the CD player home she examines it and finds that it is badly scratched. The CD player works perfectly, but its appearance is very poor. Advise Samantha as to whether or not section 14(2) of the SGA 1979 has been breached.

2) Edith buys a 24 piece tea service in a New Year Sale. Edith pays only half of the usual retail price of the tea service. When she gets home Edith discovers that several of the teacups are cracked and the handle of the teapot has come off. Advise Edith as to whether or not section 14(2) of the SGA 1979 has been breached.

Fitness for purpose (Section 14(3))

Section 14(3) of the SGA 1979 states that if the buyer expressly or impliedly makes known to the seller any particular purpose for which the goods are being bought, then there is an implied condition that the goods are reasonably fit for that purpose. This is the case whether or not the purpose made known by the buyer is the purpose for which goods of that particular type are commonly supplied.

However, section 14(3) will not apply if the circumstances show either that:

a) the buyer does not rely on the skill and judgement of the seller; or

b) it was unreasonable for the buyer to rely on the skill and judgement of the seller.

The following example shows how section 14(3) might operate. Let us assume that Hannah visits a shop and buys a cake. Before buying the cake Hannah asks the seller whether or not the cake contains nuts, explaining that she is allergic to nuts. The seller says that it does not. Relying on this, Hannah buys the cake and eats it. Hannah is made ill by the cake, which did contain nuts. Section 14(3) will have been breached even though there was nothing wrong with the general quality of the cake.

If the purpose for which goods are to be used is perfectly obvious, then the buyer does not need to state the purpose. The terms as to satisfactory quality and fitness for the buyer's purpose will both be implied.

Grant v Australian Knitting Mills [1936]

A customer who bought a pair of underpants from a shop contracted dermatitis because a chemical used in the manufacture of the underpants had not been rinsed out properly. The customer sued under section 14(3), as well as under section 14(2), because the purpose for which he bought the underpants was perfectly obvious.

Held *The buyer won under both sections.*

Griffiths v Peter Conway Ltd [1939]

A customer with abnormally sensitive skin contracted dermatitis from a tweed coat which she bought from a shop. The coat would not have affected most people.

Held *The shop were not liable under section 14(2) because there was nothing wrong with the coat. The shop were not liable under section 14(3) because the customer had not made her condition known.*

When defective goods are bought for their usual purpose it is common for the buyer to sue under both section 14(2) and section 14(3), as *Grant v Australian Knitting Mills* demonstrates. However, the terms are not implied in identical circumstances. Section 14(2) applies even if the buyer did not make any purpose known to the seller or rely in any way on the seller's skill and judgement. But it does not apply where the buyer examined the goods and ought to have noticed a defect. Nor does it apply where the defect was specifically pointed out to the buyer. Section 14(3) applies only where the buyer makes a particular purpose known to the seller and relies on the skill and judgement of the seller (although both of these matters can be done impliedly). It can apply even as regards defects which the buyer noticed or which were specifically pointed out. (If, for example, the seller wrongly said that the defect would cause the buyer no problems.)

Sale by sample (Section 15)

Section 15 provides that if goods are sold by sample the following two conditions are implied:

(a) the bulk of the goods must correspond with the sample in quality; and

(b) the bulk must be free from hidden defects, which would render the goods unsatisfactory, if these defects would not be discovered on a reasonable examination of the sample.

These two terms are implied into all sales by sample, even those which were not made in the course of a business.

Godley v Perry [1960]

A six year old boy bought a catapult which snapped in use and caused the boy to lose an eye. The boy sued the shopkeeper and won. The shopkeeper sued the wholesaler under section 15 because, before buying the catapults, he had tested a sample catapult by pulling back the elastic, and this sample had not snapped.

Held *The shopkeeper won under section 15.*

We saw earlier that a sale can be made by both sample and description, in which case the bulk of the goods must correspond with both the sample and the description.

Student Activity Questions 2.6

1) Generally second-hand cars are more expensive to buy from a garage than they are to buy privately. Why might a customer who knows little about cars be better to buy from a garage?

2) David, who knows little about cars, feels that he will get a better price from the garage if he appears to have some mechanical expertise. Before buying a car he therefore kicks the tyres, looks underneath the chassis, and examines the engine. Why might these be unwise moves?

Further Activity Questions 2.6

1) Which of the following sales are likely to be by sample?

   a) A farmer sells 100 tons of potatoes to a supermarket chain.

   b) A shopper orders a fitted carpet in a style he saw in the shop.

   c) After test driving a demonstration model, a motorist buys a new car.

   d) A shop agrees to stock a new range of pens.

   e) A householder orders a three piece suite which he saw pictured in a magazine.

2) In *Godley v Perry* the boy sued the shopkeeper and won. Under which section(s) would the boy have sued?

3) In *Godley v Perry* there was a chain of buyers.

   Manufacturer ...... supplier 1 ...... supplier 2 ...... shopkeeper ...... boy

   a) Who was the eventual loser likely to be?

   b) How would the bankruptcy of supplier 2 have affected the position?

The Supply of Goods (Implied Terms) Act 1973

As we have seen, the terms implied by the Sale of Goods Act have given excellent protection to buyers of goods since 1893. However, for many years people who acquired goods under contracts which could not be classed as contracts of sale of goods had to rely on case law for protection.

In the 1970s Parliament passed several statutes which extended the Sale of Goods Act implied terms into other types of contract.

The first of these Acts was the Supply of Goods (Implied Terms) Act 1973 (SGITA 1973), which extended the implied terms into contracts of hire-purchase. The terms implied, which are virtually identical to the terms implied by sections 12-15 of the Sale of Goods Act 1979, are contained in the following sections.

Section 8   Right to pass ownership

Section 9   Correspondence with description

Section 10   Satisfactory quality and fitness for purpose (business contracts only)

Section 11   Correspondence with sample

A contract of hire-purchase is one whereby a customer agrees to hire goods for a certain period, and is given an option to purchase the goods for a nominal sum at the end of that period.

Let us look, for example, at Mr. Smith who takes a fridge on hire-purchase from a shop. The fridge would have cost £350 to buy, but Mr Smith takes it on hire-purchase for three years at £17 a month. Until the final payment is made Mr Smith is merely hiring the fridge. The last payment he makes will include a nominal purchase price and when Mr Smith makes the final payment he then buys the fridge.

The SGITA 1973 implies terms as to ownership, description, quality, fitness and sample as soon as the hire-purchase agreement begins.

Section 10, which implies the terms as to satisfactory quality and fitness for the hirer's purpose, applies only if the owner of the goods makes the hire-purchase agreement in the course of a business. The other sections apply to all contracts of hire-purchase. In almost all hire-purchase agreements the owner will make the agreement in the course of a business.

The Supply of Goods and Services Act 1982

Part 1 of the Act

Part 1 of the Supply of Goods and Services Act 1982 (SGSA 1982) implies terms as to the right to pass ownership or possession, correspondence with description, satisfactory quality, fitness for purpose and correspondence with sample into two types of contracts. First, the terms are implied into contracts for the transfer of property in goods. Second, the terms are implied into contracts of hire. The terms are implied by the following sections.

Contracts for the transfer of property in goods

Section 2   Right to transfer the property

Section 3   Correspondence with description

Section 4   Satisfactory quality and fitness for purpose (business contracts only)

Section 5   Correspondence with sample

Contracts of Hire

Section 7   Right to hire

Section 8   Correspondence with description

Section 9   Satisfactory quality and fitness for purpose (business contracts only)

Section 10   Correspondence with sample

Under a contract of hire, a hirer is given temporary possession of goods but not ownership, by the owner of the goods. A contract will be a contract for the transfer of property in goods if it is any contract which involves the passing of ownership of goods (except a contract of sale of goods or a contract of hire-purchase). It would therefore include contracts under which goods are bartered for other goods. It would also cover the supply of goods in a contract under which services are supplied. For example, it would cover the supply of oil when a car was serviced.

Part 2 of the Act

Part 2 of the Supply of Goods and Services Act 1982 implies three terms into contracts under which a service is supplied. These terms are as follows:

Section 13   Reasonable care and skill (business services only)

Section 14   Reasonable time (business services only)

Section 15   Reasonable price

Reasonable care and skill (Section 13)

SGSA 1982 section 13 provides that:

> *'In a contract for the supply of a service where the supplier is acting in the course of a business, there is an implied term that the supplier will carry out the service with reasonable care and skill.'*

First, it is important to note that this term will only be implied where the service is supplied in the course of a business. Second, and very important, it must be realised that this term does not impose strict liability. It imposes a *tort standard of reasonable care and skill*. For example, in *Thake and another v Maurice [1986]* a patient sued a surgeon who had carried out a vasectomy which did not have the desired effect. The surgeon was not liable because he had used reasonable care and skill. (The effect of a very few vasectomies can be reversed naturally.) If the surgeon had guaranteed that the vasectomy would be successful then he would have been liable. But in the absence of such a guarantee, it is only implied that the provider of a service in the course of a business will use reasonable care and skill.

The test of whether the service provided was carried out with reasonable care and skill is objective not subjective. A person who professes to have a certain level of skill must show the level of skill which the reasonable person would expect. Professionals, such as solicitors and accountants, and tradesmen, such as plumbers and roofers, would be expected to show the level of skill which is normal in that profession or trade.

It is also important to realise that a contract can still be a contract for the supply of a service even though it is a contract under which possession of goods or ownership of goods is transferred. For example, a contract under which a motorist buys new tyres, to be fitted by the garage, is both a contract of sale of goods and a contract for the supply of a service. In such cases two sets of terms are implied. Sections 14(2) and 14(3) of the Sale of Goods Act 1979 imply terms as to satisfactory quality and fitness for purpose. Section 13 of the Supply of Goods and Services Act 1982 implies a term that the service is carried out using reasonable care and skill. So if the tyres fitted were worn at the time of sale, the buyer would sue under SGA 1979 section 14(2) because the tyres were not of satisfactory quality. If the tyres were fitted badly and came off the car, causing the driver to be injured, the driver would sue under SGSA 1982 section 13 because the tyres were not fitted with reasonable care and skill.

easonable time of performance (Section 14)

Section 14 SGSA 1982 applies only to services provided in the course of business. It provides that if no time for completion of the task was either expressly or impliedly fixed, then the service should be performed within a reasonable time.

Reasonable price (Section 15)

Section 15 SGSA 1982 provides that if no price for a service was expressly or impliedly fixed, then the customer should pay a reasonable price. This section applies to all services, whether provided in the course of a business or not.

Student Activity Questions 2.7

1) A motorist buys a new car from a garage but the car has a serious defect in the steering system. The sale was not made by description. Which section(s) of which statute gives the motorist a remedy?

... continued

2) How would your answer to question 1 be different if

a) The motorist had hired the car from a garage?

b) The motorist had bought the car from a friend, an accountant?

c) The motorist had taken the garage's car in exchange for an old caravan, without any money changing hands?

Further Activity Questions 2.7

1) Complete the following table to show which sections of which statutes would apply. Put an asterisk next to the sections which would apply only to business deals. To get you started, some of the table has already been completed.

2) Is it normal, when dealing with a professional or a tradesman, to fix the exact price in advance? Is it still necessary to do so? Is it wise to do so?

Implied item as to: / Type of transaction	Sale of Goods	Hire Purchase	Transfer of property in Goods	Hire
Right to pass ownership or possession	S.G.A. 1979 Section 12			
Correspondence with description		S.G.I.T.A. 1973 Section 9		
Quality and fitness for purpose			S.G.S.A. 1982 Section 4	
Correspondence with sample				S.G.S.A. 1982 Section 10

Table 2.1

Types of terms

If any term is breached the injured party will always have a remedy for breach of contract. The nature of that remedy will depend upon what type of term was breached

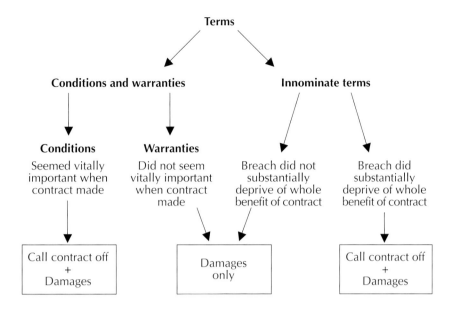

Figure 2.4 The different types of terms

Conditions and warranties

Traditionally all terms could be classified as being either conditions or warranties.

A condition is a term which seemed very important when the contract was made. (A term which went 'to the root of the contract.') If a condition is breached then the injured party can terminate the contract and claim damages.

A warranty is a term which did not seem vitally important when the contract was made. (A term which did not go 'to the root of the contract.') If a warranty is breached the injured party can claim damages but cannot treat the contract as terminated.

It might be thought that the the right to terminate a contract is of little importance if damages are always available. However, the right to terminate can be very important when one of the parties has made what has turned out to be a bad bargain.

Innominate terms

In *The Hong Kong Fir Case [1962]* the Court of Appeal invented a new category of term, the innominate or intermediate terms. In deciding whether or not breach of such a term gives the injured party the right to terminate the contract, the court does not consider how important the term seemed at the time when the contract was made. Instead, the court asks whether or not the breach deprived the injured party of substantially the whole benefit of the contract. If the breach did do this, the injured party can treat the contract as terminated and claim damages. If the breach did not do this, the injured party can claim damages but cannot treat the contract as terminated. Innominate terms have not replaced conditions and warranties. Some terms can now be classed as conditions or warranties, others are innominate terms.

There may be some uncertainty as to whether a court will classify a particular term as either a condition, a warranty or an innominate term. Generally, the position is as follows. First, a rule of law might establish that a term is a condition or a warranty. Second, the parties themselves might agree that certain terms will be conditions or warranties. The court will give effect to such an agreement. Third, if no term of the contract or rule of law stipulates that a particular term is to be either a condition or a warranty, the courts will regard the term as an innominate term. Breach of such a term will allow the injured party to terminate the contract only if the breach deprived the injured party of substantially the whole benefit of the contract.

It should also be remembered that damages will always be available for any breach of contract, whether the injured party has the right to terminate the contract or not. The subject of damages is considered in chapter 4.

The status of the statutory implied terms

The term contained in section 12(1) of the Sale of Goods Act 1979 is always a condition. If this term is breached the buyer is always therefore entitled to treat the contract as terminated and/or claim damages. The term is a condition because if the seller does not have the right to sell this amounts to a total failure of consideration. The corresponding terms contained in the SGITA 1973 section 8 and the SGSA 1982 sections 2 and 7 are also always conditions.

The term contained in section 12(2) of the Sale of Goods Act 1979 is a warranty. If this term is breached the buyer will therefore be able to claim damages but will not be entitled to treat the contract as terminated.

The terms contained in sections 13 - 15 of the Sale of Goods Act 1979 are conditions. So are the corresponding terms in the SGITA 1973 sections 9-11 and the SGSA 1982 sections 3-5 and 8-10. Where the person buying or acquiring the goods is a consumer, all of these terms are always conditions. If the terms are breached the consumer will therefore always have the right to terminate the contract and/or claim damages. However, section 15A of the Sale of Goods Act 1979 (and corresponding terms in the SGITA 1973 and in the SGSA 1982) provides that a buyer who does not deal as a consumer cannot treat the contract as terminated where breach of one of these implied terms is so slight that it would be unreasonable to allow the buyer to treat the contract as terminated. Instead, the buyer may treat the breach of condition as a breach of warranty and claim damages. Section 15A does not apply if the parties showed an intention that the person acquiring the goods should be able to treat the contract as terminated even where the breach was so slight as to make this unreasonable.

Let us look at an example, to demonstrate the effect of section 15A. Let us assume that a car dealer bought a new car from a car manufacturer and sold the car on to a consumer. The car had a very slight defect, which was just enough to mean that it was not of satisfactory quality, both when the manufacturer and when the dealer sold it. Section 14(2) of the SGA 1979 has therefore been breached as regards both sales. The consumer can treat this breach as breach of a condition and will be entitled to reject the car and treat the contract as terminated (as well as to claim damages). The car dealer will not be able to treat the contract as terminated if the breach is so slight as to make this unreasonable. However, the car dealer will be able to claim damages for breach of warranty. The car dealer would therefore have to repair the car, or have it repaired, and then claim damages from the manufacturer. These damages might reflect the cost of the repair and any profit which the dealer lost as a result of the sale to the consumer falling through.

The Sale of Goods Act 1979 section 11(4) makes one further important rule. It provides that where a seller of goods breaches a condition a buyer who has accepted the goods must treat the breach of condition as a breach of warranty. Therefore, such a buyer cannot terminate the contract but can still claim damages. Acceptance by the buyer has a technical meaning, which is examined in detail in Chapter 5.

Student Activity Questions 2.8

What rights are conferred upon a buyer of goods if the seller breaches:

(a)   A condition?

(b)   A warranty?

(c)   An innominate term?

Further Activity Questions 2.8

A retailer buys a television from a manufacturer. The retailer hires the television to a consumer for a three month period. The television was badly manufactured, so that its back casing is not tightly fitted together. The retailer could easily have tightened several screws and fixed this defect but did not do so before hiring the television to the consumer. As regards both the sale by the manufacturer and the contract of hire by the retailer, explain which sections of which statutes have been breached and the remedies available.

Exclusion clauses

Exclusion clauses, or exemption clauses as they are sometimes known, are clauses which try to exclude or limit one party's liability. Usually the liability in question will have arisen as a result of an express or implied term of a contract. However, exclusion clauses can go further and can exclude other types of liability, such as liability arising in tort.

We shall see that Parliament has restricted the effect of exclusion clauses. The following case demonstrates how unfairly exclusion clauses could operate before Parliament intervened.

L'Estrange v Graucob [1934]

A cafe owner bought a cigarette vending machine and signed a sales agreement which she did not read. A term of this agreement which was 'in regrettably small print but quite legible,' said that the machine did not need to work and that all statutory implied terms were not to apply. The machine did not work. The cafe owner sued to get her money back, claiming that section 14(2) of the Sale of Goods Act had been breached.

Held *The cafe owner failed, even though section 14(2) of the Sale of Goods Act had clearly been breached. The claimant had signed the agreement and so she was bound by it.*

Because of the unfairness of such cases Parliament felt the necessity to intervene. In 1977 it passed the Unfair Contract Terms Act (the UCTA 1977). We shall examine the UCTA 1977 later in this chapter. But when faced with an exclusion clause the first step is to consider whether the exclusion clause was a term of the contract. If the clause was not a term of the contract then it would not have any effect anyway, and it would not be necessary to consider the Act.

Is the exclusion clause a term of the contract?

It is always necessary when considering the effect of an exclusion clause in a contract to first decide whether or not the clause was a term of the contract. As we saw in *L'Estrange v Graucob*, a person who signs a document will be bound by its contents. Written, signed documents therefore present little difficulty in deciding whether or not an exclusion clause was a term of the contract. However, a person who misrepresents the effect of an exclusion clause may not be able to rely on it, even if the other party signs the document which contains the clause. An example can be seen in *Curtis v Chemical Cleaning and Dyeing Co Ltd [1951]* in which a customer who took her wedding dress to a dry cleaners was asked to sign a 'receipt'. The customer asked what it said and was told that it just covered liability for damage to beads and sequins. She signed the document, which in fact excluded all liability on the part of the dry cleaners. The wedding dress was badly stained and the dry cleaners tried to rely on their exclusion clause. They could not do so because they had misrepresented the effect of the clause

If the exclusion clause is contained in a document, such as a train ticket, which the reasonable person would think was a part of the contract then the term will be binding. If the clause was contained in a document, such as a receipt, which the reasonable person would not think contained the terms of the contract then the clause will not be binding. Sometimes what the reasonable person would have thought is obvious enough. In other cases it can be very hard to tell.

Chapelton v Barry UDC [1940]

The claimant hired a deck chair for 2d. When he sat in the chair it collapsed and he was injured. The hirers of the chair relied on an exclusion clause, which said that they were not liable for any accident or damage resulting from the hire of the deck chair. This clause had been printed on a slip of paper which the attendant issued to hirers of the chairs. It was possible to sit on a chair for an hour or two before the attendant took the money and issued the slip.

Held *The clause was not a part of the contract because it was contained in a mere receipt. The reasonable person would not have expected the terms of the contract to be contained in such a receipt.*

This case must be contrasted with *Thompson v London, Midland and Scottish Railway Co [1930]*, in which it was held that a train passenger who could not read was bound by an exclusion clause in the railway's timetables. The train ticket said that it was issued subject to the timetables, and the reasonable person would have expected to find the terms of the contract set out on the train ticket.

An exclusion clause will only be effective if it was agreed as a term of the contract, or if reasonable notice of it was given before the contract was made. A term cannot later be incorporated into a contract which has already been made

Olley v Marlborough Court Hotel [1949]

A married couple booked into a hotel for one week and paid their bill in advance. During their stay at the hotel the wife's fur coat was stolen from their room. The hotel denied liability because a notice in their room said that the hotel were not liable for lost or stolen property, unless it had been handed in to reception for safe custody.

Held *The notice was too late to be effective. The contract was made when the couple booked into the hotel.*

Thornton v Shoe Lane Parking Ltd [1971]

The claimant was badly injured in the defendants' car park, the accident being partly caused by the defendants' negligence. The claimant had driven into the car park and passed a notice at the entrance which said that cars were parked at the owner's risk. When the claimant stopped at a red light he was issued with a ticket. The ticket said on it that it was issued subject to notices displayed inside the car park. These notices, which could only be read once fully inside the car park, said that the defendants were not liable for damage to goods or for injuries to customers. The defendants denied liability for the claimant's injuries, saying that the conditions displayed inside the car park were a part of the contract.

Held *The notices inside the car park were not a part of the contract. By the time the claimant had been given the ticket which referred to these notices the contract had been made. (The contract was made by the time the claimant had no choice but to go through with the contract. That is to say, it was made when he drove past the point of no return.*

In the previous chapter we saw that a term can be implied into a contract because of a course of dealing between the parties. We considered *Kendall v Lillico*, in which the House of Lords held that an exclusion clause was a part of an oral contract. This was because the parties had often made similar oral contracts and on each occasion the seller had sent a 'sold note' containing the exclusion clause the following day. All the terms in the sold note were therefore implied into the oral contract. We also saw that terms can be implied on the basis that they are customary in a particular trade or industry. *British Crane Hire Co Ltd v Ipswich Plant Hire Ltd [1975]* provides an example. The claimant needed a crane in a hurry and made an oral contract to hire one from the defendants. This contract was made subject to all the terms in the 'Contractors' Plant Association Form' because both sides knew that whenever cranes were hired they were hired subject to the terms contained in this form.

Only if the court does decide that the exclusion clause was a term of the contract, will it move on to consider the effect of the Unfair Contract Terms Act 1977 and the Unfair Terms in Consumer Contracts Regulations 1999.

Student Activity Questions 2.9

1) Would the decision in *Olley v Marlborough Court Hotel* have been different if Mrs Olley had regularly stayed at the hotel? (Assume that the notices have been in the rooms for many years.) How would *Thornton v Shoe Lane Parking Ltd* have been different if Thornton had parked in the same car park the day before? (Assume that the notices had been clearly visible.)

2) At a self-service petrol station, would an exclusion clause be a part of the contract if:

   a) It was displayed at the entrance to the petrol station?

   b) It was displayed on the petrol pump?

   c) It was displayed above the till?

Further Activity Questions 2.9

In *Thornton v Shoe Lane Parking*, Lord Denning said that the exclusion clause on the ticket did not apply because it came after the contract was made. It follows that the offer and acceptance must have been concluded before the ticket was issued to the driver. What then was the offer, and what was the acceptance?

The Unfair Contract Terms Act 1977

Contracts covered by the Act

The sections of the UCTA 1977 which concern us apply only to business liability. This is defined by section 1 of the Act as liability which arises:

a) from things done or to be done by a person in the course of a business, or

b) from the occupation of premises used for the business purposes of the occupier.

The effect of the Act

Section 2 – Excluding liability arising from negligence

Section 2(1) provides that no contract term can exclude liability for death or personal injury arising from negligence.

Section 2(2) provides that liability for other types of damage arising from negligence, such as damage to goods, can be excluded if the term excluding liability was reasonable.

(Schedule 2 of the Act and section 11 define what reasonable means, and we will look at these later in this chapter.)

Smith v Eric S Bush [1989]

The claimant applied to a building society for a mortgage to buy a house. The building society employed the defendants to make a survey of the house. The claimant paid £40 to the building society, who agreed to supply her with a copy of the report. A disclaimer said that neither the building society nor the surveyors would be liable for any inaccuracies. The report itself also carried a similar disclaimer. The report said that the house was worth £16,000 and that no major building work was necessary. 18 months later the chimneys fell through the roof because a chimney breast had been removed without proper supports being fitted. The claimant sued the defendants for negligence.

Held *The defendants owed a duty of care to the claimant. The disclaimer which excluded liability had to be reasonable under UCTA section 2(2). It was not reasonable and so it did not apply.*

Comment *If the claimant had been killed or injured by the falling chimney breast then section 2(1) UCTA 1977 would have applied. It would not have been possible for any term to exclude liability for the death or injury. It would not therefore have been necessary to consider whether or not any term which tried to do so was reasonable.*

Whenever section 13 of the SGSA 1982 term is breached, the UCTA 1977 regards this as negligence. Therefore section 2 of the UCTA 1977 will determine the extent to which liability for breach of section 13 SGSA 1982 can be excluded, if it can be excluded at all.

Section 3 – Liability arising in contract

Section 3 protects two classes of people who make a contract:

a)   those who 'deal as a consumer'; and

b)   those who deal on the other party's written standard terms.

Before considering what protection section 3 offers, we should be clear about exactly who is protected.

The Act makes a very important distinction between a person who deals 'as a consumer' and a person who does not.

Section 12(1) tells us that a buyer or hirer deals as a consumer if:

a)   he makes the contract otherwise than in the course of business and not holding himself out to be in the course of business; and

b)   the other party to the contract does make the contract in the course of business; and

c)   if goods pass under the contract, they are a type of goods ordinarily supplied for private use or consumption.

All three of these conditions must be satisfied if a person is to deal as a consumer. For example, if a teacher buys a television from a shop the teacher would deal as a consumer. But if a teacher bought an overhead projector from a shop the teacher would only deal as a consumer if the court thought that an overhead projector was the type of goods ordinarily supplied for private use or consumption. If the teacher sold a television to a friend, the friend would not deal as a consumer. (Because the person with whom the friend is dealing, the teacher, does not make the contract in the course of a business.) When the retailer bought the television from the manufacturer the retailer did not deal as a consumer (because the retailer made the contract in the course of a business).

A person deals on the other party's written standard terms if the contract made is the same as the contract made by all the other customers of the business. Matters such as the price, and quantity may of course be different. The hire contract printed on pages 282-283 is a standard form contract.

Having decided that a person is either dealing as a consumer or dealing on the other party's written standard terms, the protection given by section 3 is as follows:

a) an exclusion clause cannot protect a party against liability for breach of contract unless this is reasonable; and

b) an exclusion clause cannot protect a party who fails to perform the contract at all, or who performs in a manner different from what was reasonably expected, unless this is reasonable.

Whether or not a person deals as a consumer is also very relevant when an exclusion clause tries to exclude liability for breach of a term implied by the SGA 1979 (or by the SGITA 1979 or by the SGSA 1982). We shall consider why shortly.

Student Activity Questions 2.10

1) Are the following purchasers dealing as consumers?

    a) John, a civil servant, buys a car from Mary, a teacher.

    b) Mary buys a new car from a dealer.

    c) The dealer buys 12 new cars from a car manufacturer.

    d) Jack, a self-employed builder, buys a cement mixer from Bill, a retired builder.

    e) Bill soon regrets having sold his cement mixer. He is bored with retirement and decides to extend his kitchen. He buys a new cement mixer from a builder's merchant, and gets trade discount by pretending that he is still in business.

2) The Unfair Contract Terms Act has not outlawed standard form contracts. Such contracts are very commonly used.

    a) Identify three types of contracts which are usually made by one party agreeing to the other's written standard terms.

    b) Is it only consumers who agree to written standard terms?

Further Activity Questions 2.10

Benjamin, a passenger on a ferry, is injured when the captain of the ferry negligently crashes into a bridge. What would be the effect of the following clauses?

a) A clause in the contract which said that the ferry operator was not to be liable for personal injuries.

b) A clause which said that the operator would not be liable for damage to passenger's luggage.

Sections 6 & 7 - Exclusion of statutory implied terms

Section 6 of the Unfair Contract Terms Act 1977 deals with exclusion of liability for breach of the terms implied by SGA 1979 sections 12-15 and the corresponding terms implied by SGITA 1973 and SGSA 1982. These implied terms were considered earlier in this chapter.

Terms as to the right to sell, right to hire etc.

Sections 6 and 7 UCTA 1977 provide that no term can exclude liability for breach of the implied term as to the right to sell, contained in section 12(1) SGA 1979. Nor can any term exclude liability for breach of the corresponding terms contained in the SGITA 1973 or the SGSA 1982.

The terms implied by sections 13-15 of the Sale of Goods Act 1979 (and the corresponding terms implied by the SGITA 1973 and the SGSA 1982) are treated differently. As regards these terms, the UCTA 1977 makes two rules. First, if the buyer deals as a consumer, none of the statutory implied terms can be excluded by any contract term. Second, if the buyer does not deal as a consumer, the statutory implied terms can be excluded, but only to the extent that the term which does exclude them satisfies the UCTA 1977's requirement of reasonableness.

One further point should be noted. A person who buys at an auction or by tender is never to be regarded as a consumer.

Section 8 Excluding liability for misrepresentations

Section 8 UCTA 1977 provides that no term can restrict liability for misrepresentation unless the term satisfied the requirement of reasonableness.

The position, therefore, is undoubtedly rather complex. The following diagram might make it more easily understood.

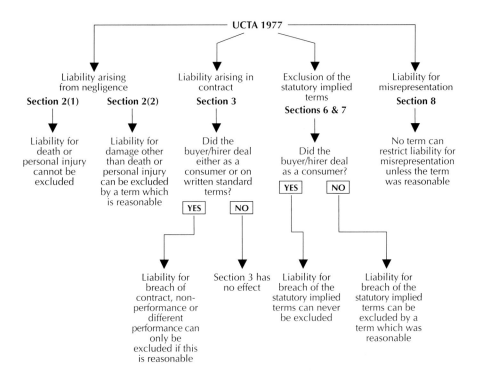

Figure 2.5 The effect of the UCTA 1977

The meaning of reasonableness

Most of the sections of the UCTA 1977 which we have considered do allow an exclusion clause to be effective if the clause satisfies the Act's requirement of reasonableness.

Section 11 says that the requirement is satisfied if:

> 'the term shall have been a fair and reasonable one to be included having regard to the circumstances which were, or ought reasonably to have been, known to or in the contemplation of the parties when the contract was made.'

Schedule 2 of the Act says that if the contract is to sell or supply any type of goods, regard must be had to the following, in deciding whether or not a term was reasonable.

a) The relative strength of the parties bargaining position relative to each other, which will include whether or not the customer could find another supplier.

b) Whether the customer was given any inducement to agree to the term, or could have made a similar contract with a different supplier without agreeing to such a term.

c) Whether the customer knew or ought to have known that the term existed.

d) If the term excludes liability unless some condition is complied with, whether or not it was reasonably practicable to comply with that condition.

e) Whether the goods were manufactured, altered or adapted at the customer's request.

Student Activity Questions 2.11

Assuming in each case that the exclusion clause had been a part of the contract, how would the following cases have been decided under the Unfair Contract terms Act 1977?

a)   *L'Estrange v Graucob* (the cafe owner's vending machine).

b)   *Chapelton v Barry UDC* (the collapsing deck chair).

c)   *Thornton v Shoe Lane Parking* (the multi storey car park).

The Unfair Terms in Consumer Contracts Regulations 1999

These Regulations replace the 1994 Unfair Terms in Consumer Contracts Regulations, which were passed to give effect to an EC directive. The Regulations do not displace the Unfair Contract Terms Act 1977, but will run alongside the 1977 Act.

The Regulations apply only to contracts made between a 'seller' or 'supplier' and a 'consumer'. (Regulation 4(1).) A consumer is defined as a person who does not make the contract in the course of a business, trade or profession. Sellers and suppliers are designed as people who supply goods or services in the course of a business, trade or profession. The Regulations' concept of a consumer is therefore very similar to the UCTA 1977's concept of a consumer. One difference is that a company can act as a consumer under the UCTA 1977 (in very limited circumstances). A company can never be a consumer for the purposes of the Regulations.

Regulation 5(1) provides that:

> 'A contractual term which has not been individually negotiated shall be regarded as unfair if, contrary to the requirement of good faith, it causes a significant imbalance in the parties' rights and obligations arising under the contract, to the detriment of the consumer.'

A term will not have been individually negotiated if the contract was drafted in advance and the consumer had no chance to influence the substance of the term. (Regulation 5(2).) This is obviously a similar concept to the UCTA 1977's concept of written standard terms. It is for the seller or supplier to prove that a term was individually negotiated (Regulation 5(4).) In deciding whether or not the requirement of good faith has been breached the court will consider all relevant matters.

If a term is regarded as unfair, then it is not binding upon the consumer, although the rest of the contact will stand if this is possible without the unfair term. (Regulation 8.)

Regulation 6 states that when deciding whether or not a term was unfair regard should be had to the nature of the goods or services supplied, all the other terms of the contract and to all the surrounding circumstances. Schedule 2 of the Regulations sets out examples of the types of terms which may be regarded as unfair. The list is far too long to be reproduced here, but includes:

> '... irrevocably binding the consumer to terms with which he had no real opportunity to become acquainted before the conclusion of the contract'; 'requiring any consumer who fails to fulfil his obligation to pay a disproportionately high sum in compensation'; and 'obliging the consumer to fulfil all of his obligations where the seller or supplier does not perform his'.

The Regulations can consider the effect of any term in a contract except a 'core' term which was written in plain and intelligible language. A 'core' term sets out the contract price and the main subject matter of the contract. The Regulations are not therefore confined to dealing with exclusion clauses. Potentially, therefore, they could have a very wide effect.

At present it is too early to say how, if at all, the Regulations will increase the protection given by the Unfair Contract Terms Act. The Regulations do not seem to add a great deal of protection. However, the language used in the Regulations is rather broad, as is often the case when Regulations are passed to give effect to an EC directive. The interpretation of this language will be the job of the courts. Until cases are decided, the meaning of the Regulations will not be entirely clear.

In addition to making unfair terms not binding upon consumers, the Regulations also allow the Director General of Fair Trading to apply for an injunction to prevent an unfair term from being used in contracts made with consumers.

Student Activity Questions 2.12

Which of the following would be regarded by the Unfair Terms in Consumer Contracts Regulations 1999 as having been made between a seller or supplier and a consumer?

a) A motor dealer orders 10 new cars from a car manufacturer.

b) John, an accountant, goes to a salon for a haircut.

c) A manufacturing company buys a new car for one of its salesmen.

d) Lucy, a postal worker, fills her car with petrol at a filling station.

e) Janice, who has inherited an extremely valuable painting, sells it to a gallery.

f) Ray, a journalist, sells his old television to his neighbour.

Further Activity Questions 2.12

Assume that in the following cases the exclusion clause had been a term of the contract. If this were the case, how would the cases have been decided under the Unfair Terms in Consumer Contracts Regulations 1999, if these Regulations had been in force at the time of the cases?

(a) *L'Estrange v Graucob.*

(b) *Olley v Marlborough Court Hotel.*

(c) *Thornton v Shoe Lane Parking Ltd.*

(d) *Chapelton v Barry UDC.*

Essential points

The nature of terms

■ The terms of a contract define the obligations which the parties to the contract have undertaken.

■ A breach of contract occurs whenever a term of the contract is breached.

■ Express terms are agreed in words by the parties to the contract.

■ Terms may be implied into a contract by either the court or by a statute.

■ The court will imply a term into a contract on the grounds that the parties must have intended the term to be a part of the contract. The term was so obvious that it did not need to be expressed in words.

■ Terms may also be implied by the court on the grounds that they are customary in a particular trade, customary in a particular locality or customary between the parties.

Terms implied by the Sale of Goods Act 1979

■ The Sale of Goods Act 1979 implies five major terms into contracts of sale of goods. The implied terms are:

• that the seller has the right to sell the goods;

• that the goods correspond to any description by which they were sold;

• that goods sold in the course of a business are of satisfactory quality;

- that goods sold in the course of a business are fit for the buyer's purpose;

- that, where goods are sold by sample, the bulk of the goods correspond with the sample in quality.

■ If a seller of goods does not have the right to sell the goods, the buyer will be entitled to reclaim all of the purchase price (and possibly also damages) on the basis that there has been a total failure of consideration.

■ If goods are sold by description then they must correspond with the description.

■ Specific goods are only sold by description where the description was an important term of the contract on which the buyer relied.

■ The terms requiring goods to be of satisfactory quality and fit for the buyer's purpose apply only where goods are sold in the course of a business.

■ Whenever a business sells goods, the goods are sold in the course of a business.

■ Goods are of satisfactory quality if they meet the standard that a reasonable person would regard as satisfactory, taking account of any description of the goods, the price (if relevant) and all the other relevant circumstances.

■ When deciding whether goods are of satisfactory quality, the following matters are aspects of the quality of the goods in appropriate cases: (a) fitness for all the purposes for which goods of the kind in question are commonly supplied; (b) appearance and finish; (c) freedom from minor defects; (d) safety; and (e) durability.

■ The term as to satisfactory quality is not implied as regards defects specifically pointed out to the buyer before the sale.

■ If the buyer examines the goods before the sale, then the term as to satisfactory quality is not implied as regards defects in the goods which the buyer's examination ought to have revealed. However, the buyer has no obligation to examine the goods.

■ If a buyer expressly or impliedly makes known to a business seller any particular purpose for which the goods are being bought, then there is an implied condition that the goods are reasonably fit for that purpose.

■ The term as to fitness for the buyer's purpose does not apply if either the buyer does not rely on the skill and judgement of the seller, or it was unreasonable for the buyer to rely on the skill and judgement of the seller.

■ Where goods are sold by sample it is implied that the bulk must correspond with the sample in quality; it is also implied that the bulk must be free from hidden defects, which would render the goods unsatisfactory, if these defects would not be discovered on a reasonable examination of the sample.

Terms implied by other statutes

■ Terms which are identical to the Sale of Goods Act implied terms are implied into contracts of hire-purchase by the Supply of Goods (Implied Terms) Act 1973.

■ Terms which are identical to the Sale of Goods Act implied terms are implied into contracts of hire, and into contracts for the transfer of property in goods, by the Supply of Goods and Services Act 1982.

■ A contract is regarded as a contract for the transfer of property in goods if goods are transferred under the contract and the contract is not a sale of goods, or a contract of hire or a contract of hire-purchase.

■ Three terms which have no equivalent in the Sale of Goods Act are implied into contracts to supply a service.

■ In a contract for the supply of a service where the supplier is acting in the course of a business, there is an implied term that the supplier will carry out the service with reasonable care and skill.

■ In a contract for the supply of a service where the supplier is acting in the course of a business it is implied that the service should be supplied within a reasonable time. This term is implied only if the contract did not expressly or impliedly fix a time for completion of the service.

■ If no price for the supply of a service was expressly or impliedly fixed by the contract, it is implied that the customer will pay a reasonable price.

Types of terms

■ A condition is a term which seemed very important when the contract was made. If a condition is breached then the injured party can treat the contract as terminated and claim damages.

■ A warranty is a term which did not seem vitally important when the contract was made. If a warranty is breached the injured party can claim damages but cannot treat the contract as terminated.

■ An innominate term is a broad term which cannot be classified as either a condition or a warranty.

■ Breach of an innominate term will always entitle the injured party to claim damages for breach of contract. The injured party will be entitled to terminate the contract only if the breach deprived him or her of substantially the whole benefit of the contract.

Exclusion clauses

■ Exclusion clauses are clauses which try to exclude or limit one party's liability for breach of contract or for liability arising in tort.

■ An exclusion clause can only exclude liability for breach of contract if it was a term of the contract or if reasonable notice of it was given before the contract was made.

■ The Unfair Contract Terms Act 1977 provides that no contract term can exclude liability for death or personal injury arising from negligence. It also provides that liability for other types of damage arising from negligence, such as damage to goods, can be excluded only if the term excluding liability was reasonable.

■ Where a party deals either as a consumer or on written standard terms, an exclusion clause cannot protect the other contracting party against liability for breach of contract unless this is reasonable.

■ Where a party deals either as a consumer or on written standard terms, an exclusion clause cannot protect another contracting party who fails to perform the contract at all, or who performs in a manner different from what was reasonably expected, unless this is reasonable.

■ Liability for breach of the statutory implied term as to the right to sell (and the equivalent terms as to the right to hire or transfer property in goods) cannot be excluded by any contract term.

■ In consumer deals, liability for breach of the statutory implied terms as to satisfactory quality, fitness for purpose, correspondence with description and correspondence with sample cannot be excluded by any contract term.

■ In non-consumer deals, liability for breach of the statutory implied terms as to satisfactory quality, fitness for purpose, correspondence with description and correspondence with sample can be excluded only by a term which is reasonable.

■ Only a term which is reasonable can restrict or exclude liability for misrepresentation.

■ The Unfair Terms in Consumer Contracts Regulations 1999 apply only to consumer contracts. The Regulations provide that a contractual term which has not been individually negotiated shall be regarded as unfair if, contrary to the requirement of good faith, it causes a significant imbalance in the parties' rights and obligations arising under the contract, to the detriment of the consumer.

End of chapter questions

Question 1

Janice, who owns a garden centre, agreed to buy a second-hand tractor from Gerald, a farmer, for £6,500. Janice also agreed to buy 100 sacks of King Edward seed potatoes from Giles, another farmer. Gerald delivered the tractor to Janice. Eighteen months later the police took the tractor away from Janice, explaining that it had been stolen from Oswald two years ago. Gerald had bought the tractor at an auction and had no idea that it was stolen. At the time when the police took the tractor away it was worth about £2,000 as Janice had used it very extensively. The seed potatoes which Giles delivered were Maris Piper not King Edwards. Janice was not very bothered about this, as she thought that customers were as likely to buy Maris Piper seed potatoes as they were to buy King Edwards. However, the day after the seed potatoes were delivered Janice saw a documentary on the television saying that Maris Piper potatoes had been linked to a certain type of cancer. In the light of the documentary Janice does not think that she will be able to sell any of the seed potatoes. Advise Janice of her legal position as regards both Gerald and Giles.

Question 2

Keith, a market trader, bought 10 portable CD players from CDMaker Ltd. The following day Keith sold 3 of these on his market stall. All 3 customers have returned the CD players which they bought to Keith's stall and demanded a refund. They claim that the CD players do not work properly as they spring open when being played. Keith finds that this is true, but that the problem can easily be fixed by tightening a screw. The customers refuse to accept this repair and are demanding their money back. Advise Keith of his legal position as regards both his customers and CDMaker Ltd.

Question 3

Manufacturer Ltd pay Service Co £2,000 to service their two boilers. After the service has been completed, Manufacturer Ltd find that neither boiler can be used. The problem with the first boiler was caused by Service Co inserting a replacement valve which did not work properly. Service Co could not have discovered in advance that the valve was faulty because it had been bought as new and looked perfectly alright. The problem with the second boiler was caused by an unknown problem. No parts were supplied or changed and Service Co say that they serviced the boiler while adhering strictly to a code of practice which is widely accepted in the boiler servicing trade. Advise Manufacturer Ltd of their legal position as regards the defects in the two boilers.

Question 4

Service Co service a boiler for Buildem Ltd. The contract is made on Service Co's new written standard terms. One term of the contract states that, 'Neither Service Co nor any of its employees can be liable in any way for any loss, injury or damage caused by faulty workmanship.' The Service Co employee who services the boiler forgets to fasten a plate securely. This problem causes the boiler to explode. The explosion badly burns the managing director of Buildem Ltd, completely destroys the boiler and causes extensive damage to Buildem Ltd's factory. Advise Buildem Ltd of their legal position.

Question 5

Satvinder is a keen ballroom dancer and often stays at the Dance Hotel. A prominently displayed notice at the entrance to the Dance Hotel states that, "All hotel guests are warned that the management cannot be held responsible for the loss of items left in hotel rooms." Satvinder leaves her handbag in her room while she goes dancing. When she returns she finds that her handbag has been stolen. A chambermaid opened Satvinder's room but then forgot to lock it. An opportunistic thief then slipped into the room and stole the handbag. Advise Satvinder of her legal position.

Task 2

A friend of yours who is visiting the country from abroad is thinking of setting up a trading company in the UK. Your friend is keen to understand English law as it relates to contractual terms, and has asked you to draft a report explaining the following matters.

(a) How the express terms of a contract come to be included in the contract.

(b) The circumstances in which a court will imply terms into a contract.

(c) The terms which are implied into contracts of sale of goods by the Sale of Goods Act 1979.

(d) Other types of contracts into which statutes imply terms similar to those implied by the Sale of Goods Act 1979.

(e) The terms which are implied into a contract to provide services by the Supply of Goods and Services Act 1982.

(f) The effect of the Unfair Contract Terms Act 1977.

(g) The effect of the Unfair Terms in Consumer Contracts Regulations 1999.

3 Misrepresentation, Mistake, Duress and Illegality

We begin this chapter by considering misrepresentation. A misrepresentation is made when a statement which is not a part of the contract, but which induced the making of the contract, proves to be false. Remedies are available to the party who was induced by the misrepresentation to make the contract. However, as we shall see, these remedies can easily be lost.

Sometimes the the parties make a contract while they are mistaken as to some fundamental fact. Depending upon the nature of the mistake made, we shall see that it is possible for a contract to be rendered void on account of a mistake having been made.

We next consider duress and undue influence. We shall see that if a party was pushed into making a contract in such a way that there was no real consent to the contract being made, the contract can be avoided by the victimised party. Finally, to conclude this chapter, we examine the grounds on which a contract may be void or illegal.

The difference between terms and representations

In Chapter 2 we saw that a contract is made up of terms and that the express terms are inserted into the contract by the parties. The offeror proposes a set of terms in the offer. If the offeree accepts the offer, the proposed terms become the terms of the contract. If any term is breached the injured party will always have a remedy for breach of contract.

Frequently, however, a person is persuaded to make a contract by a statement which is not a part of the contract. Such a statement cannot be a term, it can only be a representation. If this statement turns out to be untrue, the injured party might or might not have a remedy for misrepresentation. But to sue for misrepresentation is not the same as to sue for breach of contract. Not only are the remedies different, but the whole basis of the action is different. It is therefore necessary to distinguish terms and representations.

Written contracts

In written contracts the express terms will be contained in the written document. Statements which are not contained in the written document can only be representations.

Let us consider an example. If a person buys a car from a dealer, the terms of sale are usually spelt out in a standard form contract. When both parties sign this contract they expressly agree to all of its terms. If any of the terms are breached, then the injured party will always have a remedy for breach of contract.

But if a customer was persuaded to sign the standard form contract because the dealer made an untrue statement (perhaps saying that all the cars would be going up in price the following week, when this was not true) then the dealer has not breached a term, but has only made an untrue representation. As no term has been breached the customer will not be able to sue for breach of contract. The customer might however have a remedy for misrepresentation.

Similarly, it might have been the customer who made an untrue statement which caused the dealer to make the contract. A customer who pays with a cheque impliedly makes the statement that the cheque will be honoured. If this implied statement was untrue, because the cheque was stolen and would be dishonoured, the customer would not be breaching a term of the contract. The customer would however be making an untrue representation, and the dealer might have a remedy for misrepresentation.

So when both parties have signed a written contract, there is not too much difficulty in telling a term from a representation. Statements included in the written contract will be terms, statements not included can only be representations.

Oral contracts

Where a contract is made orally it is much harder to tell a term from a representation. It is still the case that a term is a part of the contract and a representation is not. But it can be much harder to tell exactly which statements were included in the contract.

By way of example, let us assume that a farmer, Giles, orally offered to sell his combine harvester to John for £1,000. John accepted, because shortly before the sale Giles said that the harvester had recently had a new engine fitted. After the contract was made John discovered that the harvester had not had a new engine fitted. Was Giles' statement about the new engine a term of the contract, or only a representation?

The courts decide questions such as this by looking at the opinion of the reasonable person. It asks whether the reasonable person would have thought that the parties intended the statement to be a term or a representation.

This *objective test* is necessary because once again there is no point in looking for the opinions of the parties themselves. If the court asks Giles whether he thought that the statement about the new engine was a term or a representation, Giles is likely to say that he thought it was just a representation. If the court asks John, he is likely to say that he thought it was a term.

Over the years the courts have devised various tests to decide what the reasonable person would have thought.

Strong statements are likely to be terms

The stronger the statement made the more likely it is to be a term.

Schawel v Reade [1913]

The claimant was considering buying a horse to be used for stud purposes. The defendant said, 'You need not look for anything; the horse is perfectly sound. If there was anything the matter with the horse I would tell you.' Three weeks later the claimant bought the horse, which turned out to be utterly useless for stud purposes.

Held *The defendant's statement was a term. It was so strong that it was the basis on which the offer and acceptance were made.*

The weaker the statement the more likely it is to be a representation.

Ecay v Godfrey [1947]

The claimant bought a boat, the Tio Pepe, for £750. Before selling the boat, the defendant said that the boat was sound and capable of going overseas. However, he also advised the claimant to have it surveyed before making the purchase. The claimant bought the boat, without having it surveyed, and soon discovered that it was not at all sound.

Held *The statement that the boat was sound was only a representation. It was not a part of the contract because it was a very guarded statement.*

The reliance shown to be placed upon the statement

If one of the parties *demonstrates* that the statement is considered to be vitally important then the statement is likely to be a term.

Bannerman v White [1861]

The claimant, a merchant who traded in hops, sent around a circular to all the hop farmers with whom he dealt. The circular said that the claimant would no longer buy hops which had been treated with sulphur, because the Burton on Trent brewers would not use them. When later buying a consignment of hops from the defendant the claimant asked if they had been treated with sulphur, adding that if they had he would not buy them at any price. The defendant said that they had not been treated with sulphur, but in fact they had.

Held *The defendant's statement was a term. The claimant had demonstrated that he considered the statement to be vitally important.*

The relative knowledge of the parties

A party who has more knowledge about the subject matter of the contract is likely to make terms. A party with less knowledge is likely to make representations. For example, in *Oscar Chess v Williams [1957]* a customer traded in a car to a car dealer, saying that the car was a 1948 model. In fact, the car was a 1939 model. The customer did not know this because the car's documents said that it was a 1948 model. The customer's statement was only a representation because the dealer was as well placed as the customer to know the true age of the car. By contrast, in *Dick Bentley (Productions) Ltd v Harold Smith (Motors) Ltd [1965]* a motor dealer sold a car to the claimant, saying that the car had only done 20,000 miles since having a new engine fitted. In fact the car had done 100,000 miles. The dealer's statement was a term. The dealer, with his greater knowledge of cars, had much more chance of knowing that the statement was untrue than the claimant had.

The tests we have considered are useful for distinguishing between terms and representations, but it must be remembered that they are only factors to be considered, along with all the rest of the evidence. The real test is the intentions of the parties.

Statements of opinion

Mere opinions cannot be either terms or representations. But if a party who has vastly superior knowledge makes an opinion which the other party relies on, then there may well be an implied term that this opinion was made with reasonable care and skill.

Esso Petroleum Co Ltd v Mardon [1976]

Esso's representative persuaded the claimant to take on a filling station by telling him that the station would sell 200,000 gallons of petrol a year within three years. The claimant doubted this figure but was persuaded to believe it because the Esso representative was very experienced in giving such estimates. After the contract was made it became apparent that no matter how well the station was managed it would never achieve anything like this figure.

Held *The statement about the 200,000 gallons was just an opinion, and could not therefore be either a term or a misrepresentation. But a term was implied that the opinion had been made using reasonable care and skill. As this term had been breached, the claimant was entitled to damages for breach of contract.*

Student Activity Questions 3.1

1) If a written contract is signed by both parties:

   a) Will the statements contained in the contract be terms or representations?

   b) Will oral statements which persuade a party to sign the contract be terms or representations?

2) In oral contracts:

   a) Are very strong statements likely to be terms or representations?

   b) Are statements made by the party with greater knowledge about the subject matter of the contract likely to be terms or representations?

   c) What will be the effect of one of the parties demonstrating that a certain statement was regarded as particularly important?

How a representation becomes a misrepresentation

See Figure 3.1.

A breached term always gives the injured party the right to a remedy for breach of contract. An untrue representation will lead to a remedy if it amounts to an actionable misrepresentation. If, however, the representation does not fit within the definition of a misrepresentation then it will be a mere representation and no remedy will be available.

Definition of a misrepresentation

An actionable misrepresentation is *an untrue statement of fact which induced the other party to make the contract.*

The statement must be one of fact

Statements of mere opinion are not capable of being misrepresentations.

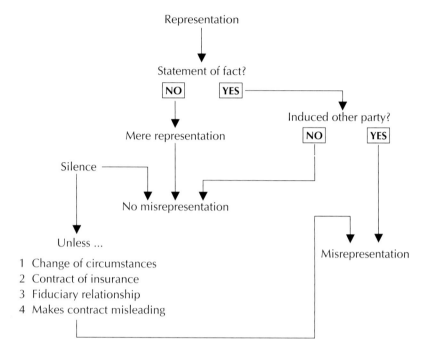

Figure 3.1   How a representation becomes a misrepresentation

Bisset v Wilkinson [1927]

The claimant bought a farm because the defendant told him that the farm would support 2,000 sheep. The claimant knew that the farm had never before been used for sheep farming. In fact the farm, no matter how well managed, could not support anything like 2,000 sheep.

Held *The statement was just an opinion and could not therefore amount to a misrepresentation.*

However, some statements of opinion imply statements of fact, as the following case shows.

Smith v Land and House Property Corporation [1884]

The claimants offered their hotel for sale, stating that it was occupied by 'Mr Frederick Fleck (a most desirable tenant)'. Before the sale went through Mr Fleck became bankrupt. The defendants discovered that for some time Mr Fleck had been badly in arrears with his rent. They refused to go ahead with the purchase of the hotel, claiming that the statement that Mr Fleck was a most desirable tenant amounted to a misrepresentation.

Held The statement was a misrepresentation. It sounded like a mere statement of opinion, but it implied facts, (such as the fact that the tenant paid the rent,) which justified the opinion.

Bowen LJ:

> '..if the facts are not equally known to both sides, then a statement of opinion by the one who knows the facts best involves very often a statement of a material fact, for he impliedly states that he knows facts which justify his opinion.'

The statement must induce the other party to make the contract

A statement can only amount to a misrepresentation if it was one of the reasons why the claimant made the contract. If a person makes a contract without checking the truth of a statement made, this suggests that the statement did induce the making of the contract.

Redgrave v Hurd [1881]

The claimant, a solicitor, advertised for a partner who would also buy the solicitor's house. The defendant answered the advertisement and was told that the practice made about £300 p.a. The claimant produced papers which he said would prove that his statement about the value of the practice was true, but the defendant did not read the papers. If he had done so he would have discovered that the practice was worthless. When the defendant did discover that the practice was worthless he refused to go ahead with the purchase.

Held The claimant's statement about the value of the practice was a misrepresentation. It could therefore be used as a defence for not going ahead with the contract. The fact that the defendant did not check the papers showed that the claimant's statement did induce the defendant to make the contract.

A person who checks the truth of a statement cannot later say that the statement induced the making a contract.

Attwood v Small [1838]

The claimant bought a mine because the defendant greatly exaggerated the capacity of the mine. Before buying the mine the claimant got his own experts to check the defendant's statement. The experts mistakenly agreed that the defendant's statement was true.

Held The statement about the mine's capacity was not a misrepresentation because the claimant did not rely on it. By appointing his own experts to check the statement, the claimant proved that he did not rely on it.

Silence as a misrepresentation

Generally silence cannot be a misrepresentation. The old rule caveat emptor (let the buyer beware) applies.

Fletcher v Krell [1873]

The claimant applied for a job as a governess without revealing that she was divorced. She would have been well aware that she stood no chance of getting the job if her secret had been discovered. The employer did not ask the claimant whether she was divorced, so she did not reveal that she was. The claimant was given a three year fixed term contract to work in Buenos Aires at a salary of £100 a year.

Held *The claimant's silence did not amount to a misrepresentation. She was therefore entitled to sue for breach of contract. (The employer had argued that the claimant had made a misrepresentation, and that this gave him a defence to being sued for breach of contract.)*

There are however four exceptions to the general rule. Silence will amount to a misrepresentation in the following circumstances.

a) If there has been a change of circumstances.

b) In contracts of insurance.

c) If there is a fiduciary relationship between the parties.

d) If the silence makes another statement misleading.

These exceptions need to be examined individually.

A change of circumstances

If a person makes a statement which is true, but due to a change of circumstances the statement becomes untrue before the contract is made, then it may be a misrepresentation not to reveal that the circumstances have changed.

With v O'Flanagan [1936]

A doctor who was selling his practice said that it had a turnover of £2,000 a year. This was true, but when the sale went ahead three months later the practice was virtually worthless because the doctor had been ill.

Held *The doctor's failure to reveal the change was a misrepresentation.*

Contracts of insurance

Contracts of insurance are contracts *uberrimae fidei* (of the utmost good faith.) In such contracts everything which could affect the price of the premium is a *material fact*. A person taking out insurance must reveal all material facts, whether asked about the matter or not.

Lambert v Co-op Insurance Society Ltd [1975]

The claimant insured her own and her husband's jewellery. She did not mention that her husband had been convicted of a small theft some years earlier. When the claimant renewed the policy she did not reveal that her husband had recently been sent to prison for 15 months for theft. The insurance company did not ask about convictions so the claimant felt no need to mention them. Over £300 worth of the insured jewellery was later stolen, and the claimant claimed on her insurance.

Held *The insurance company did not need to pay on the policy. The convictions were a material fact and the claimant should have revealed them. Not to do so amounted to a misrepresentation.*

Where there is a fiduciary relationship between the parties

A fiduciary relationship is a relationship of great trust. When the parties in such a relationship make a contract with each other, everything must be revealed. If this is not done, the silence will amount to a misrepresentation. Business examples of such fiduciary relationships include the relationships between partners, and the relationship between the promoters of a company and the company itself.

Silence makes a statement misleading

Even a statement which is literally true can amount to a misrepresentation if the statement conveys a misleading impression.

Nottingham Patent Brick and Tile Co v Butler [1886]

The defendant's solicitor, who was selling land on behalf of the defendant, was asked whether there were any restrictive covenants attached to the land. (The buyer would generally not want restrictive covenants. If there were any, they would be included in documents which the solicitor should have read.) The solicitor replied that he was not aware of any restrictive covenants. This was true, but the reason why the solicitor was not aware of any was that he had not read the documents which he should have read. The claimant agreed to buy the land but pulled out of the contract when he discovered that there were restrictive covenants.

Held *The solicitor's statement, although literally true, was a misrepresentation. Therefore the claimant was entitled to withdraw from the contract.*

Student Activity Questions 3.2

1) Can a statement of opinion be a misrepresentation?

2) Will an untrue statement of fact be a misrepresentation if it did not induce the other party to make the contract?

3) David goes for a job as a private security guard and does not reveal that he has several previous convictions for armed robbery. The security firm do not ask about previous convictions and so David, scarcely able to believe his luck, does not reveal his convictions. David gets the job. Has he made a misrepresentation?

Remedies for misrepresentation

There are three types of actionable misrepresentation. Each type gives rise to different remedies.

Types of actionable misrepresentation and their remedies

	Type of misrepresentation		
	Fraudulent	Negligent	Wholly innocent
Definition	Made: 1 knowing it was false, or 2 without belief, or 3 recklessly carelessly	Made: honestly but *un*reasonably	Made: honestly *and* reasonably
Remedies	Rescind + damages for tort of deceit (Time does not run until misrep discovered)	Rescind + damages for tort of deceit (Time runs from date of contract)	Rescind Usually no damages (Time runs from date of contract)
	RESCISSION Contract is affirmed ◄─── lost if ───► Subject matter no longer exists ↓ Third party has rights		

Figure 3.2 Types of misrepresentations and their remedies

Fraudulent misrepresentation

Fraudulent misrepresentation was defined by *Derry v Peek [1889]* , as a misrepresentation made either:

i) knowing that it was untrue; or

ii) not believing that it was true; or

iii) recklessly, not caring whether it was true or false.

A fraudulent misrepresentation allows the injured party to *rescind the contract* (call it off) and sue for *damages for the tort of deceit*. If the contract is to be rescinded this must be done within a reasonable time of the innocent party becoming aware of the misrepresentation. Damages for the tort of deceit are usually much greater than contract damages as a claim can be made for all expenses and losses caused by the deceit, even if these were not reasonably foreseeable.

Negligent misrepresentation

Section 2(1) of the Misrepresentation Act 1967 defines a negligent misrepresentation as one made honestly believing that it was true, but without reasonable grounds for such a belief.

A negligent misrepresentation allows the injured party to *rescind the contract* and to sue for *damages for the tort of deceit*. If the contract is to be rescinded this must be done within a reasonable time of the misrepresentation having been made.

Wholly innocent misrepresentation

A wholly innocent misrepresentation is one made honestly believing that it was true, with reasonable grounds for such a belief. The injured party *can rescind* but has *no right to claim damages*. However, as regards both negligent and innocent misrepresentation section 2(2) of the Misrepresentation Act 1967 allows the court to award contract damages instead of rescission where the court considers it 'equitable to do so.' It is rare for the courts to use this section to award damages for an innocent misrepresentation, but they sometimes do so when the misrepresentation was so trivial that rescission would be too drastic a remedy.

Losing the right to rescind

All three types of misrepresentation give the injured party the right to rescind. To some extent rescission is a self-help remedy. A party can rescind merely by letting the other party know that the contract is no longer regarded as binding. Rescission can also be used as a defence when sued for refusing to perform the contract, as we saw in *Redgrave v Hurd*.

The right to rescind can be lost in the following three ways.

a) If the contract is affirmed.

b) If a third party acquires rights.

c) If the subject matter of the contract no longer exists.

The contract is affirmed

The contract will be affirmed if the claimant decides to carry on with the contract after discovering the misrepresentation. The claimant might make such agreement expressly or impliedly. If the claimant does nothing for a considerable period of time the court might well take the view that the contract has been impliedly affirmed.

Leaf v International Galleries [1950]

The claimant bought a painting from International Galleries because of a non-fraudulent misrepresentation that the painting was by Constable. Five years later the claimant discovered that the painting was not by Constable and he immediately applied to the court for rescission of the contract.

Held *The claimant was too late to rescind. He had affirmed the contract by doing nothing for five years. (If the misrepresentation by the gallery had been **fraudulent**, time would only have started to run against the claimant from the moment when the misrepresentation was discovered. He would therefore have been able to rescind the contract.)*

A third party has acquired rights

A contract which can be rescinded is said to be a *voidable* contract, because one of the parties has the option *to avoid* the contract (call it off). Although a misrepresentation makes a contract voidable, it does not prevent ownership of goods sold under the contract from passing to a person who made the misrepresentation. In such a case the person making the misrepresentation will own the goods unless and until the innocent party avoids the contract. The innocent party has no obligation to avoid and may choose to affirm the contract, despite the misrepresentation, and keep what was gained under the contract.

It follows that if the misrepresentor sells the goods on to a third party *before* the contract is avoided, then the third party can keep the goods forever. This is because at the time when the goods were sold on the misrepresentor still owned the goods, and therefore still had ownership to pass on. This rule is confirmed by section 23 of the Sale of Goods Act 1979, which provides that:

> *'Where the seller of goods has a voidable title to them, but his title has not been avoided at the time of the sale, the buyer acquires a good title to the goods, provided he buys them in good faith and without notice of the seller's defect of title.'*

If however the goods are sold to the innocent third party after the contract has been avoided, then the innocent third party will get no ownership of the goods. This is because when the goods were sold on the misrepresentor no longer had any ownership to pass on, the contract having been avoided.

Cases on this matter amount to a dispute about who did what first.

Lewis v Averay [1972]

A rogue bought the claimant's car. The rogue paid with a bad cheque, pretending to be a famous actor called Richard Greene. (The rogue therefore made a fraudulent misrepresentation.) At first, the claimant was unwilling to take the rogue's cheque. However, the claimant did take the cheque when the rogue produced a Pinewood Studios pass in the name of Richard Greene, which showed the rogue's photograph. Having got possession of the car, the rogue sold it to the defendant. The defendant paid a reasonable price for the car and believed that the rogue owned it.

Held *Although the contract was voidable for fraudulent misrepresentation, the defendant gained complete ownership of it by virtue of section 23 SGA 1979. Once the car had been resold by the rogue, the claimant was too late to avoid the contract and had lost ownership of the car.*

Car and Universal Finance Co v Caldwell [1965]

A rogue bought a car with a bad cheque. The rogue sold the car to a third party who bought it in good faith. Before this second sale the original seller found out about the rogue's misrepresentation. He could not find the rogue to tell him that he was avoiding the contract, so he told the police and the AA.

Held *Telling the police and the AA. was enough to avoid the contract because it was an action which showed a definite intention to avoid the contract. The original seller therefore got the car back from the third party. If the original seller had not told the police and the AA until after the rogue had resold the car section 23 of the Sale of Goods Act 1979 would have applied, and he would never have got the car back.*

In all of these cases where a rogue buys goods with a stolen cheque one of two innocent parties is bound to suffer a loss. Either the original owner will get the goods back, in which case the third party will have paid money to the rogue in return for nothing at all, or the original owner will not get the goods back, and will therefore have been deprived of ownership of the goods in return for a worthless cheque. (It should be noticed that section 23 SGA 1979 will never operate in favour of a third party who did not buy from the misrepresentor while acting in good faith.)

Whichever of the two parties suffers the loss will be left with the right to sue the rogue for damages. However, it should be pointed out that this right is likely to be worth very little. First, the rogue might never be identified. Second, rogues who buy goods with bad cheques rarely have enough money to pay damages.

is impossible to put the parties back into their pre-contract positions

When a contract is treated as terminated for breach of a term, future performance of the contract is not required. This is the case whether or not the contract has been partly performed. However, when a contract is avoided the parties must be put back into the positions they were in before the contract was made. If this cannot be done then the contract cannot be avoided. In *Clarke v Dickson (1858)* Crompton J gave the example of a butcher who bought live cattle because a farmer had made a fraudulent misrepresentation about them. He said that once the cattle had been slaughtered and butchered rescission would not be possible. (However, tort damages could have been claimed.)

Student Activity Questions 3.3

Martha bought a cafe because the previous owner said that it had a turnover of £120,000 a year. After the first month Martha's turnover is only £5,000. The written contract made no mention of turnover.

a)   Is the statement about turnover a term of the contract?

b)   Has a misrepresentation been made? If so, what remedies would be available to Martha? In practical terms what would you advise her to do?

Mistake

When the parties make their contract, one or both of them might be mistaken as to some fundamental matter. Here we examine the types of mistake which may be made and the effect of these mistakes upon the validity of the contract. First, we consider the position where both parties make the same mistake. (This is known as common mistake.) Then we consider the position where only one of the parties makes a mistake. (This is known as unilateral mistake.)

Common mistake

There is said to be a common mistake when both of the parties freely reach agreement but do so while making the same mistake. A common mistake might be made about the *existence of the subject matter* of the contract. For example, let us assume that X Ltd agrees to buy a machine from Y Ltd. Let us also assume that at the time of the contract, unknown to both parties, the machine does not exist because it has been destroyed in a fire. Section 6 of the Sale of Goods Act provides that where there is a contract for the sale of specific goods, and the goods without the knowledge of the seller have perished at the time the contract is made, the contract is void. Y Ltd will not therefore be in breach of contract for failure to deliver the machine and X Ltd will not have to pay the contract price. If the contract had been for the sale of unascertained goods, such as 100 tons of wheat, then Y Ltd would have to find another 100 tons of wheat from elsewhere or be in breach of contract.

It is very important to note here that if specific goods which are sold cease to exist *after* the contract has been made, but before the goods have been delivered to the buyer, the contract will not be void for mistake. Generally, the buyer will have received ownership of the goods as soon as the contract was made and will therefore have to pay for the goods. If goods which have been *hired* cease to exist after the contract was made but before the hirer took possession of them the contract may well be frustrated, a matter considered in the following chapter.

A common mistake as to the *ownership of goods* will not generally make the contract void. In Chapter 2 we saw that section 12(1) of the Sale of Goods Act 1979 implies a term that the seller of goods owns the goods. A seller who does not own the goods sold will be in breach of contract, as we saw in *Rowland v Divall.*

A common mistake as to the *quality* of goods sold will not make the contract void. In *Bell v Lever Bros [1932]* Lord Atkin said:

> 'A buys B's horse; he thinks the horse is sound and he pays the price of a sound horse; he would certainly not have bought the horse if he had known, as the fact is, that the horse is unsound. If B has made no representation as to soundness and has not contracted that the horse is sound, A is bound and cannot recover back the price. A buys a picture from B; both A and B believe it to be the work of an old master, and a high price is paid. It turns out to be a modern copy. A has no remedy in the absence of a representation or warranty.'

Unilateral mistake

If the parties to the contract were at cross purposes when making the offer and acceptance there may have been no real agreement. If the reasonable person could not objectively say which of the party's views was obviously correct then there will be no contract. If the reasonable person could say that the views of one or other of the parties was obviously correct then there will be a valid contract.

Raffles v Wichelhaus [1864]

A contract was made to buy cotton as soon as it arrived on a ship called Peerless which was sailing from Bombay. In fact, two ships called Peerless were sailing from Bombay. When the contract was made the defendant was thinking of a ship called Peerless which set off in October. But the claimant was thinking of a different ship which set off in December.

Held *There was no contract because the reasonable person could not say what had been agreed. However, if the reasonable person could have said that one or other of the ships was obviously what the parties seemed to have intended then there would have been a contract to buy the cotton which arrived on that ship. (This might have happened, for instance, if one of the ships was a world famous carrier of cotton from India, while the other was an unknown ship.)*

If one of the parties knows that the other made the contract while making a fundamental mistake as to *the terms of the contract* then the contract can be void for mistake. In *Hartog v Colin & Shields [1939]*, for example, sellers of a large quantity of animal skins made a slip of the pen and offered to sell them at one third of their usual price. The buyer accepted, knowing that a mistake had been made. The contract was void for mistake because the buyers knew that the sellers had made a mistake about the terms of their offer. However, if one party knows that the other is making a fundamental mistake about the *quality of what is being sold* then the contract will not be void for mistake. For example, in *Smith v Hughes [1871]* a seller of oats showed a potential buyer a sample of the oats. The buyer thought that the oats were old oats and so he bought them. In fact they were new oats which were no use to him at all. It was held that even if the seller knew of the buyer's mistake the contract was not void for mistake. This situation differs from the examples given by Lord Atkin in *Bell v Lever Bros* because in those examples both parties were mistaken as to the quality of what was being sold. However, the outcome is the same. The contract is not void for mistake.

Mistake as to the identity of the other contracting party

This is the most important type of unilateral mistake and needs to be considered in a little more detail. Most of the cases concern a rogue who buys goods while pretending to be someone else and who pays for the goods with a bad cheque. We have already seen that a rogue who pays with a bad cheque commits a fraudulent misrepresentation which makes the contract voidable. So if the person who sells to the rogue avoids the contract in time there will be no need to argue mistake. It is when the person who sells to the rogue does not avoid in time that it becomes necessary to argue that the contract is void for mistake. If this argument is successful the person who sells to the rogue will always get the goods back because a void contract is no contract at all. No ownership of the goods ever passes to the rogue under a void contract, or to anyone else to whom the rogue sells the goods.

Whether or not a mistake as to the identity of the other contracting party will make a contract void depends upon several factors. First, it is necessary that the parties did not meet face to face when making the contract. If the parties did meet face to face then the contract will not be void for mistake. In *Lewis v Averay*, which we considered earlier in this chapter, the claimant argued that the contract was void for mistake. (If this argument had been successful the claimant would have got the car back.) The Court of Appeal rejected this argument. If the parties meet face to face then the contract will not be void for mistake.

If the parties did not meet face to face then it is possible that the contract will be void for mistake. However, this will only be the case where the innocent contracting party was mistaken as to the *identity* of the rogue. If the innocent contracting party was mistaken only as to the rogue's *attributes* then the contract will not be void for mistake. (Attributes are concerned with a person's qualities or distinguishing features. For example, one of the attributes of Darren Gough, the cricketer, is that he is a very good fast bowler. This is not the same as his identity. There are other very good fast bowlers.) The following two cases show the difference between being mistaken as to identity and being mistaken as to attributes.

Cundy v Lindsay [1878]

A rogue ordered a very large quantity of handkerchiefs from the claimants. The rogue pretended to be a reputable firm with whom the claimants had previously dealt. This firm was called Blenkiron & Co of 123 Wood Street, London. The rogue, who was called Blenkarn, disguised his signature to look like Blenkiron & Co, giving his address as 37 Wood St, where he had hired a room. The trick worked and the claimants sent the handkerchiefs to Blenkiron & Co at 37 Wood Street. The rogue sold 250 dozen of these handkerchiefs to the defendant who bought them in good faith. The claimants sued the defendant to get these handkerchiefs back.

Held *The contract was void for mistake because the claimants were mistaken as to the identity of the person with whom they made the contract. Therefore ownership of the handkerchiefs never moved away from the claimants.*

Comment *The contract was of course voidable for fraudulent misrepresentation, but the claimants had not avoided it in time. They were therefore defeated by section 23 of the Sale of Goods Act 1979, as explained above.*

Kings Norton Metal Co Ltd v Edridge, Merrett & Co Ltd [1897]

A rogue ordered goods from the claimants, who were metal manufacturers. The rogue was called Wallis, but he made the letter appear to come from Hallam & Co, Sheffield. No such company ever existed. However, the claimants sent the goods because the rogue's letter was printed on very impressive notepaper. The rogue sold the goods on to the defendants, who bought them in good faith. The claimants sued the defendants to get the goods back.

Held *The contract was not void for mistake and so the claimants were not entitled to the goods. The claimants were not mistaken about the identity of the person they were dealing with. (Unlike the claimants in* Cundy v Lindsay, *the claimants in this case had no prior knowledge of the person with whom they thought they were dealing.) They were only mistaken about the attributes of that person. They thought that they were dealing with someone who was creditworthy and respectable, whereas in fact they were not.*

Comment

i   The contract was voidable for fraudulent misrepresentation but the claimants were defeated by section 23 of the Sale of Goods Act 1979.

ii   Section 23 of the Sale of Goods Act 1979 only protects a person who buys the goods in good faith. If the defendants had known that the goods did not belong to the rogue or should have known this (perhaps the price was too cheap) then section 23 would offer no protection to them. In such a case the claimants would get the return of the goods. (iii) The rogue could have been sued for damages for the tort of deceit. However, this rogue (like most other rogues) would not have had enough money to pay any damages.

The final requirement for a contract to be void on account of a unilateral mistake as to the person is that the mistake must have been a material mistake, that is to say it must have been a mistake which would have mattered to the claimant. For example, in *Mackie v European Assurance Society [1869]* the claimant asked a friend to insure him. The claimant thought that the policy would be taken out with one particular insurance company but in fact it was taken out with another. When the claimant claimed on his insurance policy the insurers refused to pay, arguing mistake as to the person. The contract was not void for mistake. It was true that the parties did not meet face to face and that the claimant was mistaken about the identity of the other contracting party. But the contract was not void for mistake because the claimant would not have been bothered which of the two insurance companies made the contract of insurance.

Mistake as to the nature of what is being signed

If a person signs a document while making a complete mistake as to what type of document is being signed then the contract can be void for a type of mistake knows as non est factum (it is not my deed).

Saunders v Anglia Building Society [1970]

An elderly woman intended to leave her house to her nephew after her death. The nephew owed money to one Lee. To pay Lee off the nephew visited the elderly aunt with Lee, who asked the elderly woman to sign a document. Lee told her that this gave the house to the nephew but that she would be allowed to live there for the rest of her life. In fact, the document said that Lee had bought the house and paid for it. The elderly woman did not read the document because her glasses were broken. Lee mortgaged the house to the Anglia Building Society but did not pay any of the mortgage instalments. The building society applied to repossess the house.

Held *The contract was not void for non est factum because there was not a fundamental difference between what the elderly woman signed and what she thought she was signing. (Either way she was transferring her ownership of the house.) Therefore the contract was valid and the building society could repossess the house.*

Non est factum cannot be claimed by a person who was careless in signing. In *United Dominions Trust Ltd v Western [1975]* the Court of Appeal therefore held that it was not available to a person who signed a blank document for the figures to be filled in later.

Foster v Mackinnon [1869] provides a rare example of a successful plea of non est factum. An old man with very poor eyesight signed a document which he was told was a guarantee. In fact the document was a cheque. Non est factum applied and the old man was not liable on the cheque.

Student Activity Questions 3.4

1) A seller sells goods which, unknown to either the buyer or the seller, have ceased to exist before the contract was made. What is the legal position?

2) An antique dealer buys a vase for £1,000. Both the dealer and the seller believe that the vase is from the Ming period and worth about £1,000. In fact the vase is a worthless fake. The seller did not make a term or a representation that the vase was genuine. Has the dealer any remedy?

3) In what circumstances will a mistake as to the person make a contract void?

4) In what circumstances can a contract be void for non est factum?

Duress and Undue Influence

Traditionally a contract was voidable for duress only if one of the parties was forced into making it by the threat of illegal physical violence. This common law doctrine was so narrow as to be virtually useless. A person who makes a contract because of such threats is unlikely to then go to court to avoid the contract.

More recently, a doctrine of economic duress has developed. A threat of physical violence is no longer necessary. Now a party who was pushed into a contract in such a way that there was no real consent to the contract can avoid the contract. For example, in *The Universe Sentinel [1982]* shipowners were told that if they did not agree to pay money to a seaman's charity a trade union would not allow their ship to leave port. The shipowners agreed to the union's demands and their ship was allowed to sail away. The ship owners were entitled to recover the money paid to the charity on the grounds of economic duress. They had not freely agreed to pay this money, they were pushed into the contract in such a way that they did not really consent. The following case provides another example.

Atlas Express v Kafco Ltd [1989]

The defendants, a small company, agreed that the claimants would carry their products to Woolworths shops throughout the country. The price of carriage was agreed at £1.10 a carton. The first load only contained 200 cartons, not the 500 or so which the claimants had estimated. The claimants said that they would not carry any of the defendant's goods unless they were guaranteed 400 cartons a load. The defendants could not find another carrier and so they had to agree to this or they would have lost their contract with Woolworths, which was vital to them. After the cartons had been carried the defendants refused to pay the extra amount.

Held *The defendants did not need to pay. The contract was voidable on the grounds of economic duress.*

Over the years a doctrine of undue influence was developed by the courts of equity, which considered duress to be too narrow a doctrine. In certain relationships undue influence by the dominant party is presumed. A contract made between people in such a relationship will therefore be voidable, if undue influence is alleged, unless the party against whom it is presumed can show that there was in fact no undue influence. The relationships in which undue influence is presumed are as follows: doctor and patient; solicitor and client; parent and child; guardian and ward; trustee and beneficiary; and religious advisor and disciple. Even outside these relationships undue influence may be presumed where one of the parties placed great trust and confidence in the other.

Lloyds Bank v Bundy [1975]

An elderly farmer made increasingly large mortgages of his farm in order to guarantee a business which his son had started. The farmer was visited at the farm by the assistant manager of the branch of the bank where he and his son had their accounts. In December 1969 the farmer mortgaged the farm very heavily because he was told that if he did not his son's business would fail. The son's business failed anyway. When the farmer could not repay the mortgage the bank applied to repossess the farm.

Held *The mortgage taken out in December 1969 was voidable for undue influence. Therefore the bank could not repossess the farm on account of the farmer having not repaid the mortgage instalments. The farmer had grown to trust the assistant manager and placed total reliance on him. The bank should have advised the farmer to get independent legal advice before agreeing to the mortgage.*

Where there is no presumed undue influence the party alleging undue influence must prove that the contract was made because of actual pressure from the other party. I

Williams v Bayley [1866], for example, a colliery owner was allowed to have an agreement to mortgage his colliery set aside. He had only made the agreement because the other party had told him that if he did not his son would be prosecuted for fraud and transported to Australia for life. As the common law has extended the doctrine of economic duress, this type of undue influence has become much less important.

Illegal contracts

The following types of contracts are illegal at common law and therefore unenforceable.

a) Contracts to promote corruption in public life.

b) Contracts to impede the administration of justice.

c) Contracts to trade with enemy nations in time of war.

d) Contracts to commit a crime, tort or fraud.

e) Contracts tending to promote sexual immorality.

f) Contracts to defraud the Revenue.

Where a contract is unenforceable, neither side can enforce it to any extent. For example in *Miller v Karlinski [1945]* a contract was made to defraud the Revenue. The claimant sued for 10 weeks wages and £21 travelling expenses. Of the travelling expenses, £17 should have been paid as wages. The claimant and the employer agreed to say they were travelling expenses to avoid paying income tax on the £17. The Court of Appeal held that the whole agreement was unenforceable. Therefore the claimant could not recover anything, not even the proper wages or the £4 genuine travelling expenses.

Many statutes also make certain types of contracts illegal. The contracts concerned are so numerous that it is beyond the scope of this book to attempt to list them.

Contracts which contravene public policy

A contract which contravenes public policy will be void. The most important types of such contracts are contracts to exclude the jurisdiction of the courts (which we considered in Chapter 2) and contracts in restraint of trade. Contracts in restraint of trade attempt to prevent a person from working or carrying on a business. Such contracts are void unless they can be proved to be reasonable. They tend to arise where a person who sells a business agrees not to compete with the new owner. When considering whether such agreements in restraint of trade are reasonable or not the court will consider the length of time for which the agreement was to last, the extent of the area in which competition was prohibited and the type of competition which was prohibited. Contracts in restraint of trade are also found where an employee agrees not to compete with the employer's line of business after leaving the employment. A contract in restraint of trade which attempts to prevent an ex-employee from working for another employer can only be valid if it was necessary to protect trade secrets, trade connections or confidential information.

Student Activity Questions 3.5

1) In what circumstances will a contract be voidable for economic duress?

2) In what circumstances will undue influence be presumed? What is the effect of such a presumption?

3) On what grounds can a contract be illegal at common law?

4) What is a contract in restraint of trade? In what circumstances will such a contract be void?

Essential points

Terms and representations distinguished

- A term is part of a contract and if a term is breached this is breach of contract.

- A representation is a statement which persuaded another person to make a contract.

- If a representation is untrue this does not amount to breach of contract.

- A court discovers whether or not a statement is a term or a representation by asking whether a reasonable person would have thought that the parties intended the statement to be a term or a representation.

- When a contract is written, statements which are not included in the written contract will be representations rather than terms of the contract. Statements which are included in the written contract will be terms.

- The more strongly an oral statement is made, the more likely it is to be a term of the contract.

- If a person to whom an oral statement was made demonstrated that he or she considered the statement to be vitally important, then the statement is likely to be a term of the contract.

- Oral statements made by the party with the greater knowledge about the subject matter of the contract are likely to be terms of the contract. Statement made by the party with the lesser knowledge are likely to be representations.

Actionable misrepresentation

- An actionable misrepresentation is an untrue statement of fact which induced the other party to make the contract.

- Statements of mere opinion cannot amount to actionable misrepresentations.

- In order to be an actionable misrepresentation, a statement must have induced the other party to make the contract.

- Generally, silence cannot amount to an actionable misrepresentation.

- Silence can amount to an actionable misrepresentation in four circumstances: where there has been a change of circumstances; in contracts of insurance; where there is a fiduciary relationship between the parties; and where the silence makes another statement misleading.

- A misrepresentation is fraudulent if it was made either: knowing that it was untrue; or not believing that it was true; or recklessly, not caring whether it was true or false.

- A person to whom a fraudulent misrepresentation was made can rescind the contract and sue for damages for the tort of deceit.

- A misrepresentation is made negligently if it was made honestly believing that it was true, but without reasonable grounds for such a belief.

- A person to whom a negligent misrepresentation was made can rescind the contract and sue for damages for the tort of deceit.

- A wholly innocent misrepresentation is one made honestly believing that it was true and with reasonable grounds for such a belief.

- A person to whom a wholly innocent misrepresentation was made can rescind the contract but has no right to damages.

- In cases of negligent or wholly innocent misrepresentation the court has the power to award contract damages instead of rescission where it considers that it would be equitable to do so.

- A party can rescind a contract merely by letting the other party know that the contract is no longer regarded as binding.

- If a contract is rescinded the parties are restored to the positions which they were in before the contract was made.

- The right to rescind can be lost if the contract is affirmed, or if a third party has acquired rights, or if it is impossible to put the parties back into their pre-contract positions.

■ A person with the right to rescind will be regarded as having affirmed the contract if he or she does not rescind for a considerable period of time. As regards fraudulent misrepresentation, this time runs from the time when the right to rescind was discovered. As regards negligent or wholly innocent misrepresentation, this time runs from the time when the contract was made.

Mistake

■ There is a common mistake when both of the parties freely reach agreement, but do so while making the same mistake.

■ A common mistake might be as to the existence of the subject matter of the contract, or as to the ownership of goods sold or as to the quality of goods sold.

■ In general, a common mistake will not make a contract void. However, where there is a contract for the sale of specific goods, and the goods without the knowledge of the seller have perished at the time the contract is made, the contract is void.

■ Where the parties to a contract are at cross purpose as to the terms of the contract, there will be no contract if the reasonable person could not say that the view of one or other of the parties appeared to be what both of the parties intended.

■ If one party knows that the other is mistaken as to the quality of the subject matter of what is being sold this will not make the contract void. Nor will the contract be void if both parties are mistaken as to the quality of what is being sold.

■ If one party knows that the other is mistaken as to the terms of the contract, this will make the contract void.

■ A mistake as to the identity of the other contracting party can make the contract void if the parties did not meet face to face.

■ When a rogue persuades a person to make a contract by falsely claiming to be someone else, the contract will be voidable for fraudulent misrepresentation.

■ If a contract is voidable one of the parties has the right to avoid or rescind it.

■ A person who signs a document under a complete misapprehension as to what type of document it was may be able to claim that the contract is void. However, this will not be possible if the person signing the document was careless in doing so.

Duress and undue influence

■ A contract will be voidable for duress if it was made as a result of actual physical violence or the threat of it.

■ A contract may be voidable for economic duress if a person was pushed into it in such a way that there was no real consent to the contract.

■ In certain types of relationships undue influence is presumed. A contract made between people in such a relationship will therefore be voidable, if undue influence is alleged, unless the party against whom it is presumed can show that there was in fact no undue influence.

■ In relationships where undue influence is not presumed, a contract can be avoided if it can be proved that one of the parties actually exerted undue pressure which caused the other party to enter into the contract.

Illegal contracts

■ Many types of contracts are made illegal by statute.

■ Contracts to do the following matters are illegal at common law: to promote corruption in public life; to impede the administration of justice; to trade with enemy nations in time of war; to commit a crime, tort or fraud; to promote sexual immorality; or to defraud the Revenue.

■ Illegal contracts are void.

■ A contract which contravenes public policy will be void.

End of chapter questions

Question 1

Two months ago Amelia bought a small bakery for £1 million. The vendor of the bakery, Bill, told Amelia that the average monthly turnover was about £100,000. Bill offered to show Amelia the business records, which he claimed would have proved that his statement about the turnover was true. Amelia declined this offer, saying that she trusted Bill. The written contract of sale made no mention of the business turnover. Since Amelia bought the business the turnover has been only £30,000 a month. Amelia has now discovered that the monthly turnover of the business has never exceeded £45,000. Advise Amelia of her legal position.

Question 2

Cedric, a manufacturer of jewellery, received an order from a company called Acme (Superjewellers) Ltd. Cedric sent a small amount of jewellery and received prompt payment. Cedric then received a bigger order from Acme (Superjewellers) Ltd and posted jewellery worth £10,000 to Acme (Superjewellers) Ltd. Cedric did not receive payment for this and has since been informed that Acme (Superjewellers) Ltd is a fictitious company, often used as an alias by Edward, a rogue. Edward has been caught by the police and is likely to be sent to prison. The police have discovered that Frederick now has the jewellery which Cedric sent to Acme (Superjewellers) Ltd. Frederick bought the jewellery from Edward. Advise Cedric of his legal position.

Question 3

Gina, a dealer in antiques, visits the premises of Helen, another dealer. Gina buys a painting for £5,000. Helen does not make any claims about the painting. The painting turns out to be a fake and virtually worthless. Advise Gina of her legal position in the following circumstances.

a) Helen, like Gina, believed that the painting was genuine and worth about £5,000.

b) Helen had a good idea that the painting was a fake.

Question 4

Ian, a farmer, visits a seed merchant, Jim, and signs a contract agreeing to buy a ton of potatoes. Advise Ian of his legal position in the following circumstances.

a) Ian thought he was buying seed potatoes, but the potatoes delivered are not seed potatoes. Upon reading the contract which he signed Ian discovers that it describes the potatoes sold as ordinary (non-seed) potatoes. Ian knew that Jim sold non-seed potatoes, but he paid a price which would have been usual for a ton of seed potatoes. This price was about four times the usual price of non-seed potatoes.

b) Ian finds out that the contract he signed was to buy a ton of fertiliser. He signed this contract by mistake after a clerk employed by Jim took the contract away to check the VAT payable and accidentally handed Ian back the wrong contract for signature. Ian had read the contract which was taken away, ensuring that it was to buy seed potatoes, and trusted that the clerk had brought back the same contract.

Question 5

Kenny, a carpenter, put in a tender to do the carpentry work on a development which was being built in North Wales. Kenny's tender was accepted. The work was to be completed in 2 months and Kenny was to be paid £5,000. When Kenny arrived on the site he was told that there had been a mistake and another carpenter had been employed instead. Kenny was told that he could still do the work but that he would only be paid £3,500. Kenny felt that he had to accept these new terms as he had no other work available and had given up his flat so that he could move to Wales. Kenny has now finished the job on time. Advise Kenny of his legal position.

Task 3

A friend of yours who is visiting the country from abroad is considering starting a business in England. Your friend has asked you to write a report, briefly dealing with the following matters.

a) The difference between a contract term and a representation.

b) The nature of a misrepresentation.

c) The remedies for misrepresentation.

d) The types of mistake which can make a contract void.

e) The circumstances in which a contract can be voidable for duress or undue influence.

f) The types of contract which are illegal at common law.

4 Discharge of contractual liability and remedies for breach

In earlier chapters we have seen that a contract imposes obligations on the parties who made it. In the first part of this chapter we study the ways in which these obligations can be discharged, so that they no longer exist. In the second part of this chapter we examine the various remedies which are available for breach of contract.

Discharge of contractual liability

Contractual liability can become discharged in four ways; by performance, by agreement, by frustration or by breach. Each of these ways needs to be examined in turn.

Discharge by performance of the contract

In the following chapter we shall see that the Sale of Goods Act 1979 makes special rules about the performance of contracts of sale of goods. Here we are considering the position as regards contracts other than contracts of sale of goods.

In Chapter 1 we saw that a party who makes the offer of a unilateral contract promises to do something if the other party performs an act which has been requested. For example, in *Carlill v The Carbolic Smoke Ball Co* the company promised to pay any person a £100 reward if they bought a smoke ball, used it properly and caught flu. A party who makes the offer of a unilateral contract need keep the promise made only if the other party fully performs the act specified. So if Mrs Carlill had not bought the smoke ball, used it properly and caught flu, there would have been no obligation to pay her any part of the reward.

In bilateral contracts the general rule is that if one party fails to fully perform the contract the other party need not perform the contract at all. The following case demonstrates this general rule.

Cutter v Powell [1756]

Cutter had agreed to be a ship's mate on a voyage from Jamaica to Liverpool. The contract said that Cutter was to be paid £31.50, 'provided he proceeds, continues and does his duty......to the port of Liverpool'. The journey took about two months and usually ship's mates were paid about £4 a month. Cutter died after three-quarters of the voyage and therefore did not fully perform his contractual obligations. Cutter's widow sued for payment for the work Cutter had performed.

Held *The ship's captain had no obligation to pay anything because Cutter had not completely performed his contractual obligations.*

There are several exceptions to the general rule. First, part payment must be made for partial performance if the contract is regarded as *divisible* or *severable*. In *Cutter v Powell* the wording of the contract, and the fact that Cutter was to be paid a large lump sum for completing the contract, made it plain that Cutter's obligation to act as ship's mate was *entire*. That is to say, it was one obligation which was either performed or not. If a contract is divisible then it will consist of a number of separate obligations and part payment will be required for each obligation performed. Whether or not a contract is divisible or entire depends upon what the parties intended when they made the contract. In *Ritchie v Atkinson [1808]*, for example, a ship's captain agreed to carry a cargo of hemp at £5 a ton. The captain only carried half the cargo. This contract was divisible because the price was expressed per ton rather than as a lump sum for carrying the whole cargo. The captain was therefore paid for the cargo he did carry (but had to pay damages in respect of the cargo which he failed to carry). If the contract had been entire then the captain would not have been paid anything at all.

A second exception to the general rule arises where the partial performance very nearly amounted to total performance. If the partial performance can be regarded as *substantial performance* then it will have to be paid for. For example, in *Hoenig v Isaacs [1952]* the contract was to decorate and furnish a flat for £750. Defects in the work would have cost £56 to put right. The court held that there had been substantial performance and so the decorator was paid £750, but then had to pay damages of £56. By contrast, in *Bolton v Mahadeva [1972]* the contract was to install central heating in a house for £560. Defects in the work would have cost £174 to put right. The court held that there had been no substantial performance and so the installer received no payment at all.

A third exception to the general rule arises where partial performance was freely accepted by the other party. However, this acceptance must arise as a matter of choice. For example, in *Sumpter v Hedges [1898]* the claimant had agreed to build two houses for the defendant for £565. After doing work to the value of £333 the claimant was forced to stop work because he had run out of money. The defendant finished the work himself. The court held that the defendant did not have to pay the claimant for the work he had done. The defendant's act of finishing the work did not indicate that he had freely accepted the claimant's partial performance.

A final exception to the general rule arises where one of the contracting parties prevents the other from fully performing the contract. The party who is prevented from fully performing will be paid the amount deserved for the work done.

Discharge by agreement

Having made a contract, the parties are free to agree to abandon it or to vary it. However, an agreement to do either of these things must amount to another contract. All the requirements of a contract are therefore necessary. There must be an offer, an acceptance, an intention to create legal relations and consideration moving both ways. As the parties must agree to alter their legal position, there is usually no difficulty in finding the offer and acceptance or an intention to create legal relations. Generally, any problem which arises is caused by the difficulty of showing that consideration has moved from both of the parties. The following extended example, shows the possibilities.

Let us assume that John has agreed to service Jim's boiler for £1,000. Several possibilities must be considered.

i) If both of the parties agree to call the contract off before there has been any performance of it, the contract will be discharged. John has given consideration to Jim by discharging him from the obligation to pay the money. Jim has given consideration to John by discharging him from the obligation to service the boiler.

ii) If John does some of the work, and Jim agrees to pay him a proportion of the money for the work he has done, then the contract is discharged. Jim's consideration is letting John off with finishing the job. John's consideration is letting Jim off with paying the rest of the money.

iii) If John does some of the work and agrees that Jim need not pay him for this work done, then the contract is discharged. John lets Jim off with paying the money. Jim lets John off with finishing the work.

iv) If John finishes the whole job but agrees that Jim need not pay anything, the contract is not discharged. Jim has not provided any consideration for being let off the duty to pay the price.

v) If John finished the work and agreed to accept a bicycle instead of the contract price, the contract is discharged. The court will not enquire whether or not the bicycle is worth £1,000. In Chapter 1 we saw that consideration must be sufficient (worth something) but need not be adequate (worth the same amount as the other party's consideration).

vi) If John finishes the work but agrees to accept 90 per cent of the contract price, the contract is not discharged. In Chapter 1 we saw that (subject to promissory estoppel) a lesser sum of money cannot be consideration for a greater sum owed.

A party may *waive* contractual rights by indicating to the other party that the rights will not be insisted upon. If no consideration was given in return for the waiver the contract is not discharged. However, the rights which were waived can only be reintroduced by giving reasonable notice of this. Until this is done, a party cannot be in breach of contract for failure to perform a waived right.

For example, in *Charles Rickards Ltd v Oppenheim [1950]* the claimant agreed to sell the defendant a specially constructed car. The contract provided that the car was to be delivered on 20 March. The claimant did not deliver on time and the defendant kept asking him for delivery. The defendant then said that if the car was not delivered by 25 July he would refuse to accept delivery. The claimant tried to deliver the car in October, but the defendant refused to accept delivery. The court held that the defendant was entitled to refuse to accept delivery. The defendant had waived his right to receive delivery on 20 March, but had given reasonable notice that delivery had to be made by 25 July. If the claimant had tried to deliver at any time before 25 July the defendant would have been bound to accept the delivery.

Discharge by frustration

A contract may become frustrated if it becomes impossible to perform, illegal to perform or radically different from what the parties contemplated. Before we examine these three grounds on which a contract may be frustrated, it is important to notice that we are talking about a valid contract becoming illegal, impossible or radically different. If a contract is impossible to perform when it is made then it may be void for mistake. If a contract is illegal to perform at the time when it is made then it is an illegal contract and will therefore be void. If the contract was, at the time of making the contract, radically different from what the parties intended then it may be void for mistake. Both mistake and illegal contracts were considered in the previous chapter.

If a contract becomes *impossible to perform* then it will be frustrated.

Taylor v Caldwell [1863]

A music hall was hired out for four days. Before these days came around the music hall was accidentally burnt down.

Held *The contract was frustrated.*

If a party who has contracted to perform the contract personally dies or becomes too ill to perform the contract will be impossible to perform. It will therefore be frustrated. (The contract was not frustrated in *Cutter v Powell* because the doctrine of consideration only evolved around the year 1850.)

Where a contract becomes *illegal to perform* it will be frustrated. For example, in the *Fibrosa case [1943]* a contract to supply machinery to Poland was frustrated when Germany occupied Poland. Great Britain was at war with Germany, and it is illegal to supply an enemy-occupied country.

A contract will be frustrated if it becomes *radically different from what the parties intended* when they made the contract.

Krell v Henry [1903]

King Edward VII was about to be crowned. In celebration, a huge coronation procession was to pass through London on 26 and 27 June. The defendant agreed to hire a room from the claimant for these 2 days for £75. The written contract did not state the purpose of this. However, both parties understood that the sole purpose was that the defendant and his friends could view the coronation procession from the room. The King was ill and so the coronation procession was cancelled. The claimant sued the defendant for the contract price.

Held *The defendant did not have to pay because the contract had become frustrated.*

In a similar case, *Herne Bay Steamboat Co v Hutton [1903]*, the defendant had agreed to hire a steamboat for two days in order to cruise around the fleet and to watch the naval review. The King's illness caused the naval review to be cancelled. The contract was not frustrated. Performance of the contract was different from what the parties intended, but it was not radically different. (The defendant could still have cruised around the fleet.)

Rules about frustration

Before we examine the effects of a contract becoming frustrated, there are several points about frustration which we should notice.

If a contract states that it should be performed in a certain way then it will be frustrated if it becomes impossible to perform in that way. For example, if a contract states that a cargo should be carried on a particular ship then it will be frustrated if that ship sinks. This is the case even if other ships could carry the cargo just as well.

A contract will not become frustrated merely because it becomes more difficult to perform. For example, in *Davis Contractors Ltd v Fareham UDC [1956]* a contract to build 78 houses in 8 months was not frustrated when a shortage of labour and materials meant that the contract took 22 months to perform. The builders should have considered that there might be shortages of labour and materials before agreeing to do the job.

If the parties to the contract foresee that there might be difficulties and set out in the contract what should happen if these difficulties arise, the courts will give effect to what has been agreed. Clauses which make such provisions are known as *force majeure* clauses. For example, if in *Davis Contractors Ltd v Fareham UDC* the parties might have included a force majeure clause dealing with what the position should be if there turned out be a shortage of labour and materials. Such a clause might have stated that if there was a shortage of labour and materials then the contract would be frustrated. Or it might have said that if there was a shortage of labour and materials the contract should not be frustrated but the builder should be given more time to do the work and paid more money. Whatever the force majeure clause agreed, the court would have enforced the clause.

If only one of the parties knows that the frustrating event might happen (or should have known this) then that party cannot claim frustration. For example, in *Walton Harvey Ltd v Walker & Homfrays [1931]* a hotel owner who had agreed to let the claimant put advertisements on his hotel could not claim that the contract was frustrated when the hotel was compulsorily demolished. The hotel owner was in breach of contract because he knew that the hotel might be compulsorily demolished and the advertisers did not know this. Nor will a contract be frustrated if the frustrating event was the fault of either party. For example, if in *Taylor v Caldwell* it had been the fault of the music hall owner that the music hall had burnt down then the contract would not have been frustrated.

Lease of land cannot be frustrated because a lease is more than a contract, it creates an interest in land.

The legal effect of frustration

As soon as the frustrating event happens the contract comes to an end. The Law Reform (Frustrated Contracts) Act 1943 then makes the following rules.

i)   Money owing under the contract ceases to be payable.

ii)   Money which has already paid under the contract can be recovered. However, the court has a discretion to allow some of this money to be kept to cover expenses incurred.

iii)   If one of the parties has received a valuable benefit under the contract the court can order that a fair amount is paid to compensate for this.

Example

X Ltd has agreed to supply Y Ltd with 1,000 toy guns. The contract price was £2,000 and half of this was paid in advance. Parliament passes a statute making the sale of toy guns illegal. The contract is therefore frustrated. Y Ltd do not need to pay the £1,000 which has not yet been paid. Y Ltd can recover the £1,000 already paid.

However, the court could allow X Ltd to keep some of this money to compensate for expenses incurred. If 100 toy guns had already been delivered then the court could order that Y Ltd make a payment for these. This payment might be ten per cent of the contract price (because ten per cent of the guns have been delivered) but would not necessarily be so. The amount payable, if anything, is at the court's discretion.

Discharge by acceptance of breach

In Chapter 2 we considered the extent to which a party is entitled to treat a contract as discharged on account of the other party's breach of contract. (See conditions, warranties and innominate terms.) In addition, if a party shows an intention not to be bound by the contract this is known as a repudiation of the contract. A repudiation allows the other party to treat the contract as terminated. For example, if Jack contracted to service X Ltd's boiler for £1,000 and then told X Ltd that he was not going to do the job, X Ltd would be discharged from their contractual liability. X Ltd could therefore employ someone else to service their boiler and Jack could not change his mind and insist that he still had a contract to do the job. (X Ltd could also sue Jack for damages for breach of contract.)

When one of the parties repudiates the contract before the time for performance of the contract is due this is known as an anticipatory breach. The injured party can either accept the breach or keep the contract open. If the breach is accepted the injured party can treat the contract as terminated and sue for damages. If the anticipatory breach is not accepted the contract is still alive. The position then depends upon whether the anticipatory breach becomes an actual breach (because the contract is not performed when performance becomes due). If it does not become an actual breach (because the contract is properly performed in time) then there is no problem. If it does become an actual breach the injured party can sue for damages for breach of contract. The following case demonstrates these principles.

Hochster v De La Tour [1853]

In April 1852 the defendant contracted to employ the claimant as a courier for a 3 month period which was to begin on 1 June. On 11 May the defendant told the claimant that he was not in fact going to employ him. The claimant immediately sued for damages.

Held *The claimant was entitled to sue for damages because he had accepted the anticipatory breach. The claimant did not need to wait until the breach became an actual breach (which it would have done on 1 June).*

In *Hochster v De La Tour* the claimant could have chosen to wait until the anticipatory breach became an actual breach. If the defendant had changed his mind, and decided to employ the claimant after all, there would have been no breach of contract and no problem. If the defendant did not change his mind, and did not employ the claimant after all, then there would have been an actual breach on 1 June. However, there is a slight risk in waiting until an anticipatory breach becomes an actual breach. The contract might become frustrated, as the following case shows.

Avery v Bowden [1856]

The defendants contracted to supply the claimant's ship with a cargo. The cargo was to be supplied at Odessa within 45 days. When the claimant's ship reached Odessa the defendant repeatedly told the claimant that no cargo would be delivered. The claimant kept his ship in Odessa, hoping that the defendant would change his mind. The Crimean War broke out before the 45 days had expired.

Held *The outbreak of war frustrated the contract (because Odessa had become controlled by the enemy) and so the right to sue had been permanently lost.*

Student Activity Questions 4.1

1) In what four ways can a party's contractual liability be discharged?

2) On what three grounds can a contract be frustrated?

3) What is the effect of a contract becoming frustrated?

4) What is an anticipatory breach of contract?

5) What options are available to a party who is faced with an anticipatory breach of contract?

Remedies for breach of contract

Refusal to perform the contract

We have already seen that in some circumstances a party will be able to refuse to further perform the contract on account of the other party's breach of contract. We have seen that this will be possible if the other party repudiates the contract or breaches a condition of the contract. It will also be possible if the other party breached an innominate term in such a way that this deprived of substantially the whole benefit of the contract. (See conditions, warranties and innominate terms in Chapter 2.)

Damages

Any breach of contract always allows the injured party to sue for damages. Contract damages are intended to put the injured party into the same position as if the contract had been performed. It follows that if the the injured party has suffered no loss as a result of the breach only nominal damages will be available. Nominal damages are damages in name only, perhaps 5p or £1.

Remoteness of damage

When a contract is breached, substantial damages can only be claimed in respect of losses which fall within one of the two rules in *Hadley v Baxendale [1854]*. Other losses are regarded as too remote.

Rule 1 allows damages for a loss if the loss arose naturally from the breach of contract, in the usual course of things.

Rule 2 allows damages for a loss if the loss can reasonably be supposed to have been within the contemplation of the parties when they made the contract.

The following case shows how the two rules work.

Victoria Laundry v Newman Industries [1949]

The claimants agreed to buy a second-hand boiler from the defendants. The defendants knew that the boiler was to be used immediately in the claimants' laundry. They also knew that there was a big demand for general laundry services at this time. The defendants delivered the boiler 20 weeks late. Two claims for damages were made by the claimants. First, they claimed £16 a week, which represented the extra profit they could have made by doing more general laundry work with the new boiler. Second, they claimed £262 a week which had been lost on account of the claimants not being able to use the boiler to fulfil a very profitable contract to dye army uniforms.

Held *The claimants were entitled to the £16 a week, under the first rule in* Hadley v Baxendale. *The £262 was not available under either rule. (It would have been available under the second rule in* Hadley v Baxendale *if the claimants had told the defendants that such a very profitable contract would be lost if the boiler was not delivered on time.)*

Having decided that a loss is within one of the two rules in *Hadley v Baxendale*, it must then be decided how much the damages should be.

Amount of damages

If the contract is a sale of goods, the Sale of Goods Act 1979 sets out rules which determine the amount of damages payable. These rules are examined in Chapter 5.

In contracts other than contracts of sale of goods the damages are quantified on the basis that they are intended to put the injured party in the same position as if the contract had been properly performed. Damages will therefore be available for putting right defects caused by the breach of contract. They will also be available for any other losses, as long as these were caused by the breach of contract and were within one of the rules in *Hadley v Baxendale*. If the defendant's breach of contract causes the claimant to pay damages to a third party, these damages paid are also recoverable.

Example

Jerry agrees to service Z Ltd's boiler for £1,000. Jerry knows that Z Ltd need the boiler to operate their laundry. Z Ltd tell Jerry that the service must be finished on time because otherwise Z Ltd will be in breach of a very profitable contract to do laundry for Y Ltd. Jerry performs the service so badly that Z Ltd's boiler cannot work at all. Jerry cannot fix the problem. Z Ltd hunt around for someone else to fix the boiler. The only person they can find is Tom, who fixes the boiler one week after Jerry should have fixed it. As Z Ltd could not do the laundry for Y Ltd they are themselves in breach of contract and will have to pay Y Ltd £2,000 damages. Jerry will have to pay damages to Z Ltd as follows. (i) The cost of Tom putting right the fault which Jerry caused. (ii) The amount of ordinary business profit lost by Z Ltd as a consequence of not being able to use the boiler for one week. (iii) The profit Z Ltd would have made if they had been able to perform their contract with Y Ltd. (iv) The amount of damages which Z Ltd had to pay to Y Ltd.

In the above example, Z Ltd might have incurred even more losses if they had not hunted around to find someone else to fix the boiler. However, if they had not hunted around to find someone else they could not have claimed more damages. A party who suffers a loss as a result of breach of contract must take all reasonable steps to *mitigate* (reduce) the loss. No substantial damages can be claimed in respect of a loss which could have been mitigated by taking reasonable steps.

Brace v Calder [1895]

The claimant was employed by a partnership of four people for a fixed two year period. The partnership was dissolved when two of the partners left. The two remaining partners immediately agreed to employ the claimant on exactly the same terms as he had previously been employed. The claimant refused this offer and sued for breach of contract.

Held *There had been a breach of contract because the four partners had not employed the claimant for the full two year period. However, the claimant was entitled only to nominal damages (from the original partners). He should have mitigated his loss by accepting the alternative employment.*

Damages are generally not available for injured feelings or disappointment. However, where the contract was to provide the claimant with enjoyment and relaxation (as in the case of a holiday) it is possible that damages can be awarded for disappointment and distress caused by a breach of the contract.

Agreed damages

Sometimes, a term of the contract will fix the amount of damages payable in the event of breach of contract. Damages agreed in this way are classified as being either *liquidated damages* or *penalties.*

If the amount of damages fixed is the amount which the parties genuinely believed that the loss would be, then the damages agreed are liquidated damages. The amount of damages fixed by the term will then be the amount of damages awarded, no matter what the actual loss turned out to be.

If the amount of damages fixed is not the amount which the parties genuinely believed that the loss would be, then the damages agreed will be a penalty. A penalty is ignored and damages are calculated as if the term setting out the penalty had not existed. Penalties are often put into a contract by the party with the greater bargaining power, to try to terrorise the other party into performing the contract.

Example

John, a builder, agrees to build a new shop which is to be completed by 1 March. A term of the contract states that if the shop is not completed on time then the damages payable by John will be £500 a week for every week that the shop is not completed. John completes the work 10 weeks late. If, when the parties made the contract, they thought that the actual loss to the shop owner would be £500 a week, then the agreed damages are liquidated damages. John would therefore have to pay £5,000 damages, no matter how much his breach of contract actually cost the shop owner. If, when the parties made the contract, they did not think that the actual loss in the event of breach would be £500 a week, then the term will be a penalty. The penalty will be ignored and damages will be calculated in the usual way to compensate the shop owner for the actual loss suffered.

A contract might agree that interest on damages should be paid at a certain rate. If the parties do not make such an agreement then the court will order that interest is payable from the date when the claim arose.

The following figure gives an overview of damages for breach of contract.

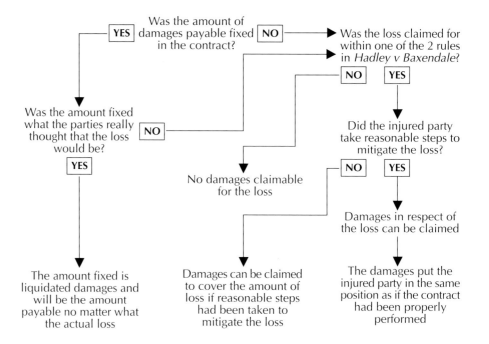

Figure 4.1 An overview of damages for breach of contract

Student Activity Questions 4.2

1) What are the two rules in *Hadley v Baxendale*? Why are the two rules important?

2) If a loss caused by a breach of contract is not too remote, how does a court assess the actual amount of damages payable in respect of that loss?

3) What is meant by mitigation?

4) If an amount of damages payable in the event of breach is specified in the contract itself, will a court always award this amount of damages in the event of the contract being breached?

An action for the contract price

When a seller sues for the contract price this is not the same thing as suing for damages. When a claim is made for the payment of a debt the amount claimed is said to be *liquidated.* As the claim is not for damages, the rules on remoteness, mitigation and quantification of damages will not apply. For example, let us assume that X agreed to build an office for Y for £70,000 and completed the job properly. If Y does not pay the contract price then X can sue for it. The rules on remoteness, mitigation and quantification of damages will not apply. So there will be no need to consider the rules in *Hadley v*

Baxendale, and X does not need to take any steps to reduce his loss. Nor will a court need to make calculations to find the amount being claimed.

The Sale of Goods Act 1979 lays down the circumstances in which a seller of goods can sue for the contract price. These rules are examined in Chapter 5.

The Late Payment of Commercial Debts (Interest) Act 1998 gives small businesses the right to claim interest when a commercial debt arising from the supply of goods and services to another business is paid late. A small business is defined as one with fewer than 50 full-time employees (or their part-time equivalents).

Interest becomes payable under the Act from a date which the supplier and purchaser expressly or impliedly agreed. If no such date is fixed, interest becomes payable 30 days after the supplier performed his obligations under the contract, or 30 days after the purchaser was given notice of the debt, whichever is the later. The rate of interest is currently set at 8% above the base rate. After 1 November 2002 it is proposed that all businesses will have the right to claim interest under the Act.

The effect of the Act cannot be avoided by means of a contractual term unless there is a 'substantial' remedy available for the late payment of the debt. It is only possible for a contractual term to postpone the time at which a debt is created to the extent that the term satisfies the UCTA 1977 requirement of reasonableness. (The UCTA requirement of reasonableness was examined in Chapter 2.)

Specific performance

Specific performance is an equitable remedy which arises when a court orders a person to actually perform the contractual obligations undertaken. For example, if X agreed to sell an antique vase to Y but then refused to go through with the contract, Y might ask the court for an order of specific performance. If such an order was made by the court X would be ordered to go through with the contract and to let Y have the vase. Disobeying such a court order would put X in contempt of court and liable to a fine or imprisonment.

Specific performance is rarely ordered by a court. It will not be ordered where damages would provide a good enough remedy. It will not therefore be ordered to make a seller hand over new mass-produced goods which could be obtained from another seller. Specific performance can be ordered where a seller refuses to hand over unique goods (such as an antique vase). All plots of land are regarded as unique and so specific performance will be ordered where a seller of land refuses to perform the contract.

As specific performance is an equitable remedy, it is only available at the court's discretion. The remedy will not be ordered in the following circumstances. First, where the claimant has behaved inequitably (unfairly). This reflects an old saying that, 'He who comes to Equity must come with clean hands'. Second, specific performance will not be ordered to enforce a contract which required personal services to be provided (such as a contract of employment). Third, it will not be ordered where to order it would cause excessive hardship to the defendant. Fourth, it will not be ordered for or against a minor (person under 18).

Injunction

An injunction is a court order which requires a person to do or not to do a certain thing. An injunction can be ordered, as an equitable remedy, to prevent a party from breaching a contract. However, an injunction will not be ordered where an award of damages would give a satisfactory remedy. In cases where specific performance could not be ordered, an injunction will not be ordered if it would have the same effect as an order of specific performance.

Warner Bros Pictures Inc v Nelson [1936]

An actress, Bette Davis, made a contract with the claimants. She agreed that she would act for the claimants, and not act for anyone else, for a two year period. The actress intended to act for another company. The defendants sought an injunction to prevent this.

Held *An injunction was ordered to prevent the actress from breaching her contract by acting for another company. This did not amount to an order of specific performance of a personal service contract because the claimant was not compelled to act for the defendants. She could have earnt a living in some other way.*

Two special types of injunctions may be ordered, but only in very limited circumstances. A *Mareva injunction* prevents a person from moving assets out of the jurisdiction of the English courts. An *Anton Pillar injunction* allows the claimant to take away or photocopy documents which the defendant might destroy. Both of these injunctions are granted only in very exceptional circumstances.

Rectification

Rectification is an equitable remedy which arises when a contract which has been concluded orally is then written down. If what is written down does not accurately reflect what the parties agreed orally, the court can allow the written document to be rectified (put right).

Quantum meruit (the amount he deserves)

A party who receives a quantum meruit payment is paid the amount deserved for work done. Such a right can arise in three circumstances. First, if the other contracting party prevented further performance of the contract. Second, if the other contracting party voluntarily accepted partial performance of the contract. Third, if the contract did not provide how much should be paid.

Time limits on remedies

The Limitation Act 1980 makes the following rules about the time span within which a remedy for breach of contract must be claimed.

A simple contract (one not made by a deed) must be sued upon within six years of the right to sue arising. The right to sue will arise when the contract is breached. A claim for personal injuries must be made within 3 years of the right to sue arising. Where a contract is made by a deed a claim must be made within 12 years of the right to sue arising. Time does not run against minors until they reach the age of 18. Time does not run against a victim of a fraud until the fraud is, or should have been, discovered. Where the claim is for a debt, any written acknowledgment of the debt's existence, will cause the time period to begin again.

The time limits set out in the Limitation Act 1980 do not apply to equitable remedies. However, an equitable remedy will not be granted to a party who has delayed unreasonably in asking for the remedy.

Student Activity Questions 4.3

1)   How does an action for the contract price differ from an action for damages?

2)   What is an order of specific performance?

3)   How can an injunction be a remedy for breach of contract?

4)   What is the time limit for making a claim for breach of a simple contract?

ssential points

Discharge of contractual liability

- Contractual liability can become discharged in four ways; by performance, by agreement, by frustration or by breach.

- The general rule is that if one party fails to fully perform the contract the other party need not perform the contract at all.

- Despite the general rule, part payment must be made for partial performance in four circumstances: if the contract is regarded as divisible or severable; if the partial performance very nearly amounted to total performance; if the partial performance was freely accepted by the other party; or if one of the contracting parties prevents the other from fully performing the contract.

■ Contractual obligations may be discharged by agreement, as long as both partie give some consideration to the other in return for being released from thei contractual obligations.

■ A contract may become frustrated if it becomes impossible to perform, illegal to perform or radically different from what the parties contemplated when the made the contract.

■ A contract will not become frustrated merely because it becomes more difficul to perform.

■ A contract comes to an end as soon as it is frustrated.

■ When a contract is frustrated the Law Reform (Frustrated Contracts) Act 194 makes the following rules: money owing under the contract ceases to be payable money already paid under the contract can be recovered, although the court ha a discretion to allow some of this money to be kept to cover expenses incurrec a party who has received a valuable benefit under the contract may be ordere to pay a fair amount for the benefit.

■ If a contracting party shows an intention not to be bound by the contract this known as a repudiation of the contract.

■ When one of the parties repudiates the contract before the time for performanc of the contract is due this is known as an anticipatory breach.

■ A party faced with an anticipatory breach of contract may either accept th breach and sue at once, or may keep the contract open.

■ If a party faced with an anticipatory breach keeps the contract open, there wi be no breach if the contract is properly performed when performance become due. If the contract is not properly performed at the time when performanc becomes due then the anticipatory breach will become an actual breach c contract.

Remedies for breach of contract

■ A party will be able to refuse to further perform the contract if a condition breached. A party will also be able to refuse to further perform the contract if a innominate term is breached and this breach deprived him or her of substantial the whole benefit of the contract.

■ A party will not be able to refuse to further perform the contract if a warranty breached. Nor will a party be able to refuse to further perform the contract if a innominate term is breached and this breach does not substantially deprive hi or her of the whole intended benefit of the contract.

■ Any breach of contract always allows the injured party to sue for damages.

4 Discharge of contractual liability and remedies for breach

■ Contract damages are intended to put the injured party into the same position as if the contract had been performed. Therefore, if the the injured party has suffered no loss as a result of the breach only nominal damages will be available.

■ Substantial damages can only be claimed in respect of losses which fall within one of the two rules in *Hadley v Baxendale*. Other losses are regarded as too remote.

■ *Hadley v Baxendale* rule 1 allows damages for a loss if the loss arose naturally from the breach of contract, in the usual course of things.

■ *Hadley v Baxendale* rule 2 allows damages for a loss if the loss can reasonably be supposed to have been within the contemplation of the parties when they made the contract.

■ Substantial damages cannot be claimed in respect of a loss which could have been mitigated by taking reasonable steps.

■ Damages are generally not available for injured feelings or disappointment.

■ If the contract fixes the amount of damages payable, and the amount is what the parties genuinely believed that the loss would be, then the damages agreed are liquidated damages. The amount of the liquidated damages will then be the amount of damages awarded, no matter what the actual loss suffered.

■ If the contract fixes the amount of damages payable, and the amount is not what the parties genuinely believed that the loss would be, then the damages agreed will be a penalty. A penalty is ignored and damages are calculated as if the term providing for the penalty did not exist.

■ When a seller sues for the contract price or a debt this is not the same thing as suing for damages. Therefore the rules on remoteness, mitigation and quantification of damages will not apply.

■ Specific performance is a discretionary equitable remedy which arises when a court orders a person to actually perform the contractual obligations undertaken.

■ Specific performance will not be ordered where damages would provide a satisfactory remedy.

■ An injunction is a court order which requires a person to do or not to do a certain thing and can be ordered, as an equitable remedy, to prevent a party from breaching a contract.

■ An injunction will not be ordered where an award of damages would give a satisfactory remedy.

■ The Limitation Act 1980 provides that a simple contract (one not made by a deed) must be sued upon within six years of the contract being breached. A claim for personal injuries must be made within 3 years of the right to sue arising.

End of chapter questions

Question 1

Giles, a poultry farmer, agreed to supply Export Ltd with 5,000 turkeys. The contract sa that the turkeys were for export to Ruritania and had to meet Ruritanian health standard The contract price was £15,000. £5,000 was paid in advance and £10,000 was to l paid once all the turkeys had been delivered. After 1,000 turkeys had been delivere Great Britain declared war on Ruritania. Advise Giles of his legal position.

Question 2

TeaSell Ltd, a retailer of high class teas, contracted last year to buy one ton of Darjeelir tea from TeaGrow Ltd. The tea was to be delivered on 1 November. This year the weath in Darjeeling has been very bad and the annual tea crop has been disastrous. TeaGro Ltd had expected to grow ten tons of Darjeeling but has only managed to harvest one to On 1 September TeaGrow Ltd wrote to TeaSell Ltd, saying that it would not be able supply the ton of Darjeeling tea which it had agreed to sell. The letter explained th TeaGrow Ltd had no other existing contracts to sell the tea to anyone else, but that th price of Darjeeling teas has increased so substantially that it would be able to get a muc better price from another buyer. Advise TeaSell Ltd of the following matters.

a) Whether TeaGrow Ltd has committed a breach of contract.

b) Whether TeaSell Ltd could prevent the sale of the one ton of Darjeeling tea to anoth buyer.

c) Whether TeaGrow Ltd could be ordered to deliver the one ton of Darjeeling tea TeaSell Ltd, as agreed in the contract.

d) If TeaGrow Ltd do not deliver the tea, whether a claim for damages could be mac in respect of the following losses.

   i) Ordinary business profits lost by TeaSell Ltd as a consequence of their not bei able to sell Darjeeling tea to regular customers.

   ii) The loss of a very profitable contract to sell Darjeeling tea to a specialist cafe.

   iii) Damages which TeaSell Ltd has had to pay because the lack of Darjeeling te caused TeaSell Ltd to breach a contract to sell tea to a tea shop.

   iv) The managing director of TeaSell Ltd having a heart attack, and spending all his money on private health care. The heart attack was caused by the stress TeaGrow Ltd breaching their contract with TeaSell Ltd.

Task 4

A friend of yours from abroad is considering setting up business in England. Your friend would like to know the ways in which contractual liability can be discharged and the remedies available for breach of a contract. Write a report for your friend, briefly explaining the following matters.

a) How contractual obligations can be discharged by performance.

b) How a contract can be discharged by agreement between the contracting parties.

c) The ways in which a contract can become frustrated.

d) The legal position when a contract is frustrated.

e) The meaning of an anticipatory breach of contract, and the remedies available to a party faced with an anticipatory breach.

f) How a court decides whether or not a loss caused by a breach of contract is too remote for damages to be claimed in respect of the loss.

g) How a court quantifies the amount of damages payable for breach of contract.

h) What is meant by mitigation of a loss.

i) Whether the courts will apply a clause in a contract which sets out the amount of damages payable in the event of a breach of contract.

j) What is meant by specific performance of a contract.

k) How an injunction can be a remedy for breach of contract.

l) What is meant by a quantum meruit payment, and the circumstances in which a contracting party will be entitled to a quantum meruit payment.

m) The time limits within which a claim for breach of contract must be brought.

5 The Sale of Goods Act 1979

In this chapter we consider important rules laid down by the Sale of Goods Act 1979. This is not the first time that we have come across the Sale of Goods Act. In Chapter 2 we examined sections 12-15 of the Act, which imply statutory terms into contracts of sale of goods. Before examining the nature of the statutory implied terms, we first considered the definition of a contract of sale of goods. If you have forgotten this definition you should re-read it. You should also once more work your way through Student Activity Questions 2.2. It is necessary to remember the definition of a contract of sale of goods because the rules which we consider in this chapter apply only to contracts of sale of goods. Similar rules do not apply to other types of contracts.

The passing of ownership and risk

The purpose of a contract of sale of goods is to pass ownership of the goods to the buyer in return for payment of the price. The Sale of Goods Act 1979 sets out rules which determine exactly when ownership does pass. It can be important to know exactly when ownership passes for two main reasons. First, the goods might become lost or damaged. The party who owned the goods at the time of the loss or damage will generally have to bear the loss. Second, either the buyer or the seller might become insolvent. The rights of the solvent party will depend upon whether or not ownership had passed at the time of the insolvency.

The goods become lost or damaged

Section 20 of the SGA 1979 provides that, unless the buyer and seller have agreed otherwise, the risk of the goods being lost or damaged remains with the seller until ownership of the goods passes to the buyer. Once ownership of the goods has passed to the buyer then the risk of loss or damage passes to the buyer. The parties might of course agree that the rule set out in section 20 should not apply, but this rarely happens. So if the goods are accidentally lost or damaged, the loss will usually fall upon the person who has ownership of the goods. It is worth noticing straight away that ownership of the goods is not the same thing as possession of the goods. Section 20 provides that the risk passes with ownership whether the goods have been delivered to the buyer or not.

If ownership has passed from the seller to the buyer at the time when the goods become lost or damaged, the position is straightforward. The loss will fall upon the buyer, who will have to pay the full price of the goods (if the price has not already been paid).

If ownership has not passed to the buyer at the time when the goods become lost or damaged, then the loss will fall upon the seller. However, the legal position will then depend upon whether the contract was for the sale of specific or unascertained goods. Specific goods are defined by section 61 of the Act as goods which have been identified and agreed upon at the time of sale. For example, if a second-hand car is sold this is a sale of specific goods. (Both the buyer and the seller have identified the car and agreed that it is that particular car, and no other, which is being sold.) Unascertained goods are goods which have not been identified and agreed upon at the time of sale. For example, if 100 tons of wheat are sold, where the buyer and seller have not identified any particular 100 tons of wheat as the subject matter of the contract, this is a sale of unascertained goods.

If specific goods are lost or damaged before ownership and risk have passed to the buyer, the seller is in breach of contract. Obviously, the seller cannot deliver lost goods. Nor can the seller deliver damaged goods because the buyer will be entitled to reject these goods on account of their being of unsatisfactory quality. Therefore the buyer will not need to pay the price and accept the damaged goods. If the buyer has already paid some of the price of lost or damaged goods the seller will have to refund the amount paid. The buyer will also be able to sue the seller for damages for non-delivery. In practice, a buyer might choose to accept damaged goods, but at a much reduced price. The strength of the buyer's legal position would put strong pressure on the seller to accept the reduced price.

If unascertained goods are lost or damaged before ownership has passed to the buyer, then the legal position will be the same if the seller cannot find replacement goods which match the contract description. However, the seller could still properly perform the contract by acquiring other goods which match the contract description and by delivering these goods to the buyer. A seller who does this will not be in breach of contract. The buyer will therefore have to accept the goods and pay the full price.

Example 1

> B agrees to buy a two year old lorry from S for £12,000, and pays a deposit of £2,000. The lorry is damaged by vandals before ownership has passed to B. B need not accept the damaged lorry because it is not of satisfactory quality. B has a right to sue S for damages for non-delivery and need not pay the £10,000 which has not yet been paid. B can also recover the £2,000 which has been paid.

Example 2

B agrees to buy 1,000 barrels of oil (unascertained goods) from S. While S still has ownership of 1,000 barrels of oil which he intended to supply to B, this oil is destroyed in a fire. If S can acquire another 1,000 barrels of the same type of oil before the date of delivery is due then S can deliver this oil to B, who must accept it and pay the full contract price. If S cannot acquire another 1,000 barrels of the same type of oil before delivery is due, then S is in breach of contract. B need not pay the price and can recover any amount of the price already paid. B can also sue S for damages for non-delivery.

If the loss of the goods or the damage to them was the fault of a particular person the legal position would be the same, except that the party who owned the goods at the time of the loss or damage would be able to claim damages from the person who caused the loss or damage. So if in Example 2 it was X's fault that the oil was destroyed then S could sue X for damages to compensate for all the loss suffered.

Figure 5.1 shows an outline of the legal position where goods which have been sold have become lost or damaged. It assumed that the parties have not agreed to separate the risk from the ownership and that the loss or damage was not the fault of either party. (If the loss or damage is the fault of either the buyer or the seller, the party at fault will have to bear the loss.)

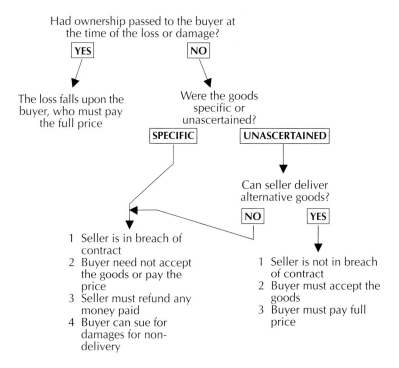

Figure 5.1   *The importance of the passing of ownership where the goods become lost or damaged.*

Insolvency of the buyer or the seller

If the *seller* becomes insolvent *before* the ownership of the goods has passed to the buyer then the seller's liquidator will have no duty to deliver the goods to the buyer. If the goods have already been delivered to the buyer then the seller's liquidator will be able to reclaim the goods from the buyer. The buyer will not have to pay for the goods, because ownership has not passed to the buyer. However, a buyer who has paid any or all of the price can only claim against the seller's liquidator as just another unsecured creditor. In practice, this means that the buyer will certainly not get back all money which has been paid and may get none of this money back.

If the *seller* becomes insolvent *after* the ownership of the goods has passed to the buyer then the buyer, as owner of the goods, can keep the goods. The seller's liquidator will, however, be able to sue the buyer for any amount of the price which has not yet been paid.

If the *buyer* becomes insolvent *before* the ownership of the goods has passed, then the seller need not deliver the goods to the buyer and could reclaim the goods if they had already been delivered. If the buyer has already paid any part of the price then the buyer's liquidator can reclaim this amount from the seller. However, if the buyer's liquidator chooses to pay the seller the full price then the seller must deliver the goods. (The contract is not automatically terminated on account of the buyer having become insolvent.)

If the *buyer* becomes insolvent *after* the ownership of the goods has passed then the buyer's liquidator will be entitled to keep the goods. The seller can retain any part of the price which has already been paid, but can only sue for any outstanding amount as an unsecured creditor. (The seller is therefore most unlikely to receive payment in full, receiving anything at all.)

Example 1

S has sold 100 tons of corn to B for £2,000 and B has paid £200 in advance. Before ownership has passed to B, S becomes insolvent. S's liquidator has no obligation to deliver the goods and could reclaim the goods if they had already been delivered. B has no obligation to pay the £1,800 which has not yet been paid. However, B can only reclaim the £200 already paid as an unsecured creditor of S.

Example 2

S has sold 100 tons of corn to B for £2,000 and B has paid £200 in advance. After ownership has passed to B, but before the rest of the price has been paid, B becomes insolvent. S cannot reclaim the goods from B's liquidator as ownership had passed to B. S can keep the £200 already paid and can sue B's liquidator for the remainder of the price (£1,800) as an unsecured creditor.

Figure 5.2 shows an outline of the legal position where either the buyer or the seller have become insolvent.

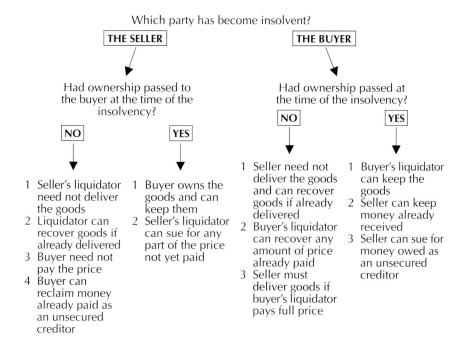

Figure 5.2 *The importance of the passing of ownership where the buyer or seller becomes insolvent.*

Student Activity Questions 5.1

Are the goods sold in the following contracts specific or unascertained goods?

1   Stuart often gives Bill a lift to work in his car. Bill agrees to buy this car for £5,000.

2   Belinda telephones Samantha and asks Samantha if she can get hold of any King Edward potatoes. Samantha says that she has not got any King Edwards at the moment, but that she can get up to 100 tons at short notice. Belinda asks how much 10 tons would cost. Having been given a price, Belinda agrees to buy 10 tons of King Edward potatoes.

3   Bert telephones Sam and asks if he can get hold of any onions. Sam says that he has got five bags of onions sitting in his warehouse but that he will not be able to get any more. Bert agrees to buy the 5 bags of onions which Sam now has.

4   Does the risk of loss of the goods or damage to the goods always pass from the seller to the buyer at the same time as the ownership passes?

..... continued

5   Sam has sold a ton of potatoes to Bert for £90. Bert becomes insolvent before ownership of the potatoes has passed to him. Bert had already paid £45 at the time of his insolvency, but the potatoes had not been delivered to him. What is Sam's legal position?

6   Belinda has bought a ton of carrots from Samantha for £120. After ownership has passed to Belinda, Samantha has become insolvent. Belinda had paid half the price at the time of Samantha's insolvency. What is Belinda's legal position?

The Sale of Goods Act rules on the passing of ownership

Sections 16-20 of the Sale of Goods Act 1979 lay down rules which determine exactly when the ownership of goods should pass from the seller to the buyer.

Passing of ownership of specific goods

We have already seen that specific goods are goods which are identified and agreed upon at the time of sale. We have also seen that specific goods are contrasted with unascertained goods, which are not identified and agreed upon at the time of sale.

Having decided that the goods sold are specific, the next step is to apply sections 17 and 18 of the SGA 1979. Section 17, which takes precedence over section 18, provides that ownership of specific goods passes when the parties intend it to pass. Section 17 also provides that the intention of the parties can either be a term of the contract or can be inferred from the conduct of the parties or the circumstances of the case.

Example

On 7 July B agrees to buy S's tractor (specific goods). A written contract is drawn up and one of the terms states that ownership is to pass to B on 2 September. Ownership will pass on 2 September, even though an application of section 18 might have come to a different conclusion. Section 17 takes precedence over section 18.

If section 17 does not show when the parties intended the ownership to pass, then the first four rules set out in section 18 will have to be applied. As we shall see, the rules deal with different types of specific goods.

Rule 1 - Specific goods in a deliverable state

Section 18 Rule 1 provides that where specific goods in a deliverable state are unconditionally sold ownership passes to the buyer at the time of the contract, even if the time of delivery and payment are postponed.

Goods are in a deliverable state when the seller has nothing more to do to the goods themselves. Goods could be in a deliverable state even if they needed to be packed. Goods would not be in a deliverable state if the seller had to overhaul them before the buyer was to take delivery.

Example of Rule 1

Tarling v Baxter [1827]

S sold a haystack to B on 6 January. The contract provided that B was to pay the price on 4 February and the haystack was not to be moved until 1 May. The haystack was burned down on 20 January.

Held *Ownership had passed to the buyer on 6 January.*

Rule 2 - Specific goods which the seller must put into a deliverable state

Section 18 Rule 2 provides that where there is a contract for the sale of specific goods and the seller is bound to do something to the goods to put them into a deliverable state, ownership passes when the seller has done the thing and the buyer has notice that it has been done.

Example of Rule 2

Underwood Ltd v Burgh Castle Sand and Cement Syndicate [1922]

On 20 February S sold a 30 ton engine to B. The contract obliged S to detach the engine from a concrete casing and to put it on a train. (This would take over 2 weeks.) While the engine was being loaded on the train it became damaged.

Held *Ownership had not passed to B at the time of the damage. The engine was not in a deliverable state at the time of sale. S was obliged to free the engine and put it on a train in order to put it into a deliverable state. Ownership would only pass to B when S had done these things and had told B that they had been done. (It was not the great weight of the engine which prevented it from being in a deliverable state. A ship which the seller has finished building could be in a deliverable state, even though it might weigh many thousand tons.)*

Rule 3 - Goods to be weighed, measured or tested by the seller to find the price

Rule 3 applies where the seller is to weigh, measure or test the goods, in order to find the price. It provides that in such a case ownership is not to pass until the goods have been weighed, measured or tested and the buyer has been informed of this.

It is important to notice two things here. First, the rule applies only where the weighing etc is to be done by the seller. Second, the weighing etc must be required in order to find the price.

Example of Rule 3

B visits S's scrap yard and sees a heap of copper. It is agreed that B will buy the heap of copper at £100 a ton and that S will weigh the heap to see how much B has to pay. The ownership will pass when S has weighed the heap and told B that this has been done. (If it had been agreed that B would weigh the copper, then Rule 1 would have applied. Ownership would therefore have passed to B as soon as the contract was made.)

Rule 4 - Goods delivered on approval, sale or return or other similar terms

Goods are delivered on approval where the buyer has a choice as to whether or not to buy the goods delivered. Goods are delivered on sale or return where it is understood that the buyer is going to try to resell the goods. If the buyer cannot resell the goods then they will be returned to the seller. Where goods are delivered on approval, sale or return or other similar terms, then the ownership passes to the buyer in the following circumstances:

❑ When the buyer signifies approval.

❑ When the buyer does an act which adopts the transaction. (An act which would prevent the buyer from returning the goods to the seller, such as selling the goods on to another buyer or consuming the goods.)

❑ When the buyer keeps the goods for longer than a time limit fixed by the contract.

❑ If no time limit is fixed by the contract, when the buyer keeps the goods for more than a reasonable time.

Example of Rule 4

S delivers goods to B, a shopkeeper, on sale or return. B sells the goods to a customer. This is an act adopting the transaction. Therefore the ownership passed to B as soon as the goods were sold on. B then immediately passed ownership to the customer under section 18 Rule 1.

Risk, mistake and frustration

We have already seen that section 20 of the SGA 1979 provides that, unless the parties have agreed otherwise, the risk passes from the seller to the buyer at the same time as ownership of the goods passes. So it is possible for the parties to separate risk and ownership, but unless this is done the two pass together.

Section 6 provides that where there is a contract for the sale of specific goods, and the goods without the knowledge of the seller have perished at the time when the contract is made, the contract is void. Goods will have perished if they are stolen or destroyed. Goods will also be regarded as having perished if they become damaged to the point where they can no longer be regarded as the same thing, in a business sense, as the goods which were sold.

Example

> S agrees to sell a combine harvester (specific goods) to B. Unknown to S, the combine harvester had been destroyed in a fire half an hour before the contract was made. The contract is rendered void by section 6. Therefore S will have no obligation to deliver the goods and will not be in breach of contract for failure to do so. B will have no obligation to pay the price and can recover any amount of the price already paid.

Section 7 provides that where there is an agreement to sell specific goods and subsequently the goods, without any fault on the part of the seller or buyer, perish before the risk passes to the buyer, the agreement is avoided.

There are several points to notice about this section. First, the perishing of the goods must not be the fault of the buyer or the seller. (If it is the fault of either party that party will bear the loss.) Second, the goods must perish *after* the contract to sell has been made but *before* the risk has passed. Assuming that the parties have not agreed to separate risk and ownership, section 7 cannot therefore operate when section 18 Rule 1 applies. (Because risk and ownership will pass to the buyer at the same time, that is to say when the contract is made.) Section 7 can operate when section 18 Rules 2 and 3 apply. When section 7 does apply, the rules set out in the Law Reform (Frustrated Contracts) Act 1943, which we considered in Chapter 4, do not apply.

Example

> S agrees to sell a machine tool to B. The contract obliges S to overhaul the machine before delivery is made. The contract will be governed by section 18 Rule 2 because it is a sale of specific goods to be put into a deliverable state by the seller. After the contract has been made, but before S has overhauled the machine, the machine is destroyed in a fire. (The fire was not caused by the fault of either S or B.) Section 7 provides that the contract is frustrated. Therefore S is not in breach of contract for failure to deliver the machine. B need not pay the price and can recover any amount of the price which has already been paid. Other losses, such as time spent by S on trying to free the machine, lie where they fall. (That is to say, no compensation can be claimed in respect of them.)

The following figure shows the rules on the passing of ownership in contracts for the sale of specific goods.

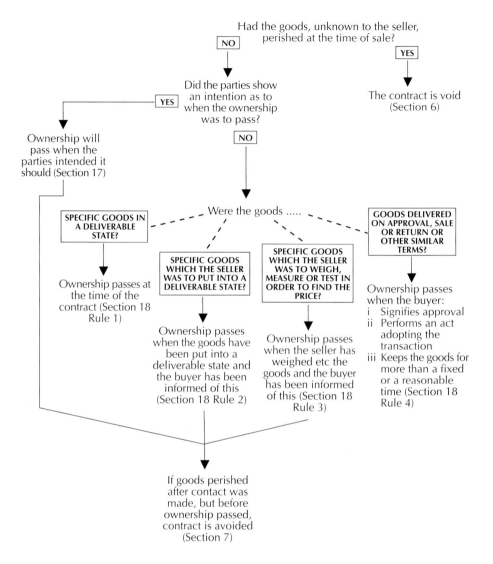

Figure 5.3   The time at which ownership of specific goods passes from the seller to the buyer

Passing of ownership of unascertained goods

Section 16 SGA 1979 provides as follows:

> *[Subject to Section 20A below] Where there is a contract for the sale of unascertained goods no [ownership] in the goods is transferred to the buyer unless and until the goods are ascertained.*

The first thing to notice about section 16 is that it does not tell us when the ownership of unascertained goods does pass. It merely says that the ownership cannot pass until the goods have become ascertained. Unascertained goods which have been sold become ascertained when they are identified as the particular goods which are to become the subject matter of the contract. Once the goods have become ascertained, section 17 will apply and the property will pass when the parties intended it to pass. If section 17 does not show when the ownership is to pass then section 18 Rule 5 will apply.

Section 18 Rule 5 says that the ownership of unascertained goods will pass when goods which match the contract description, and which are in a deliverable state, are unconditionally appropriated to the contract. Goods are unconditionally appropriated to the contract when they are earmarked as the particular goods to be delivered, in such a way that the seller can be taken to have decided that those goods, and no others, were to become the buyer's property. If the seller could still substitute other goods then an unconditional appropriation has not been made.

The unconditional appropriation must be done either by the seller with the buyer's agreement or by the buyer with the seller's agreement. (But a court will be generally be fairly willing to infer that either the buyer or the seller agreed to the unconditional appropriation.) It is important to notice that if the goods are unascertained *at the time of the contract* then the governing rules are section 16, 17 and 18 Rule 5. Once the goods become ascertained you do not switch to section 17 and section 18 Rules 1-4. It is also important to realise that the appropriate sections must be applied in the correct order. First section 16, then section 17, then section 18 Rule 5.

Example

> S sells 100 tons of wheat (unascertained goods) to B. The parties did not show any intention as to when ownership was to pass. S delivers 100 tons of wheat to a carrier to take to B. First, section 16 provides that ownership cannot pass until the goods are ascertained. The goods became ascertained when they were identified as the particular goods to be used in performance of the contract. Second, if the parties had shown an intention as to when the ownership should pass then this intention would have been given effect by section 17 (as long as the goods had become ascertained). Third, as the parties did not shown an intention as to when ownership was to pass, section 18 Rule 5 would apply. Ownership would therefore have passed when the 100 tons of wheat were delivered to the carrier to take to B. This would have been an unconditional appropriation of the goods to the contract and B would be taken to have agreed to it.

Undivided shares in unascertained goods which were a specified quantity of an identified bulk

Sections 20A and 20B of the Sale of Goods Act 1979 were introduced into that Act by the Sale of Goods (Amendment) Act 1995. Before sections 20A and 20B were introduced, the rules on the passing of ownership of unascertained goods could operate very unfairly when a buyer had bought and paid for goods which formed part of an identified bulk. The following case demonstrates this unfairness.

Re Wait [1927]

S owned 1,000 tons of wheat which was on board a certain ship. S sold 500 tons of this wheat to B, who paid the price in full. Before the ship arrived in port, S became insolvent.

Held *The contract was for the sale of unascertained goods because the 500 tons which B had bought had not been identified and agreed upon at the time of sale. (It was just any 500 tons out of the 1,000 tons.) As the sale was of unascertained goods, section 16 provided that ownership could not pass to B until the goods became ascertained. The goods had not become ascertained at the time of S's insolvency and so ownership of the goods could not have passed to B. Therefore B could only hope to claim his money back from S's liquidator as an unsecured creditor.*

When we examined section 16 earlier, we saw that it begins by saying that it is subject to section 20A. Section 20A allows a buyer who has bought a specified quantity of an identified bulk to become a co-owner of the whole bulk even before his share of the bulk is ascertained. However, the section is limited and will only apply if the following conditions are satisfied.

1   The buyer must have bought a specified quantity of unascertained goods which form part of a bulk. (Goods form part of a bulk if they are contained in a defined space or area and all the goods are interchangeable with all the other goods.)

2   The bulk must have been either identified in the contract or identified by later agreement between the parties. For example, the sale of 20 tons of the 100 tons of wheat currently stored in S's warehouse would be within section 20A if it was made plain that B was buying 20 tons out of that particular 100 tons. But if S happened to have 100 tons of wheat in his warehouse, an agreement by S merely to sell B 20 tons of wheat would not be within section 20A at the time of the contract. (It could come within section 20A if the parties subsequently identified that the 20 tons was to be taken from the 100 tons in S's warehouse.)

3   The buyer becomes co-owner of the whole bulk as soon as the price is paid, but only in proportion to the amount of the price of the whole bulk which has been paid.

Example

Re Wait can be used as an example of how section 20A operates. If the facts of the case were to arise today, section 20A would apply because the conditions which it sets out have been satisfied. (B bought and paid for a specified quantity of unascertained goods which formed part of a bulk which was identified in the contract.) Therefore, as soon as B paid the price of his 500 tons he would become a 50% co-owner of the whole bulk of 1,000 tons. (Because he has paid 50% of the price of the whole 1,000 tons.) If B had paid only half the price of his 500 tons, he would have become a 25% co-owner of the whole bulk of 1,000 tons. (Because he would have paid 25% of the price of the whole bulk.)

Where several buyers become owners in common of a bulk, through the operation of section 20A, Section 20B allows the seller to deliver to each buyer the appropriate share of the bulk. Section 20B provides that all the buyers who became co-owners are taken to have agreed to this. When a delivery is made to a buyer under section 20B, section 18 Rule 5 operates to pass ownership in the goods delivered to that particular buyer. When ownership passes to this buyer, the other buyers are given an increased percentage ownership of the remaining bulk.

Example

> Steve has 100 lawn mowers in his warehouse. Steve sells 50 of these to Bill and 30 to Ben. The conditions set out in section 20A are satisfied and Bill and Ben both become co-owners of the 100 lawn mowers. (Bill has 50% ownership and Ben has 30% ownership.) Steve delivers 50 of the lawn mowers to Bill. Bill becomes owner of these 50 lawn mowers, (and loses all co-ownership of the other 50) under section 18 Rule 5. (Goods matching the contract description, and in a deliverable state, have been unconditionally appropriated to the contract.) Section 20B provides that Ben must assent to this delivery to Bill. As Steve has only 50 lawn mowers left, Ben becomes a 60% owner of these 50 lawn mowers.

Sections 6 and 7 have no application to contracts for the sale of unascertained goods. However, section 20 does apply to such contracts and so the risk will pass with ownership of the goods, unless the parties have agreed otherwise.

Figure 5.4 shows the rules on the passing of ownership in contracts for the sale of unascertained goods.

Student Activity Questions 5.2

Sally sells goods to Beryl. When will ownership pass to Beryl if the goods were:

a) specific goods in a deliverable state;

b) specific goods to be put into a deliverable state;

c) specific goods which Sally was to measure in order to find the price;

d) specific goods which Beryl was taking on sale or return;

e) unascertained goods which did not form part of an identified bulk;

f) goods which were a specified quantity of unascertained goods which formed part of a bulk which was identified in the contract?

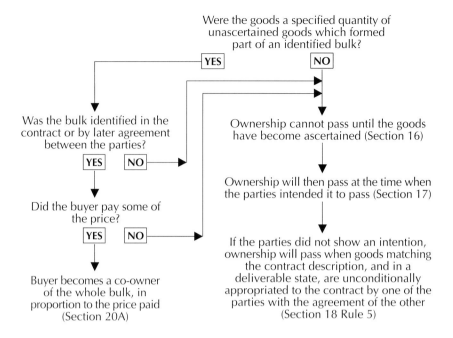

Figure 5.4   The time at which ownership of unascertained goods passes from the seller to the buyer

Duties of the buyer and seller

The seller has one duty – to deliver the goods. The buyer has three duties – to accept the goods, to take delivery of them and to pay the price. The seller's duty to deliver the goods and the buyer's duty to pay the price are said by section 28 to be concurrent conditions unless the parties agree that they should not be. The effect of section 28 is that if the seller is not ready and willing to deliver the goods the buyer need not pay the price, and that if the buyer is not ready and willing to pay the price the seller need not deliver the goods. Section 28 is concerned with the parties' willingness to deliver and pay. It does not require that payment and delivery actually take place at the same time.

The seller's duty to deliver

If the contract was for the sale of specific goods, then the seller must deliver those specific goods. If the contract was for the sale of unascertained goods, then the seller can deliver any goods which match the contract description.

Example

Stephen agrees to sell his car (specific goods) to B1 and 10 tons of Basmati rice (unascertained goods) to B2. Stephen must deliver the specific car sold, and no other, to B1. Stephen can deliver any 10 tons of Basmati rice which match the contract description to B2.

The delivery of goods is concerned with passing possession of goods, not with passing ownership. (We have already examined the circumstances in which ownership will pass.) Delivery will usually be made physically. However, delivery to the buyer can also be made in the following ways.

❒ By delivering the goods to a carrier who is to take the goods to the buyer.

❒ By delivering a 'document of title' such as a bill of lading to the buyer.

❒ By delivering the means to control the goods to the buyer. For example, a seller could deliver a car by giving the buyer the keys to the car.

❒ By getting a third party who has possession of the goods (such as a warehouse keeper) to acknowledge that the goods are now held on behalf of the buyer.

❒ Where the buyer already has possession of the goods, by allowing the buyer to retain possession.

Place of delivery

Section 29 of the SGA 1979 provides that:

1) *Whether it is for the buyer to take possession of the goods or for the seller to send them to the buyer is a question depending in each case on the contract, express or implied, between the parties.*

2) *Apart from any such contract, express or implied, the place of delivery is the seller's place of business if he has one, and if not, his residence; except that, if the contract is for the sale of specific goods, which to the knowledge of the parties when the contract is made are in some other place, then that place is the place of delivery.*

First, then section 29(1) makes it plain that the parties might either have agreed that the seller will take the goods to the buyer, or that the buyer will fetch the goods from the seller. But if no such agreement has been made, then section 29(2) will apply. As regards unascertained goods, section 29(2) provides that the place of delivery is the seller's place of business or, if the seller has no place of business, the seller's home. This is also true of specific goods - with one exception. If both parties know that the specific goods are in some other place, that place is the place of delivery.

Example

> Stan, a garage owner in London, agrees to sell a Jaguar which is standing on the fore-
> court of his garage to B1. Stan also agrees to sell a Bentley to B2. Both Stan and B2
> know that the Bentley is standing in a warehouse in Huddersfield. The place of
> delivery of the Jaguar is Stan's place of business, his garage. The place of delivery of
> the Bentley is the warehouse in Huddersfield. B1 must therefore come to Stan's garage
> to collect the Jaguar. B2 must go to the warehouse in Huddersfield to collect the
> Bentley. Stan fulfils the duty to deliver both cars by making them available for collec-
> tion by B1 and B2.

It can be seen that in the Sale of Goods Act the word 'delivery' has a technical sense and
is not used in its everyday sense. If I buy a washing machine from a shop then the shop
fulfils its duty to deliver by allowing me to collect the machine. (For this reason, shops
can charge extra for physical delivery to the buyer's house.)

Time of delivery

If the contract fixes a time for delivery then delivery must be made at this time. If no time
for delivery is fixed, then delivery must be made within a reasonable time. The amount
of time which is reasonable will depend upon all the circumstances of the case.

In Chapter 2 we saw that a breach of warranty entitles the injured party to damages, but
not to terminate the contract. We also saw that a breach of condition allows the injured
party to claim damages and/or to terminate the contract. Section 10(2) of the SGA 1979
states that whether late delivery is a breach of condition or a breach of warranty depends
upon all the circumstances of the case. In commercial contracts any time fixing delivery
is likely to be regarded as a condition.

Bowes v Shand [1877]

A cargo of rice was sold. The contract stated that the rice was to put on board a certain ship during March or April 1874. 87% of the rice was put on board the correct ship in February 1874. The remainder of the rice was put on board in March.

Held *The buyers could reject the whole cargo of rice and terminate the contract, even though the value of the rice was unaffected by the early shipment. A condition of the contract had been breached.*

Delivery of the wrong quantity

If the seller delivers to the buyer a lesser quantity of goods than the contract required, section 30 of the SGA 1979 gives the buyer a choice: the buyer may either reject the goods (and sue the seller for damages for non-delivery); or accept the goods, pay for them at the contract rate and sue the seller for damages for non-delivery of the shortfall.

Example

> S agrees to sell 100 tons of wheat to B for £1,500. S delivers only 90 tons of wheat. B can reject the 90 tons and sue S for non-delivery. Alternatively, B can accept the 90 tons, pay S £1,350 and sue S for damages for non-delivery of the 10 tons which were not delivered.

If the seller delivers a quantity of goods which is greater than the contract called for, section 30 gives the buyer three options. First, the buyer may reject all of the goods and sue the seller for damages for non-delivery; second, the buyer can accept the quantity of goods which should have been delivered and pay the contract price; third, the buyer may accept the whole quantity of goods delivered and pay for them at the contract rate.

Example

> S agreed to sell B 100 tons of wheat for £1,500. S delivers 110 tons of wheat. B can either: reject the delivery and sue S for damages for non-delivery; accept 100 tons and pay the contract price of £1,500; accept all 110 tons and pay £1,650.

A deviation in the quantity delivered can be ignored if it was so slight that it could be regarded as 'a trifle'. For example, in *Shipton Anderson & Co v Weil Bros [1912]* the buyer tried to reject a delivery of 4,950 tons of wheat because the delivery was 55 pounds overweight. The buyer could not reject because the deviation was so slight as to be a trifle.

Delivery by instalments

Section 31 of the SGA 1979 provides that the buyer does not have to accept delivery by instalments unless the contract provided for delivery by instalments. If this were not the case, a seller who delivered less than the contract required could later top the delivery up.

If a contract does provide for delivery by instalments difficulties arise where the seller breaches a condition by delivering one defective instalment. Can the buyer reject just that one instalment? Or can the buyer terminate the whole contract? Section 31 provides that the answer depends upon whether the seller's breach, in delivering the defective instalment, was a repudiation of the whole contract. If it was a repudiation of the whole contract the buyer can treat the whole contract as terminated and sue for non-delivery as regards all future instalments. If delivering the defective instalment was not a repudiation of the whole contract, the buyer cannot treat the whole contract as repudiated. (The buyer can still refuse to accept the one defective instalment and sue for damages for non-delivery of that particular instalment.) In deciding whether or not a defective delivery of one instalment was a repudiation of the whole contract section 31 says that regard must be had to the terms of the contract and the circumstances of the case. The two most important circumstances will be (i) the percentage of the contract to which the breach related, and (ii) the likelihood of the breach being repeated. The following two cases provide examples of these tests being applied.

Maple Flock Ltd v Universal Furniture Products Ltd [1934]

100 tons of waste wool was sold, delivery to be made by instalments of one and a half tons each. The first fifteen instalments delivered were satisfactory. The sixteenth instalment was defective because it contained 8 times more than the legal limit of chlorine. By the time the buyers noticed this defect, two more satisfactory instalments had been delivered.

Held The buyers could not treat the whole contract as terminated. The breach was unlikely to be repeated and affected only a small percentage of the whole contract.

Robert Munro & Co Ltd v Meyer [1930]

1,500 tons of bone meal were sold, delivery to be by 10 instalments. After 600 tons had been delivered the buyers discovered that all of the meal so far delivered had been deliberately mixed with cocoa husks.

Held The buyers could treat the whole contract as terminated. The breach concerned a large percentage of the contract and indicated that future deliveries might also be defective.

The buyer's duty to pay the price

Section 8 sets out the way in which the price of the goods may be fixed.

> 1) *The price in a contract of sale may be fixed by the contract, or may be left to be fixed in a manner agreed by the contract, or may be determined by the course of dealing between the parties.*
>
> 2) *When the price is not determined as mentioned in subsection (1) above the buyer must pay a reasonable price.*
>
> 3) *What is a reasonable price is a question of fact dependent on the circumstances of each particular case.*

If there appears to be a contract of sale of goods but the price cannot be found, then the contract will be void for lack of agreement. However, section 8 shows that even where the parties do not expressly agree the price, or agree how the price should be fixed, the price usually can be found. First, a course of dealing between the parties might fix the price, under section 8(1). For example, let us assume that B, a plumber, frequently buys a particular type of copper piping from S, a plumber's merchant. The first few times B makes such purchases the price is agreed at £1 a foot. If B rings up and orders another 100 feet of this type of piping, without mentioning the price, then the course of dealing which has taken place between the parties will fix the price at £100.So if S has changed the price, this change must be communicated to B before it will become effective. Second, where the price is not fixed by section 8(1), section 8(2) provides that a reasonable price must be paid. So, to extend the example just considered, even if S and B had never previously dealt with each other, the price would still be fixed. Section 8(2) would require that B pay a reasonable price. A court could calculate this price by considering all the circumstances (section 8(3)). The court would therefore hear evidence as to what a plumber's merchant such as S would usually charge a plumber for 100 feet of this type of pipe.

The buyer's duties to accept the goods and take delivery of them

The buyer's duty to accept the goods requires the buyer not to reject the goods without a justifiable reason for doing so. Such a rejection of the goods could be made either before or after the goods had been delivered. If the buyer does wrongfully reject the goods the seller can sue for damages for non-acceptance. The buyer also has a duty to take delivery of the goods if requested to do so by the seller. (This duty is concerned with the buyer physically taking possession of the goods.)

Student Activity Questions 5.3

1) Bruce visits Sally's shop and agrees to buy a new washing-machine. Nothing is agreed about delivery. Where will the place of delivery be? How will Sally fulfil her duty to deliver the goods?

2) Sheila sold 10 tons of coal to Brian and 10 tons of coke to Bashir. Sheila only delivered 9 tons of coal to Brian but delivered 11 tons of coke to Bashir. What options are open to Brian and Bashir?

3) Sheila agrees to deliver goods to Brian by ten instalments. The second instalment is defective because the goods delivered are not of satisfactory quality. How will a court decide whether or not Brian has the right to treat the whole contract as terminated?

Remedies of the buyer and seller

The buyer's remedies

The Sale of Goods Act 1979 gives the buyer the right to sue for damages if the seller either fails to deliver the goods or if the seller breaches a warranty. If the seller repudiates the contract or breaches a condition the buyer will be able to treat the contract as terminated. However, once the buyer has accepted the goods the right to treat the contract as terminated for breach of condition will be lost. The right to damages will, however, remain even after the goods have been accepted. Acceptance is therefore an important matter which needs to be considered in some detail.

Acceptance by the buyer

If the seller has breached a condition, or if the seller has repudiated the contract, then the buyer has a right to reject the goods and to terminate the contract. This right to reject can be exercised even if the buyer has taken delivery of the goods and even if ownership of the goods has passed to the buyer. A buyer who rejects the goods does not need to return the goods physically to the seller. All the buyer has to do is let the seller know that the goods are rejected, and to make them available for collection by the seller. If the buyer does properly reject the goods then the seller can be sued for damages for non-delivery. A buyer with the right to reject the goods may choose instead to accept the goods and to sue the seller for damages for breach of warranty. (Section 11(2).)

Section 11(4) of the SGA 1979 provides that a buyer who has accepted the goods will no longer be able to treat the contract as terminated and to reject the goods, even if the seller has breached a condition. The buyer's right to damages will remain. The rule in section 11(4) applies whether the breach of condition was caused by delivering the wrong quantity of goods or by delivering goods of the wrong quality.

Section 35 SGA 1979 sets out three ways in which the buyer can be deemed to have accepted the goods. These ways are as follows.

(i)   The buyer indicates to the seller that the goods are accepted.

(ii) After the goods have been delivered to the buyer, the buyer does any act which is inconsistent with the seller still owning the goods. For example, if the buyer physically altered the goods or consumed them this would be regarded as acceptance, because to do these things would be inconsistent with the seller still owning the goods. If the buyer resells the goods to a sub-buyer, or gets a third party to repair the goods, either of these actions could amount to acceptance. However, reselling the goods or getting them repaired will not amount to acceptance unless the buyer has had a reasonable opportunity to examine the goods.

(iii) The buyer keeps the goods for more than a reasonable time, without letting the seller know that the goods are rejected.

Example

> Billy buys a second-hand car from Sarah's garage. The car is not of satisfactory quality and therefore section 14(2) SGA 1979 has been breached. This breach is a breach of condition and so Billy can reject the car and terminate the contract, as well as claim damages. Billy can reject the car even though it has been delivered to him and even though ownership has passed to him. If Billy told Sarah that he was aware of the defects but was still accepting the car, then he could still claim damages but could not reject the car. Similarly, Billy could not reject the car if he had sprayed it a different colour or if he waited six months before letting Sarah know that he was rejecting it.

When goods are delivered to a buyer who has not already examined the goods, the buyer cannot lose the right to reject by indicating to the seller that the goods are accepted, unless the buyer has had a reasonable opportunity to examine the goods. For example, when goods are delivered, buyers often sign a delivery note saying that the goods are in perfect condition and that they are accepted. Signing such a note cannot amount to acceptance until the buyer has had a chance to examine the goods to see if they conform with the contract.

Partial rejection

If goods are delivered to the buyer and some of the goods conform to the contract whilst others do not, the buyer has three options.

First, the buyer can reject all of the goods and sue the seller for non-delivery.

Second, the buyer can accept only the goods which do conform to the contract. (The goods which do not conform to the contract can be rejected and the seller can be sued for non-delivery in respect of these goods.)

Third, the buyer can accept all of the goods which do conform to the contract and also accept some of the goods which do not. (The seller can be sued for non-delivery in respect of those goods which are rejected. The seller can also be sued for breach of warranty of quality as regards the goods which did not conform to the contract but which were accepted.)

However, there is no right of partial rejection where the goods form part of one commercial unit. For example, a buyer who bought a set of encyclopaedias and accepted one volume would not be able to reject later volumes which were badly printed. (The buyer would be able to claim damages for breach of warranty of quality.)

The buyer's right to damages for non-delivery

The buyer's right to sue for non-delivery arises in the following three circumstances.

i)   Where the seller wrongfully neglects to deliver the goods.

ii) Where the seller wrongfully refuses to deliver the goods.

iii) Where the seller breaches a condition and the buyer decides to treat the contract as terminated and rejects the goods. (A buyer who has received possession of the goods, but who is treating the contract as terminated on account of the seller's breach of a condition, and is therefore rejecting the goods, must make the goods available for collection by the seller.)

Section 51(2) repeats the first rule in *Hadley v Baxendale* by providing that the measure of damages for non-delivery is the estimated loss directly and naturally arising in the ordinary course of events from the seller's breach of contract.

Where there is an available market for the goods section 51(3) provides that the amount of damages is generally to be the difference in price between the contract price and the market price of the goods at the time when the goods should have been delivered. There will be an available market for the goods if the goods were not unique, if a different seller of such goods could be found, and if the price of such goods could be fixed by supply and demand. There is no market price for second-hand cars as they are regarded as unique goods.

A buyer who has a right to claim damages for non-delivery, can also refuse to pay the contract price and can recover any amount of the price which has already been paid.

Example

> On 6 July S agrees to sell B 10 tons of coal for £1,000, delivery to be made on 1 December. B pays £100 in advance. S refuses to deliver on 1 December. B can recover the £100 already paid. If there was an available market for coal of this type on 1 December, and the market price for 10 tons of such coal was £1,500, B's damages would usually be £500. If on 1 December the market price of this type of coal was either £1,000 or £750, B's damages would generally be nominal. (That is to say no substantial damages could be claimed.)

If goods are delivered late, but the buyer chooses to accept the goods, damages will be assessed on ordinary contract principles. (Which were considered in Chapter 4.) The buyer might be able to claim for loss of profit and for loss caused by the difference in the price of the goods when they were delivered and the price at the time when they should have been delivered.

Damages for breach of warranty

The buyer may claim damages for breach of warranty in the following three circumstances.

i)   Where the seller breaches a warranty.

ii) Where the seller breaches a condition and the buyer chooses to treat this as a breach of warranty.

iii) Where the seller breaches a condition which the buyer is compelled (by reason of having accepted the goods) to treat as a breach of warranty.

In all three of these circumstances the buyer cannot reject the goods, but can sue for damages for breach of warranty. If the buyer has not already paid the full price, the amount which would be claimable as damages can be deduced from the amount of the price which is still owing.

Section 53(2) provides that the damages for breach of warranty should be calculated using the first rule in *Hadley v Baxendale*. Section 53(3) provides that where the breach is a breach of warranty of quality the buyer's damages are generally to be the difference between the goods in the state they were in at the time of delivery and the amount they would have been worth if the warranty had not been breached.

Example

B buys a tea service from a shop for £150. The tea service is not of satisfactory quality because several of the cups are chipped. B does nothing about this for six months and is therefore deemed to have accepted the goods. B no longer therefore has the right to treat the contract as terminated. B then claims damages. If the tea service would only have been worth £50 at the time of delivery, on account of the tea cups being chipped, B's damages will generally be £100.

Specific performance

Section 52 SGA 1979 provides that a buyer might be able to claim specific performance of the contract where the seller breaches an obligation to deliver specific or ascertained goods. In Chapter 4 we examined the very limited circumstances in which an order of specific performance will be made.

Student Activity Questions 5.4

1) What is the significance of a buyer of goods having accepted the goods?

2) In what three ways can a buyer of goods be deemed to have accepted the goods?

3) In what circumstances will a buyer of goods have the right to sue for damages for non-delivery?

4) In what circumstances will a buyer of goods be entitled to sue for damages for breach of warranty?

The seller's remedies

If the buyer breaches a contract of sale of goods the seller will always be entitled to a remedy. The remedies available are classed as either real remedies or personal remedies. The real remedies are taken against the goods, whereas the personal remedies give the seller the right to sue the buyer.

The personal remedies of the seller

The Sale of Goods Act 1979 gives the seller two personal remedies against the buyer. These remedies are to sue for the price or to sue for damages for non-acceptance.

The right to sue for the price

Section 49 of the SGA 1979 provides that the seller can only sue the buyer for the price if either the contract fixed a definite date for payment, or if the ownership of the goods has passed to the buyer.

Colley v Overseas Exporters Ltd [1921]

Unascertained goods were sold. The contract provided that ownership should pass when the goods were loaded on board a ship which the buyer had a duty to nominate. The buyer breached a condition of the contract because he did not nominate an effective ship. This caused the goods to be left lying around on a dockside. The seller sued the buyer for the contract price.

Held *The seller was not entitled to the price. The contract had not fixed a definite date for payment and ownership of the goods had not passed to the buyer. (This case is not as harsh on the seller as it might seem. The seller could sue the buyer for damages for non-acceptance.)*

We saw in Chapter 4 that a seller who sues for the price is suing in debt and so has no duty to mitigate the loss.

Damages for non-acceptance

The seller can sue for damages for non-acceptance if the buyer wrongfully refuses or neglects to accept the goods. The right to sue for damages for non-acceptance is not affected by whether or not the ownership of the goods has passed to the buyer.

Section 50(2) provides that the amount of damages is generally the loss directly and naturally resulting in the ordinary course of events from the buyer's breach of contract. This restates the first rule in *Hadley v Baxendale* and allows the seller to recover damages in respect of matters such as profit lost on account of the buyer not having accepted.

Section 50(3) provides that where there is an available market for the goods the seller's damages are generally assessed as the difference between the contract price and the market price of the goods when the goods ought to have been accepted or when the buyer refused to accept.

Example

> On 1 December S agrees to sell 10 tons of coal to B for £1,000, delivery to be made on 1 February. On 1 February S tries to deliver but B refuses to accept the coal, saying that it does not match the contract description. In fact, the coal delivered did match the contract description. B has therefore wrongfully refused to accept the goods. S can sue for damages for non-acceptance. On 1 February there is an available market for this type of coal. If on 1 February the market price of this type of coal is £90 per ton, S's damages will generally be assessed at £100 (10 x £10). If the market price on 1 February is either £110 a ton or £100 a ton, S would generally be entitled only to nominal damages

Section 54 allows the seller to recover additional damages to cover matters such as storing the goods, insuring the goods or the cost of setting up a sale to a different buyer.

Damages for refusing to take delivery on time

Where the buyer does accept the goods, but accepts them late, the seller can sue for damages for refusing to take delivery. Section 37 allows for this where the seller is ready and willing to deliver the goods, and requests the buyer to take delivery, but the buyer refuse to do this. It provides that the seller can sue for any loss caused by the buyer's refusal to take delivery and for a reasonable charge for care and custody of the goods. This section compensates the seller for incidental losses incurred, such as looking after the goods, but not for the loss of the bargain.

Seller's right to terminate the contract

The seller has the right to terminate the contract if the buyer repudiates the contract. A buyer who shows an unwillingness to be bound by the contract will be regarded as having repudiated the contract. A seller who rightfully terminates can sue for damages and (possibly) for the contract price.

Example

> Simon has sold a lorry to Barry for £20,000. After the contract was made, but before the lorry has been delivered, Barry told Simon that he had changed his mind. He told Simon not to bother delivering the lorry and that the price would not be paid. Barry has repudiated the contract. Simon can terminate the contract and sue Barry for damages for non-acceptance. If ownership of the lorry had passed to Barry, or if the contract fixed a definite date for payment, Simon could sue for the price.

The real remedies of the unpaid seller

In addition to the personal remedies already explained, an unpaid seller of goods has three real remedies which allow action to be taken against the goods sold. These remedies are available only to an unpaid seller. Section 36 of the Act defines an unpaid seller as (a) a seller who has not been paid, or to whom the buyer has not tendered, the whole of the purchase price; or (b) a seller who has received a dishonoured cheque (or other negotiable instrument) as payment for the goods. The fact that the seller has given the buyer credit will not prevent the seller from being an unpaid seller.

The three remedies which might be available to an unpaid seller of goods are: a lien over the goods; the right to stop the goods in transit; and the right to resell the goods.

The unpaid seller's lien

Section 41 provides that the unpaid seller's lien allows an unpaid seller to retain possession of the goods (even if ownership has passed to the buyer or the goods should have been delivered) in the following three circumstances:

a) where the goods have been sold without any stipulation as to credit; or

b) where the goods have been sold on credit but the term of credit has expired; or

c) where the buyer has become insolvent.

By exercising the lien, the unpaid seller is not terminating the contract but merely exercising a self-help remedy. As soon as the price is paid by the buyer, or by the buyer's liquidator, the lien will be lost and the seller will be obliged to hand over possession of the goods. A lien can be particularly useful when a buyer has become insolvent before the goods have been delivered. Notice that a lien cannot be claimed where the buyer has been granted credit, unless the credit term has expired.

Example

B buys a combine harvester from S for £58,000. The combine harvester was specific goods in a deliverable state and therefore under section 18 Rule 1 ownership passed to B as soon as the contract was made. B is not given credit. B pays half of the price but S refuses to give up possession of the combine harvester until the full price is paid. S has a right to do this. S is an unpaid seller and is exercising the right of lien. B then pays the rest of the price and S loses the lien. S must therefore now allow B to take possession of the combine harvester.

Section 43 provides that an unpaid seller can lose a lien in three ways. First, by waiving the right to the lien (that is to say, by voluntarily surrendering the right to it). Second, by delivering the goods to a carrier to take to the buyer without reserving the right of disposal of the goods. Third, by allowing the buyer to lawfully gains possession of the goods. The seller's retaining possession of the goods is therefore the key to the lien.

The right of stoppage in transit

We have seen that the seller's lien is lost once the goods are delivered to a carrier who is to take them to the buyer. If the buyer has become insolvent, and only if the buyer has become insolvent, section 46 may give the seller the right to stop the goods in transit. The effect of stoppage in transit is that the seller will recover possession of the goods from the carrier. This is likely to be very important because if the goods are delivered to the buyer the buyer's liquidator will be entitled to keep them. The seller would then be reduced to making a claim as an unsecured creditor. If stoppage in transit is achieved the buyer' liquidator would have the option of enforcing the contract, but the seller would have to be paid the full price of the goods. To achieve stoppage in transit the unpaid seller mus let the carrier know that this is being done *before the carrier delivers the goods to th buyer.* As soon as the goods are delivered to the buyer the right to stoppage in transit wi be lost.

Example

> Stephen has sold 12 new cars to B Ltd. The contract price is £90,000. B Ltd has paid a deposit of £9,000. The cars are handed over to British Rail for delivery to B Ltd. (Therefore ownership passes to B Ltd by virtue of section 18 Rule 5.) Stephen then hears on the radio that B Ltd has become insolvent. Stephen phones British Rail and tells them that he is effecting stoppage in transit. British Rail must return the cars to Stephen, who must pay the cost of this. B Ltd's liquidator can enforce the contract, and so gain possession of the cars, but only by paying Stephen the rest of the price (£81,000). If B Ltd's liquidator does not enforce the contract, Stephen will have to refund to the liquidator the £9,000 already received.

Stoppage in transit is only possible where the carrier is not the agent of either the buye or the seller. If the carrier is the buyer's agent then delivery will have been made to th buyer. If the carrier is the seller's agent stoppage in transit is not necessary, as the ager should anyway obey the seller's instructions to bring the goods back. Stoppage in trans and the right to a lien apply only where the ownership has already passed to the buye Where ownership has not already passed, section 39 gives an unpaid seller a very simil right to withhold delivery until the full price is paid.

The right to resell the goods

Once ownership of the goods has passed to the buyer, the seller no longer has the rig to sell the goods to a different buyer. The goods no longer belong to the seller. Howeve in three circumstances section 48 of the SGA 1979 gives an unpaid seller the right resell the goods without breaching the contract with the original buyer. The three circun stances in which the right of resale arises are as follows.

1) Where the goods are perishable and the buyer does not pay the price, or tender th price, within a reasonable time.

2) Where the unpaid seller gives the buyer notice of an intention to resell the goods an the buyer does not pay the price within a reasonable time.

3) Where a term of the contract expressly gives the unpaid seller a right to resell th goods.

It should be noticed that the buyer's insolvency does not give the unpaid seller the right to resell. The buyer's liquidator might choose to pay the full price and enforce the contract.

Example

> S sells a ton of bananas to B for £400. B is not granted credit. S asks for the price but B does not pay it. S exercises a lien over the bananas and refuses to let B have possession of them. S tells B that the bananas must be paid for as they are beginning to over ripen. B still does not pay the price or tender it. S can resell the bananas to B2, without breaching the contract with B1.

If the seller exercises the right of resale this terminates the contract with the original buyer. If the seller resells the goods for a higher price than was agreed with the original buyer then the seller can keep the profit. If the seller resells the goods at a lower price than was agreed with the original buyer then the original buyer must compensate the seller for this loss. The seller must return to the original buyer any part of the price which has been paid.

Reservation of title (ownership) by the seller

Section 19 gives the seller the right to retain ownership of goods sold until some condition (almost always that the buyer has paid the full price) is fulfilled. A clause in a contract which says that the ownership of the goods is not to pass until some condition has been fulfilled is called a reservation of title clause, or a reservation of ownership clause.

Example

> S sells his second-hand car to B, who takes delivery of the car. A term of the contract states that ownership of the car is not to pass to B until the full price is paid. Normally, ownership would have passed at the time of the contract because the goods were specific goods in a deliverable state (section 18 Rule 1). However, ownership will not pass to B until the full price is paid. So if B becomes insolvent, S will be able to reclaim possession of the car from B's liquidator because S is still the owner of the car. S would then have to refund to B's liquidator any part of the price which B had already paid. If there had been no reservation of title clause B's liquidator would have been entitled to keep the car (it would have been B's property at the time of B's insolvency) and S could only have claimed for the price as an unsecured creditor.

The law on reservation of title is very complex, but the following points should be noted.

1) Section 25 gives a buyer who has possession of the goods, but who has not yet acquired ownership, the power (but not the right) to pass ownership to a sub-buyer who buys the goods in good faith, and who takes possession of the goods.

Example

> S sells 200 tons of wheat to B1. The wheat is delivered to B1. A reservation of title clause states that B1 is not to own the wheat until the full price has been paid. B1 sells the wheat to B2, who does not know of the reservation of title clause. B2 takes possession of the wheat. B1 becomes insolvent without having paid any of the price to S. S cannot recover the wheat from B2 or make any claim against B2. S can make a claim against B1's liquidator for the price of the wheat.

2) A reservation of title clause cannot be effective once the goods sold have been manu-factured into other goods.

Re Peachdart Ltd [1983]

S supplied leather to B Ltd. The contract contained a reservation of title clause. B L *manufactured the leather into handbags. B Ltd then became insolvent.*

Held *S could not reclaim the leather or the handbags, even though the reservation of tit* *clause said that S could do either of these things. S could only make a claim against L* *liquidator as an unsecured creditor.*

3) A reservation of title clause will be effective to allow the seller to reclaim the goo if the buyer still has the goods and they have not been manufactured into oth goods. This is the case even if the buyer has become insolvent.

4) A reservation of title clause which states that if B sells the goods any money receive by B belongs to S is unlikely to be effective.

Student Activity Questions 5.5

1) In what circumstances can a seller of goods sue the buyer for the price?

2) Is it possible for a seller of goods to sue the buyer for damages for non-acceptance if ownership of the goods has already passed to the buyer?

3) What are the three real remedies which might be available to an unpaid seller?

4) How is an unpaid seller defined?

5) What is a reservation of title clause?

Essential points

Transfer of ownership of the goods

- The purpose of a contract of sale of goods is to pass ownership of the goods to the buyer in return for payment of the price

- Unless the buyer and the seller have agreed otherwise, the risk of the goods becoming lost or damaged remains with the seller until ownership of the goods passes to the buyer.

- Ownership of specific goods passes from the seller to the buyer when the parties intend it to pass. If no intention can be found, the first four rules in section 18 of the Sale of Goods Act will apply.

- Rule 1 provides that where specific goods in a deliverable state are unconditionally sold, ownership passes to the buyer at the time of the contract, even if the times of delivery and payment are postponed.

- Rule 2 provides that where there is a contract for the sale of specific goods, and the seller is bound to do something to the goods to put them into a deliverable state, ownership passes when the seller has done the thing and the buyer has notice that it has been done.

- Rule 3 applies where the seller is to weigh, measure or test the goods, in order to find the price. It provides that in such a case ownership is not to pass until the goods have been weighed, measured or tested and the buyer has been informed of this.

- Where goods are delivered on approval, on sale or return or on other similar terms, then the ownership passes to the buyer in the following circumstances: when the buyer signifies approval; when the buyer does an act which adopts the transaction; when the buyer keeps the goods for longer than a time limit fixed by the contract; or if no time limit is fixed by the contract, when the buyer keeps the goods for more than a reasonable time.

- Where there is a contract for the sale of specific goods and the goods without the knowledge of the seller have perished at the time when the contract is made, the contract is void.

- Where there is an agreement to sell specific goods and subsequently the goods, without any fault on the part of the seller or buyer, perish before the risk passes to the buyer, the agreement is avoided.

- Where there is a contract for the sale of unascertained goods no ownership in the goods is transferred to the buyer unless and until the goods are ascertained. (The only exception to this rule is in section 20A, which allows a buyer who has bought a specified quantity of an identified bulk to become a co-owner of the whole bulk even before his share of the bulk is ascertained.)

- Once unascertained goods have become ascertained ownership passes when the parties intend it to pass. If the parties do not show an intention as to when ownership should pass it will pass when goods which match the contract description and which are in a deliverable state, are unconditionally appropriated to the contract. The appropriation must be done by one of the parties to the contract with the express or implied consent of the other party.

Duties of the buyer and the seller

- The seller has a duty to deliver the goods.

- If the seller delivers to the buyer a lesser quantity of goods than the contract required the buyer may either: reject the goods (and sue the seller for damages for non-delivery); or accept the goods, pay for them at the contract rate, and sue the seller for damages for non-delivery of the shortfall.

- If the seller delivers a quantity of goods which is greater than the contract called for the buyer may either: reject all of the goods (and sue the seller for damages for non-delivery); or accept the quantity of goods which should have been delivered and pay the contract price; or accept the whole quantity of goods delivered and pay for them at the contract rate.

- If no time for delivery is fixed then the goods must be delivered within a reasonable time.

- The buyer has three duties: to accept the goods, to take delivery of the goods and to pay the price.

Remedies of the buyer and seller

- A buyer who has accepted the goods will not be able to reject the goods even if the seller has breached a condition of the contract. (The buyer will have the right to claim damages if any term of the contract is breached.)

- The buyer can be deemed to have accepted the goods in three ways: by indicating to the seller that the goods are accepted; by doing an act which is inconsistent with the seller's continuing ownership; or by keeping the goods for more than a reasonable time without letting the seller know that they have been rejected.

- The buyer can claim damages if the seller does not deliver the goods or if the seller breaches a warranty.

- The seller can sue for the contract price only if the contract fixed a definite date for payment or if ownership of the goods has passed to the seller.

- If the buyer wrongfully refuses to accept the goods the seller can sue for damages for non-acceptance.

- An unpaid seller is given three real remedies. These are to exercise a lien over the goods, to stop the goods in transit or to resell the goods.

- A seller is an unpaid seller if the buyer has not paid or tendered the whole of the purchase price or if the seller has taken a dishonoured cheque as payment for the goods.

- It is possible for a seller of goods to reserve ownership of the goods until the buyer has paid the full price of the goods. If this is done, ownership remains with the seller even though the buyer may take possession of the goods.

End of chapter questions

Question 1

Sid, who has owned and run a bicycle shop for many years has decided to retire. Bryony intends to open a bicycle shop shortly. Sid invites Bryony to his shop to see if she wants to buy any of his stock. Bryony visits Sid's shop on Monday and agrees to buy the following things.

a) A Super Deluxe Velocipede Mark 2 bicycle, which Sid is repairing. Sid agrees that he will finish the repairs within 2 days and that this bicycle will then be available for collection by Bryony.

b) All the paraffin stored in Sid's tank, at a price of £1 a gallon. It is not known how much paraffin is in the tank and Sid is to measure the paraffin to discover the price which Bryony must pay.

c) 3 of the 6 Velocipede Mark 1 bicycles which are stored in Sid's basement.

d) Sid's computer, on which he keeps track of all his business dealings.

e) A tricycle, which Bryony is to test ride. If Bryony likes the tricycle she will let Sid know and she will then buy it. If she does not like the tricycle she will return it within two weeks.

Bryony does not take any of the goods with her, except for the tricycle. On Monday night Sid's shop is burnt down by a stray firework and all of the contents of the shop are destroyed. Advise Bryony, who has decided that she does not want to buy the tricycle, of her legal position.

Question 2

On 1 March Bertha agrees to buy 100 bags of potatoes from Susan. The price is £200 and it is agreed that Susan will deliver the potatoes in one month's time, when she has herself bought them from a farmer. Bertha pays £20 of the price in advance. She is given credit as regards the rest of the price, which is to be paid on 1 September.

a) Where would the place of delivery of the potatoes be?

b) What would the legal position be if Susan did not deliver the potatoes on time?

c) What would the legal position be if Susan delivered 120 bags of potatoes, instead of 100 bags?

d) What would the legal position be if Bertha made it plain that she was not going to take delivery of the potatoes or pay for them?

e) If delivery was to be made in 10 instalments, what would Bertha's position be if the second instalment contained many rotten potatoes?

f) If no price had been fixed, would there be a contract? If so, how would the price be fixed?

g) What remedies would be available to Bertha if she took delivery of the potatoes and stored them and, six months later, discovered that they had been rotten at the time of delivery?

h) What would the legal position be if Bertha took delivery of the potatoes and immediately discovered that they were rotten?

i) In what circumstances could Susan sue Bertha for the £180 of the price which has not yet been paid?

j) Is Susan an unpaid seller?

k) Would Susan have a right to a lien? If Susan did have a right to a lien, what would this right amount to?

l) In what circumstances would Susan have a right to stop the goods in transit? How would she do this and what would the effect of doing it be?

m) In what circumstances would Susan have the right to resell the potatoes to a different buyer?

n) If Susan delivered the potatoes to Bertha, what would be the effect of a reservation of title clause in the contract?

Task 5

A friend of yours who is visiting the country from abroad is thinking of setting up a trading company in the UK. Your friend is keen to understand English law as it relates to the sale of goods, and has asked you to draft a report explaining the following matters.

a) How a contract of sale of goods is defined.

b) The time at which ownership of the goods sold is transferred from the seller to the buyer.

c) The duties of the buyer and the seller in a contract of sale of goods.

d) The remedies available to the buyer and the seller should a contract of sale of goods be breached.

6 The Tort of Negligence

In the first four chapters of this book we considered the general law of contract. In Chapter 5 we considered the special rules which apply to one particular type of contract, a contract of sale of goods. In this chapter we consider a different type of liability, liability in tort. Before considering specific rules about particular torts we first need to consider the differences between liability in contract and liability in tort. We then examine in some detail the major principles of the tort of negligence. The chapter ends with a consideration of the liability of occupiers of premises and the liability of manufacturers of unsafe products.

Contract and Tort

A tort can be defined as 'a civil wrong which is not a breach of contract.' This definition makes it plain that civil liability can be broadly classified into two types: liability arising in contract and liability arising in tort. In previous chapters we have studied the law of contract and have seen that liability under a contract is liability *voluntarily undertaken*, and for which something was given in return. For example, if Business A makes a contract to buy a computer system from Business B, then both the decision to buy and the decision to sell will have been freely made. In addition, both sides will have made a bargain. That is to say that the liabilities which they assumed under the contract will have been given in exchange for the rights which they gained under the contract

Liability in tort is not undertaken voluntarily. It is *imposed by the courts* who have decided that certain types of behaviour give rise to tortious liability. If a person injures someone else by such behaviour the injured person may sue. For example, if a driver runs over a pedestrian while driving badly then the injured pedestrian will be able to sue the driver for the tort of negligence. The driver has no choice about whether or not to accept such liability, the courts will impose it. Nor will the driver have received any benefit in return for accepting the liability. It will have arisen not as a result of a bargain, but as a consequence of having committed a tort.

Another difference is that *liability in contract is generally strict*, whereas *liability in tort is based on fault*. For example, In Chapter 2 we saw that section 14(2) of the Sale of Goods Act 1979 requires that goods sold in the course of a business must be of satisfactory quality. This contractual liability is strict. A shop which sells packaged goods which are not of satisfactory quality is liable for breach of contract even though it was not the shopkeeper's fault that the goods were unsatisfactory, and even if the shopkeeper could not have discovered that they were. But liability in tort is only imposed when a person's conduct does not match up to an objective, reasonable standard. So a driver who runs over a pedestrian will only be liable if he or she drove badly and failed to take reasonable care. If it cannot be shown that the driver drove badly then there will be no liability, no matter how severe the pedestrian's injuries.

Contract remedies and tort remedies

Both the breaching of a contract and the commission of a tort give rise to liability in damages. However, the purpose of contract damages is not the same as the purpose of tort damages. Both of course are designed to compensate. As we have seen, contract damages achieve this by putting the injured party in the position he or she would have been in *if the contract had been properly performed*. Tort damages achieve it by putting the injured party in the position he or she would have been in *if the tort had never been committed*.

Let us assume that one business agreed to deliver a new machine to another business but delivered the machine one month late. The business buying the machine would be entitled to damages for breach of contract. These damages would be calculated by considering how much it cost the business buying the machine that the computer system had not been delivered on time. Such damages might include an amount for profit lost as a result of the machine not being available, or for the cost of employing extra workers who were needed to do the work which the machine was meant to do.

A pedestrian who was run over by a negligent driver would be awarded tort damages. The purpose of these damages would be to put him or her in the same position as if the tort had not been committed. The damages might include an amount for matters such as pain and suffering, for lost wages and perhaps for damage to clothes. These losses would all be recoverable because if the pedestrian had not been negligently run over, none of the losses would have arisen.

It should however be pointed out that the two methods of assessing damages will often arrive at the same result. If an employee loses two months wages as a result of the contract of employment being breached, the damages awarded would compensate for this loss on the basis that if the contract had been properly performed the employee would have received the wages. If an employee loses two months wages as a result of being negligently run over by a car driver, the same compensation would be awarded in respect of the lost wages on the basis that if the tort had not been committed the employee would have earned the wages.

Student Activity Questions 6.1

1) John goes to a large department store to buy a cooker. Would he have the right to sue in contract, or in tort, if:

   a) The cooker did not work properly?

   b) He injured his back after slipping on a pool of oil which was lying on the shop floor?

2) If a customer bought a new cooker from a shop and the cooker did not work properly, would the shop still be liable if it was not the shop's fault that the cooker did not work properly?

3) If a customer in a shop was injured by slipping on a pool of oil, would the customer need to show that the shop had failed to take reasonable care in exposing customers to the risk of injury?

Negligence

In order to establish the tort of negligence the claimant must prove three things:

a) that the defendant owed him or her a duty of care;

b) that the defendant breached that duty; and

c) that a foreseeable type of damage resulted from the breach.

That a duty of care was owed

The following case is the foundation of the modern law of negligence.

Donoghue v Stevenson [1932]

The claimant and her friend visited a cafe. The claimant's friend bought some ice cream and a bottle of ginger beer for the claimant. The claimant poured some ginger beer over the ice cream and ate some of this mixture. When the claimant's friend poured out the rest of the ginger beer the remains of a decomposed snail fell out of the bottle. The contamination of the ginger beer caused the claimant to suffer gastro-enteritis and the sight of the snail caused her to suffer nervous shock. The claimant could not sue the cafe which had sold the ginger beer because she had no contract with the cafe. Instead she sued the manufacturer of the ginger beer, claiming that the manufacturer owed a duty of care to customers. The manufacturer denied that any such duty was owed.

Held *(By a 3:2 majority) The claimant won. Manufacturers owe a duty of care to see that their customers are not injured by their products.*

Lord Atkin:

> 'You must take reasonable care to avoid acts and omissions which you can reasonably foresee would be likely to injure your neighbour. Who, then, in law is my neighbour? The answer seems to be – persons who are so closely and directly affected by my act that I ought reasonably have them in contemplation as being so affected when I am directing my mind to the acts or omissions which are called in question.'

Using this famous 'neighbour speech,' the courts have established certain recognised *duty situations.* For example it is well established that road users owe a duty of care to other road users and pedestrians. Similarly, manufacturers and repairers owe a duty of care to their customers, and professional advisers owe a duty of care to their clients. When a new situation arises the courts decide whether or not a duty of care is owed by considering how similar the new situation is to situations where the courts have earlier decided that duty is or is not owed.

Breaching the duty

Merely owing a duty of care is not enough to give rise to liability for the tort of negligence. Every car driver owes a duty of care to many people. The driver is not liable to be sued by such people unless he or she injures them by breaching the duty of care which is owed.

A duty of care will be breached if the defendant does not take the care which a reasonable person would take in all the circumstances. This is an *objective* standard. It is no defence that the defendant was doing his or her incompetent best. Notice the contrast with criminal law here. Most *mens rea* demand that the accused deliberately does wrong.

A higher standard of care is expected of professional people. They must show the degree of care which a reasonably competent person in that profession would show.

A duty of care owed will not have been breached unless it could reasonably have been foreseen that the defendant's actions would cause injury.

Roe v Minister of Health [1954]

In 1947 the claimant was paralysed by an anaesthetic used by a hospital. The anaesthetic was kept in glass ampoules which were stored in disinfectant. Traces of disinfectant had seeped through the glass ampoules into the anaesthetic and this disinfectant had caused the paralysis.

Held *The defendant was not liable because in 1947 no-one knew that fluid could permeate glass. Of course a hospital would have been liable if a similar accident had occurred after this fact had become known. The court, Lord Denning said, 'must not look at the 1947 accident with 1954 spectacles.'*

In deciding whether or not a duty has been breached, the courts tend to attach particular importance to four factors.

a) The *likelihood of the claimant suffering harm.*

b) The *potential seriousness of injury which the claimant was likely to suffer.*

c) The *cost of making sure that no harm was caused.*

d) The *usefulness of the defendant's actions.*

The first two factors are weighed against the second two. If the first two are greater than the second two then it is likely that the duty will have been breached. If they are smaller it is likely that it will not.

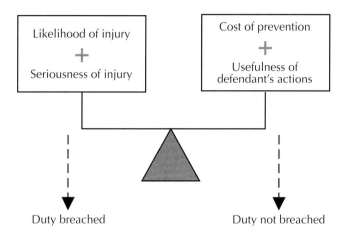

Figure 6.1 Breach of a duty of care: factors to be taken into account

This sounds rather complicated, but the following two cases illustrate that it is relatively straightforward.

Bolton v Stone [1951]

A cricket ball was hit right out of a cricket ground and struck and injured the claimant. The ball cleared a 7 foot high fence built on a 10 foot high bank. The claimant was 22 yards beyond the fence, about a hundred yards from the wicket. About half a dozen balls had been hit out of the ground in the previous thirty years.

Held *The duty was not breached. A and B, (the likelihood of harm and the potential seriousness of injury,) were much smaller than C and D, (the cost of preventing the accident.)*

The usefulness of playing cricket was not much of a factor in this case. However it was accepted that people need to take recreation and that cricket is a traditional type of English recreation.

Paris v Stepney Borough Council [1951]

The claimant, who had the use of only one eye, was told by his employers to hamme and grind the underneath of a vehicle. He was not given protective goggles and whil hammering lost the use of his good eye when this was pierced by a shard of metal.

Held *The duty was breached. A and B (The likelihood of harm and the potential seriou ness of injury) were much greater than C and D (the cost of preventing the accident an the usefulness of working without goggles.)*

The usefulness of the defendant's actions tends to be an important factor in cases wher the defendant acted in an emergency.

Watt v Hertfordshire CC [1954]

A fire station received a call that a woman was trapped under a heavy vehicle about 25 yards away from the station. The officer in charge set off immediately, ordering that lorry should be loaded with heavy lifting gear and that it should follow as soon a possible. The lifting gear was loaded on to the back of the lorry, but it could not be lashe down. When the lorry braked one of the firemen travelling with the lifting gear wa injured.

Held *The fire authority was not negligent. The risk to the firemen had to be balance against the purpose to be achieved.*

Denning LJ:

> *'If this accident had happened in a commercial enterprise without any emergency, there could be no doubt that the [fireman] would succeed. But the commercial end to make profit is very different from the human end to save life and limb. The saving of life and limb justifies the taking of considerable risk.'*

The thing speaks for itself (previously known as *res ipsa loquitor*)

As negligence is a civil action the burden of proof is on the claimant to prove his or he case on a balance of probabilities. Sometimes the claimant will not be able to prove i precisely in what way the defendant was negligent. In *Donoghue v Stevenson*, for instance the claimant would not have been able to prove exactly how the defendants were negl gent in allowing the snail to get into the bottle of ginger beer.

By claiming that the thing speaks for itself, the claimant can *reverse the burden of proo* so that the defendant must prove that the damage was not caused by his or her failure t take reasonable care.

The claimant will be able to say that the thing speaks for itself only if the following thre conditions are satisfied:

a) the defendant must have been in control of the thing that caused the damage;

b) the accident must be the kind of accident which would not normally happen withou carelessness; and

c) the cause of the accident must be unknown.

Ward v Tesco Stores [1976] provides an example. A customer in the defendants' super-market slipped on yoghourt which had been left on the floor. The defendants would have breached the duty of care they owed to customers if the yoghourt had been on the floor for an unreasonable time, but not otherwise. The claimant did not know how long the yoghourt had been on the floor. The defendants were able to prove that they swept the supermarket floor five or six times a day. The Court of Appeal held that the duty of care which the defendants owed to the claimant had been breached. The claimant could not prove that the defendants were at fault but had showed that something had happened which, in the absence of any explanation, made it more likely than not that the defen-dants were at fault. This meant that the defendants were liable unless they could prove that they were not at fault, which they could not do.

Student Activity Questions 6.2

Applying the four factors which the courts take into account, decide whether or not the duty of care was breached in the following cases. The actual decisions are avail-able on this book's Website.

1) *Haley v London Electricity Board [1965]*

    Electricity Board workers dug a 60 foot trench in the pavement and left warning signs at both ends of the trench. They also laid a long-handled hammer across one end of the trench and picks and shovels across the other. The head of the hammer was on the pavement and the other end of the hammer was resting on railings two feet high. These precautions would have been quite sufficient for ordinarily sighted people. But the claimant, who was blind, tripped on the hammer and banged his head on the pavement. As a result of this accident he became almost totally deaf. The claimant was not himself negligent, his white stick passed over the hammer.

    Held ... ?

2) *Latimer v AEC Ltd [1953]*

    During an abnormally heavy rain storm, the floor of a factory became flooded. This caused an oily cooling mixture to escape from a channel in the floor and to mix with the water. As a result the factory floor became very slippery. The employer put down sawdust to make the floor less slippery. A workman was trying to load a heavy barrel on to a lorry in an area of the factory which had not been treated with sawdust. He slipped and injured himself. As there was not enough sawdust to cover all areas of the floor, the only way to make sure that no-one was hurt would have been to close the factory down. This would have meant 4,000 workers missing the night shift.

    Held ... ?

A foreseeable type of damage resulted from the breach of duty

In order to recover damages for the tort of negligence the claimant must prove that the defendant's breach of duty *caused* the loss for which damages are being claimed. Furthermore, the claimant must prove that the loss was a type of loss which would *foreseeably* follow from the defendant's breach.

Causation

The claimant can only recover damages in respect of a loss if it can be proved that the loss was caused by the defendant's actions. Generally, the courts use a 'but for' test in assessing this. That is to say, they ask whether the claimant would have suffered the loss but for the defendant breaching the duty. If the claimant would not, then this suggests that the defendant's breach of duty caused the loss. If the claimant would have suffered the same loss even if the defendant had not breached the duty, then the defendant will not be liable for the loss. For example, in *Barnett v Chelsea Hospital [1969]* a patient who visited a hospital suffering from vomiting was negligently turned away by a doctor and died from arsenic poisoning. The patient would have died anyway, even if the doctor had given him all possible treatment, and so the hospital was not liable for the patient's death.

To prove that the defendant caused the loss, the claimant must show that there was a chain of causation between the defendant's breach of duty and the claimant's loss. This chain must not be broken by a new act intervening (previously known as novus actus interviens).

The Orepesa [1943]

A ship called the Orepesa was negligently navigated and this caused it to damage another ship. The captain of the other ship decided to approach the Orepesa in a lifeboat to discuss the best way to save his ship. The lifeboat overturned in the heavy sea and several crew members were drowned. Their relatives sued the owners of the Orepesa.

Held *The owners of the Orepesa were liable. The actions of the captain of the other ship did not break the chain of causation because they were reasonable in all the circumstances.*

Unreasonable actions will break the chain. So if one of the lifeboat crew had drowned after deciding to swim to the Orepesa then the chain would have been broken and the owners of the Orepesa would not have been liable for his death.

Reflex actions will not break the chain of causation. In *Carmarthenshire CC v Lewis [1955]* a lorry driver was killed when he swerved to avoid running over a 4 year old boy. A primary school had been negligent in letting the boy get out onto the road. The school was liable for the driver's death. The driver's reflex action of swerving the lorry did not break the chain of causation.

Foreseeability

In order for damages to be claimed for a loss, the loss must have been a *type of loss or injury* which was a foreseeable consequence of the defendant's breach of duty. The extent of the loss does not need to be foreseeable, nor does the precise way in which it arose.

The Wagon Mound [1961]

The defendants negligently spilt a large quantity of furnace oil into Sydney harbour. The claimants' wharf was about 600 feet away, but the oil soon spread there. The oil was lying on top of the water and so the claimants were advised to stop welding on their wharf. The claimants later carried on welding when they were advised that this was safe. A spark from a welding torch set fire to a large bale of cotton which was floating in the water. This bale ignited the oil and extensive damage was caused to the claimants' wharf. The defendants did not know, and could not have been expected to know, that furnace oil floating on water could be ignited.

Held Even though the defendants had negligently spilt the oil, they were not liable for the damage which the fire caused. Fire was not a foreseeable type of damage. Therefore the defendants were not liable for any fire damage. If a claim had been made for pollution by oil then the defendants would have been liable for this, because this was a foreseeable type of damage.

As long as a certain type of damage is foreseeable, then the defendant will be liable for all damage of that type. So the 'egg shell skull' rule holds that if a certain amount of injury to the person was foreseeable then the defendant will be liable for much greater injury suffered by a particularly sensitive claimant. For example, in *Smith v Leech Brain [1962]* the defendants' negligence caused the claimant to suffer injury when a drop of molten metal splashed onto his lip. Unknown to anyone, the claimant was particularly prone to cancer. The injury to his lip caused him to develop cancer, from which he died. The defendants were liable for the claimant's death, even though a burnt lip would not have caused death in many cases.

Damages can be awarded for psychiatric injury, which is generally known as 'nervous shock'. However, the courts are cautious in awarding damages for nervous shock.

Economic loss

As a matter of policy, tort damages for pure 'economic' loss are not recoverable. Loss is economic loss if it is not an injury to the person or damage to property. (In Chapter 4 we saw that damages for breach of contract can be claimed for pure economic loss.) If economic loss is connected to a physical injury or damage to property then damages can be claimed for it. (For example, if a person is physically injured and therefore loses wages on account of having to have time off work.) But in cases where the only loss suffered is economic loss, damages cannot generally be claimed. The following case provides an example.

Weller v Foot and Mouth Research Institute [1966]

The defendants negligently allowed foot and mouth disease to escape from their labora tory. Foot and mouth disease seriously affected the health of livestock and when outbreaks occurred livestock could not be moved. The claimants were auctioneers o livestock. They lost a great deal of money because they could not conduct any auction until the outbreak was cleared up.

Held *The claimants could not recover damages for their lost profit as the lost profit wa pure economic loss.*

Damages

It has already been stated that the purpose of tort damages is to put the injured party int the position he or she would have been in if the tort had not been committed.

Where the loss consists of damage to goods the amount of damages will usually be th cost of repairing or replacing the goods. A claim might also be made for not being abl to use the goods until they could be repaired or replaced. Such a claim might include a amount for lost profit.

Damages for personal injuries

Whenever damages are claimed in respect of personal injuries, the law makes a distinc tion between special damages and general damages. (This distinction is made whethe the personal injury was caused by a breach of contract or by a tort.) When a claim made for *special damages*, the amount of money claimed in respect of a loss can b calculated exactly because the claimant can itemise the loss and prove that it arose. Bu when a claim for *general damages* is made, the amount of damages claimed in respec of a loss cannot be itemised and proved exactly, but will be assessed by the judge wh hears the case.

As special damages can be calculated exactly, they could be claimed for the followin matters: loss of earnings before the case came to trial; the cost of private medical care u to the time of the trial; and money lost by other people (such as relatives) who hav provided services which became reasonably necessary on account of the injury to th claimant. In most cases, special damages are agreed between the parties, as either allow able or not, before the case comes to court. If this is not agreed, the judge will rule o which claims are to be allowed.

As general damages cannot be calculated exactly, they could be claimed for th following matters: pain and suffering, whether it was endured before the trial or likely arise in the future; loss of amenities, which means the loss of ability to do things due physical or mental disability (the younger the claimant the higher these damages a likely to be, especially if they prevented the claimant from pursuing a hobby or a spo which had previously been enjoyed); and loss of future earnings.

In Chapter 4 we saw that nominal damages (damages in name only) can be awarded for a breach of contract. Such damages can also be awarded to a claimant who has proved that a tort has been committed, but only if the tort is one which does not require the claimant to prove actual loss. Nominal damages cannot therefore be awarded in cases of negligence. However, contemptuous damages can. These damages would be very small because the court did not approve of the claimant's behaviour or because the court thought very little of the claim being made.

A claimant has a duty to take all reasonable steps to mitigate (reduce) the loss suffered. Damages cannot be claimed for a loss which could have been mitigated by taking reasonable steps. However, if a reasonable attempt to mitigate the loss actually increases the loss, the claimant can recover damages to cover this increased loss.

Defences to negligence

Contributory negligence

Contributory negligence is not a complete defence, but reduces the damages payable to the claimant. Individual damages for personal injuries can run to well over a million pounds, and any percentage reduction could amount to a great deal of money.

The Law Reform (Contributory Negligence) Act 1945 section 1 provides that:

> *'Where any person suffers damage as the result partly of his own fault and partly of the fault of any other person.....the damages recoverable....shall be reduced to such an extent as the court thinks just and equitable having regard to the claimant's share in the responsibility for the damage.'*

The following case provides an example of contributory negligence.

Froom v Butcher [1975]

A motorist was injured by an accident which was not in any way his own fault. He suffered injuries to his head, chest and finger. If he had been wearing a seat belt, (which in those days was not compulsory,) the injuries to his head and chest would have been avoided altogether.

Held *The damages in respect of the head and chest injuries were reduced by 25%. The damages for injury to his finger were not reduced as these would have arisen even if the claimant had been wearing a seat belt.*

Contributory negligence is concerned with the claimant's contribution to the injury caused by the accident. The claimant's behaviour after the tort has been committed cannot amount to contributory negligence. However, if the claimant unreasonably makes matters worse after the tort has been committed, the damages awarded can be reduced to take account of this. For example, if a claimant suffered moderate injuries because of the defendant's negligence, but suffered much more serious injuries as a consequence of unreasonably failing to get medical treatment, damages would only be awarded in respect of the moderate injuries which should have been suffered. The defendant should have mitigated the loss by seeking medical treatment.

Volenti non fit injuria (to one who volunteers no harm is done)

It is a complete defence to show that the injured person voluntarily assumed the risk which caused the injury. The defence is known by its Latin name, volenti non fit injuria. It often defeats employees who are injured as a result of not following safety procedures. The following case provides an example.

ICI Ltd v Shatwell [1965]

Experienced shot firers were badly injured when they tested detonators without taking the proper safety precautions. They sued their employer, who did not know that the safety precautions had not been adopted.

Held *The employer had a complete defence. The injured workers had voluntarily assumed the risk which injured them.*

Volenti non fit injuria will not apply if the claimant was injured while reasonably trying to carry out a rescue. For example, in *Haynes v Harwood [1935]*, a policeman was injured when he tried to save some children from a runaway horse. The policeman could claim for his injuries, even though they were caused by his decision to try to save the children.

Exclusion of liability for negligence

In Chapter 2 we saw that section 2 of the Unfair Contract Terms Act 1977 deals with the exclusion of liability for negligence. We saw that section 2(1) of the Act provides that no contract term or notice can exclude or restrict liability for death or personal injury resulting from negligence. We also saw that section 2(2) provided that liability for loss or damage other than death or personal injury can be excluded, but only to the extent that this was reasonable.

Student Activity Questions 6.3

1) A claimant is injured as a result of a duty of care being breached. If a claim for damages is to be successful, to what extent must the injury suffered have been foreseeable?

2) What is pure economic loss? To what extent can damages be recovered for economic loss caused by a breach of a duty of care?

3) What is the difference between special and general damages?

4) How can contributory negligence affect an award of damages?

5) What is meant by volenti non fit injuria?

Negligent misstatement

Negligent misstatement is not a tort in its own right. It is a branch of
Liability for negligent misstatement was first considered by the H
following case.

Hedley Byrne & Co Ltd v Heller and Partners Ltd [1963]

*The defendants were merchant bankers. A certain company, E Ltd, banked with the
defendants. The claimants were considering giving credit to E Ltd. The claimants asked
their own bank to find out whether E Ltd was a good credit risk. The claimants' bank
therefore asked the defendants whether E Ltd were a good credit risk. The request was
made in confidence. The defendants replied that E Ltd were creditworthy. The letter
which said this was headed, 'For your private use and without responsibility on the part
of the bank or its officials'. The claimants' bank passed on to the claimants the information that E Ltd were considered creditworthy. Relying on this, the claimants extended
credit to E Ltd. However, they lost a great deal of money because E Ltd went into liquidation before repaying this money. The claimants therefore sued the defendants, arguing
that the defendants had been negligent in wrongly saying that E Ltd were creditworthy.*

Held *The defendants were not liable because their letter had made it plain that they gave
their advice without responsibility. This prevented a duty of care from arising. If they had
not made this plain, the defendants would have been liable for their negligent misstatement.*

Hedley Byrne & Co Ltd v Heller and Partners Ltd is an important case because the House
of Lords made it plain that liability for negligent misstatements could exist, and that this
liability could arise even in respect of pure economic loss. However, this liability will
only arise where there is a *special relationship between the parties*. There will only be a
special relationship if the claimant could reasonably and foreseeably expect to be able to
rely on the defendant's advice. There is no requirement that the defendant should receive
anything in return for the advice. It is necessary that the claimant asked for the advice or
had a right to receive it.

In *Caparo Industries plc v Dickman [1990]* the House of Lords held that the relationship
between individual members of a company and the company auditor was not close
enough to amount to a special relationship. The company's auditors said in their auditors' report that the company had made a profit of £1.2 million, whereas in fact it had
made a loss of £0.4 million. The claimant was a shareholder in the company and, in
reliance on the auditors' report, made a successful take-over bid for the company. The
claimant had no claim against the auditors. (The auditors do owe a duty of care to the
company and to the company members as a whole.)

ccupiers' Liability

Occupiers of premises owe a duty of care to all lawful visitors, and a separate duty of care to trespassers. Almost all businesses must occupy some premises, and so almost a are potentially liable. Any person with control of the premises can be liable as an occupier. It follows that there might be more than one occupier in respect of the sam premises. People who have control of movable structures, such as vehicles or ladder can also be liable as occupiers.

Lawful visitors

Any person who comes on to premises with either express or implied permission of th occupier will be a lawful visitor. Express permission is given in words. It can be mor difficult to tell when implied permission has been given. It will, however, have bee given if the court finds that there was an agreement (not made in words) that the perso is allowed to be on the premises. So delivery drivers or service mechanics would be a much lawful visitors on the premises of a business as would invited visitors such a important customers. People who have a statutory right to be on premises, such as mete readers and policemen, are lawful visitors.

The Occupier's Liability Act 1957 section 2 requires occupiers of premises to take:

> 'such care as in all the circumstances of the case is reasonable to see that the
> visitor will be reasonably safe in using the premises for the purposes for which
> he is invited or permitted by the occupier to be there.'

This standard of care is very similar to the standard required in the tort of negligence. I some ways the statute has just extended the tort of negligence to cover injuries to lawfu visitors on premises.

The standard is not an absolute one. It varies with all the circumstances. Some people such as children, can he expected to be less careful than others, and a higher duty therefore owed to them. Others, such as contractors, can be expected to look out fc themselves rather better than most people, especially if they have been warned of particular danger. Consequently they are owed a lower duty.

Notices which warn of danger might mean that the occupier is not liable, but only if the enable the lawful visitor to be reasonably safe in visiting the premises. Notices which g further than mere warnings, and which try to restrict liability for injury to lawful visito will be subject to the Unfair Contract Terms Act 1977. In Chapter 2 we saw that sectio 2(1) of that Act provides that liability in respect of death or personal injury caused b negligence can never be excluded. We also saw that section 2(2) provides that liabili for damage other than death or personal injury can be excluded, but only by a term c notice which is reasonable. As far as the UCTA 1977 is concerned, liability under th Occupier's Liability Act 1957 is liability in negligence.

Damages can only be claimed in respect of injuries or losses which were of a reasonably foreseeable type. Volenti non fit injuria can be a complete defence and contributory negligence can reduce the amount of damages awarded.

Non lawful visitors

Any person who enters the premises other than as a lawful visitor will do so as a non lawful visitor. Frequently such non lawful visitors will be trespassing children, and the courts have recognised that even trespassers need considerable protection from inherently dangerous things such as live railway lines.

Section 1(3) of the Occupiers' Liability Act 1984 extends a statutory duty of protection to trespassers. The occupier owes the duty to take *such care as is reasonable* to see that the trespasser is not injured. The duty arises if three conditions are met:

a) the occupier knows or ought to know that a danger exists;

b) the occupier knows or ought to know that the trespasser is in the vicinity of the danger; and

c) the risk is one against which the occupier could, in all the circumstances of the case, reasonably be expected to offer the trespasser some protection.

Liability under the Occupier's Liability Act 1984 can only arise for personal injuries. The Unfair Contract Terms Act 1977 does not apply to the duty of care created by the 1984 Act. Notices and signs can therefore have the effect of excluding liability, even for death or personal injury. However, notices will only have this effect if they reasonably give notice of the danger concerned or reasonably discourage people from taking the risks which injure them. It seems likely that warning signs cannot protect an occupier who knows that the condition of the land or the activities of the trespasser mean that the trespasser is likely to be injured. Nor can liability be excluded for conduct which intentionally or recklessly causes injury.

The Consumer Protection Act 1987 Part I

In 1985 a European Community Directive ordered all Member States to pass legislation to introduce the concept of *product liability*. The United Kingdom passed the Consumer Protection Act to comply with this Directive.

Under Part I of the Act, a claimant who is injured by an unsafe product will be able to sue the manufacturer of the product (and possibly others) without having to prove the tort of negligence.

When we considered the tort of negligence we saw that manufacturers owe a duty of care to their customers. Earlier in this chapter when we considered *Donoghue v Stevenson* we saw that in that case the manufacturers of the ginger beer were liable to Mrs Donoghue because they breached the duty of care which they owed her.

However, negligence is a difficult tort to establish. The manufacturers of the ginger beer would not have been liable if they could have proved that they had taken all reasonable care.

Under the Consumer Protection Act liability is strict. This means that, in the absence of one of the defences listed in the Act, consumers injured by a product will always gain damages from the producer of the product if the product was less safe than could reasonably be expected. The defences available are, as we shall see, narrow and specific.

Who may sue?

The Act gives the right to sue to any person who is injured by a product, *the safety of which was 'not such as persons generally are entitled to expect.'*

For over a hundred years the Sale of Goods Act required that goods sold by a business were of merchantable quality. As we have seen, this requirement has been replaced by a requirement that the goods be of satisfactory quality. If a buyer of goods is injured because goods sold by a business were not of satisfactory quality the Sale of Goods Act 1979 will provide the buyer with a remedy. But privity of contract restricts the remedies offered by the Sale of Goods Act to the buyer of the goods. The Consumer Protection Act now gives a similarly high level of protection to anyone injured by unsafe goods. (The effect of privity of contract is considered at the end of this chapter.) The Consumer Protection Act is not concerned with the general quality of the goods.

Who is liable?

The Consumer Protection Act 1987 places liability on the 'producer' of the product, and sections 1 and 2 define the producer as including:

a) The *manufacturer* of the product.

b) The *extractor* of raw materials.

c) *Industrial processors* of agricultural produce.

d) *'Own branders'* who add their label to products which they did not produce

e) Anyone who *imports* the product *into the EC.*

If more than one of these people are liable they are *jointly and severally liable.* This means that the injured person can sue any or all of them. Retailers who are not own-branders will not be liable under the Act. (Retailers who sold an unsafe product would be liable for breach of section 14(2) of the Sale of Goods Act 1979.)

Defective products

Section 3 says that products can be regarded as defective if their safety is not such as persons generally are entitled to expect. Products include not only finished products but also component parts of another product and raw materials. For example, a new car is a product, but so is the battery in the car and the rubber from which the tyres were made.

The court will consider all the circumstances when deciding whether or not the *objective* standard which the Act requires has been breached. The Act does however mention a number of factors to be considered, including the following.

a)   The way in which the product was marketed.

b)   Instructions and warnings issued with the product.

c)   What might reasonably be expected to be done with the product.

d)   The time at which the product was supplied.

This last factor is designed to give some protection to manufacturers producing new products. These are not to be considered unsafe just because later products were safer. (This is linked to the controversial 'development risks' defence, which is considered below.)

Damage suffered

Section 5 of the Act allows a claimant to claim damages for *death or any personal injury* caused by the unsafety of the product.

Damage to *property* is only claimable if it causes an individual to suffer a loss of more than £275. The loss may be made up of damage to several items.

Damage to the product itself is not recoverable. Nor is damage to other products supplied with the product. Nor can a claim be made in respect of loss of or damage to business property.

For example, let us assume that Mr and Mrs A are bought a toaster as a wedding present. The toaster catches fire and burns Mr A's hand. The kitchen work surface is damaged and the toaster itself is destroyed. Under the Act damages could be claimed for the injury to Mr A and for all of the damage to the work surface as long as that amounted to more than £275. Damage to the toaster itself could not be claimed under this Act. The buyer of the toaster could claim back the price of the toaster under the Sale of Goods Act 1979 (because section 14(2) of that Act would have been breached).

Compensation for injury, death and damage to goods must be claimed within 3 years of the loss becoming apparent. In addition, there is an absolute time limit of ten years after the date when the product was supplied. This means that a person injured by a product more than ten years after buying it will have no remedy.

Contributory negligence on the part of the claimant can reduce the damages.

Defences

Under the Act *liability is strict* and this means that the claimant does not need to prove fault. Nor can liability be excluded by any contract term or notice. There are however certain defences available, as listed below.

a) That the defect was caused by *complying with EC or UK legislation.*

b) That the product was not supplied or manufactured *in the course of a business.* For example, a person who made jam as a hobby would not be liable under this Act if the jam poisoned a person who consumed it. (They might of course be liable under the tort of negligence.)

c) That the defect in the product did not exist *when the product was put onto the market.*

d) A *supplier of a component* will have a defence if the unsafety arose because the manufacturer of the finished product misused the component.

e) The *development risks defence* gives a defence to a producer if he can show that when he produced it the state of scientific and technical knowledge was 'not such that a producer of products of the same description as the product in question might be expected to have discovered it.'

This is a controversial defence. It would have meant that the victims of the drug Thalidomide would not have had a remedy because when the drug was created scientists were not aware of its danger. (For the same reason the drug manufacturers would not have been liable in the tort of negligence.) The Government in power when the Act was passed included the development risk defence because it thought that not to do so would make the manufacture of drugs and certain other products so hazardous as to be economically impractical.

Ultimately, the balance to be struck between the interests of drug manufacturers and drug users is a matter of politics.

Privity of contract

The doctrine of privity of contract holds that a contract is private between the parties who made it. Anyone who did not make the contract cannot sue on the contract or be sued on it. The Contracts (Rights of Third Parties) Act 1999 has created an exception to the privity rule. However, the rule is perhaps best understood if it is considered before the effect of the 1999 Act is considered. The following case provides a classic example of the privity rule.

Tweddle v Atkinson [1831]

William Guy and John Tweddle made a contract with each other that William Guy would pay the claimant £200 and in return John Tweddle would pay the claimant £100. (The claimant was the son of John Tweddle who was marrying the daughter of William Guy.) The contract between William Guy and John Tweddle said that the claimant should be able to sue either of them to enforce the contract. John Tweddle paid the money he had promised to pay but William Guy died before paying the money he had promised. The claimant sued William Guy's personal representatives to make them pay. (The personal representatives took over William Guy's affairs and would have had exactly the same obligation to pay as William Guy would have had.)

Held *The claimant could not sue on the contract because he did not make the contract.*

It might be thought that the solution would have been for John Tweddle (who did make the contract) to sue William Guy's personal representatives to enforce the contract. John Tweddle could have done this but he would only have been entitled to damages for breach of contract. As we have seen, contract damages are designed to put the injured party who made the contract into the position he or she would have been in if the contract had been properly performed. As John Tweddle would have been in no better financial position if the contract had been properly performed, only nominal damages would have been awarded to him.

Privity could cause particular injustice when one person bought unsafe goods or services on behalf of another. The following case provides an example.

Daniels v White and Tarbard [1938]

Mr Daniels bought a bottle of lemonade. Both Mr and Mrs Daniels drunk the lemonade, which was contaminated with carbolic acid. They were both injured by this and both sued the manufacturers of the lemonade for the tort of negligence. Mr Daniels also sued the retailer of the lemonade for breach of contract.

Held *The manufacturers were not liable for the tort of negligence. They showed that they operated a 'fool proof' system and so it could not be proved that they had failed to take all reasonable care. Mr Daniels succeeded in his claim for breach of contract. The retailer had to pay damages to compensate Mr Daniels for his injuries, but did not have to pay damages in respect of Mrs Daniel's injuries. (The damages for breach of contract were only to compensate for the loss caused to Mr Daniels.) Mrs Daniels could not sue the retailer for breach of contract because she had no contract with the retailer.*

In *Jackson v Horizon Holidays Ltd [1980]* the Court of Appeal allowed a husband who had booked a holiday for himself and his wife to recover substantial damages when the holiday was disastrous. Lord Denning, one of the judges in the Court of Appeal, said that the husband could recover damages to compensate for his own disappointment and for that of his wife. This decision was strongly criticised by the House of Lords in a later case and so it must be regarded as incorrect. As regards package holidays, the Package Travel, Package Holidays and Package Tours Regulations 1992 now provide that damages can be awarded to holidaymakers who do not get the holiday contracted for, even if they did not themselves make the contract. However, these Regulations are confined to package holidays and do not change the principles of the general law of contract.

The Contracts (Rights of Third Parties) Act 1999 has changed the privity rule but not abolished it. The Act provides that a third party can in some circumstances sue on a contract which he or she did not make. However, this is only the case if the contract expressly provided that the third party should be able to sue, or if the contract was made for the third party's benefit. A contract will only be regarded as having been made for the third party's benefit if the third party is expressly identified in the contract. Applying the Act to *Daniels v White and Tarbard* we can see that the Act would not have allowed Mrs Daniels to sue on the contract with the retailer unless Mr Daniels had expressly identified Mrs Daniels as a person for whose benefit the contract was being made.

The following examples demonstrate the present day position as regards product liability.

Example 1

John buys a toaster from a shop. The toaster explodes, injuring John and damaging his kitchen. John made the contract with the shop. The shop is in breach of section 14(2) of the Sale of Goods Act 1979. John can sue the shop for breach of contract and will recover damages for his injuries and the damage to his kitchen. John can also recover the price of the toaster from the retailer.

Example 2

John buys a toaster as a Christmas present for Mary. John tells the retailer that the toaster is being bought for Mary and asks the retailer to deliver it to her house. The toaster explodes, injuring Mary and damaging her kitchen. The Contracts (Rights of Third Parties) Act 1999 allows Mary to sue the retailer just as if she made the contract. She will therefore recover damages for her injuries and the damage to her kitchen. John or Mary can recover the price of the toaster from the retailer.

Example 3

John buys a toaster as a Christmas present for Mary. John does not tell the retailer that the toaster is being bought for Mary. The toaster explodes, injuring Mary and damaging her kitchen. Privity will prevent Mary from suing the retailer because she has no contract with the retailer. The Consumer Protection Act 1987 will allow Mary to sue the manufacturer of the toaster to claim damages for her injuries. Mary will also

be able to use the Consumer Protection Act to claim damages for all the damage to her kitchen if this amounts to damage of more than £275. (If the damage to Mary's kitchen does not exceed £275, it is possible but most unlikely that Mary could sue the manufacturer of the toaster for the tort of negligence to recover damages.) John can recover the price of the toaster from the retailer but cannot recover damages on Mary's behalf. If John does not recover the price of the toaster from the retailer Mary will have no right to do so or to sue the retailer for damages.

Student Activity Questions 6.4

1) In what circumstances can a person owe a duty of care in respect of negligent misstatements?

2) What duties of care do occupiers of premises owe to lawful visitors and to trespassers?

3) In what way might the Consumer Protection Act 1987 Part I help a person who suffers loss or injury which was caused by an unsafe product?

4) Explain the privity rule and how it has been affected by the Contracts (Rights of Third Parties) Act 1999.

Essential points

Contractual and tortious liability compared

- Liability in contract is generally strict, liability in tort is almost always based on fault.

- The parties to a contract choose to undertake liability, liability in tort is imposed by the courts.

- Contract damages are designed to put the injured party into the same position as if the contract had been properly performed.

- Tort damages are designed to put the injured party into the same position as if the tort had never been committed.

The tort of negligence

- In order to establish the tort of negligence, a claimant must prove:

  a) that the defendant owed him or her a duty of care;

  b) that the defendant breached this duty; and

  c) that a foreseeable type of loss or damage resulted from the breach of duty.

- As long as the type of damage suffered was a foreseeable consequence of the breach of duty, the precise extent of the damage does not need to have been foreseeable.

- Loss which is not connected to an injury to the person, or to damage to property, is classed as pure economic loss. Damages cannot be recovered for pure economic loss caused by negligence.

- In personal injuries cases, claims for special damages are made in respect of losses which can be itemised and proved as causing a definite calculable loss. Claims for general damages are made in respect of losses which cannot be itemised and proved as causing a definite calculable loss.

- Contributory negligence by the claimant can reduce the claimant's damages.

- It is a complete defence for the defendant to prove that the claimant was injured by a risk which he or she freely and voluntarily chose to accept.

Negligent misstatement

- A defendant can become liable for a negligent misstatement which caused the claimant to suffer loss, even if the loss suffered was purely economic loss.

- A claim for negligent misstatement can be made only where the claimant and the defendant are in a special relationship.

- There will only be a special relationship between the claimant and the defendant if the claimant could reasonably and foreseeably expect to be able to rely on the defendant's advice.

Occupiers' Liability

- Occupiers of premises owe a duty of care to all lawful visitors, and a separate duty of care to trespassers.

- Any person with control over premises can be liable as an occupier.

- The duty owed to lawful visitors is to see that the lawful visitor is reasonably safe in using the premises for the purpose which he or she is invited or allowed to be on the premises.

- The duty owed to non lawful visitors is to take such care as is reasonable to see that the trespasser is not injured. (Non lawful visitors can only claim damages in respect of personal injuries.)

The Consumer Protection Act 1987 Part 1

- The CPA Part 1 imposes on manufacturers strict civil liability for injuries caused by unsafe products which they manufactured.

- Liability under the CPA is strict. However, it arises only where the safety of a product is not such as persons generally are entitled to expect.

- Liability under the CPA arises in respect of death or personal injury. It also arises for damage to property but only if this damage amounts to more than £275.

- The CPA is concerned only with product safety. It provides no remedy where a product is merely defective.

Privity of contract

- Where a product bought from a business is defective the buyer will be able to claim back the purchase price (and possibly damages as well). Such a claim is a claim in contract.

- Generally, privity of contract prevents anyone other than the buyer from suing for breach of the contract which the buyer made.

- The Contracts (Rights of Third Parties) Act 1999 allows a third party (a person who did not make the contract) to sue on the contract in limited circumstances.

- The 1999 Act only allows a third party to sue on a contract if the contract expressly provided that the third party should be able to sue, or if the contract was made for the third party's benefit.

End of chapter questions

Question 1

Alan was walking along the pavement when an HGV lorry reversed out of Bodgit Ltd's premises and ran him over. The lorry was being driven by the managing director of Bodgit Ltd, Billy. Billy did not have a licence to drive HGV vehicles. He was driving the lorry in order to free up a car parking space and did not realise that it was in reverse gear. Alan suffered two broken legs and concussion. His injuries kept him off work for two months. Advise Alan of his legal position.

Question 2

Cathy visits a shop and buys two pre-packed sandwiches. The sandwiches were made by a local company which supplied many local shops with sandwiches. Cathy and her friend Dinah shared the sandwiches. Both Cathy and Dinah were made seriously ill as the sandwiches were contaminated with rat poison. Advise Cathy and Dinah of their legal positions.

Question 3

The premises of Bodgit Ltd are often in a dangerous state. Last week two people were injured while on the premises. Edward, an accountant employed by Bodgit Ltd, broke his elbow when he slipped on an oil spillage on some stairs. The oil had been spilt on the stairs four hours earlier. No orders to clear the spillage had been given, although all employees had been warned to take care while using the stairs. Francine, who is 7 years old, was injured while playing on partially completed buildings which are standing on Bodgit Ltd's premises. A friend of hers pushed her over and she fell into an exposed barrel of preservative chemical. The chemical caused severe injuries to Francine's skin. The managing director of Bodgit Ltd knew that children had been breaking in and playing on the building site. Last week he had put up a prominent sign, which read, "NOTICE WARNING TO PARENTS. THIS SITE CONTAINS HAZARDOUS BUILDINGS AND DANGEROUS SUBSTANCES. KEEP OUT. " Advise Bodgit Ltd of any liability they might have to Edward or Francine.

Task 6

A friend of yours is contemplating starting a small business manufacturing garden benches to be sold to local garden centres. Your friend has asked you to draw up a report briefly explaining the following matters.

a) The matters which need to be proved in order to establish that the tort of negligence has been committed.

b) The extent to which liability in negligence can be reduced or extinguished.

c) The extent to which occupiers of premises can incur liability to visitors and to non visitors who are injured while on the premises.

d) The circumstances in which the Consumer Protection Act 1987 Part I can impose liability on manufacturers.

e) The meaning of privity of contract, and the extent to which the Contracts (Rights Third Parties) Act 1999 has limited the effect of privity.

7 Business organisations 1

This is the first of two chapters which consider the law relating to business organisations. In this chapter we consider the characteristics of business organisations and the ways in which business organisations are formed. In the following chapter we consider the rights and liabilities of members of business organisations, the ways in which business organisations can be wound up and the relative advantages and disadvantages of trading either as a company or as a partnership.

The characteristics of business organisations

We begin this chapter by considering the characteristics of companies, partnerships, limited liability partnerships and sole traders.

Characteristics of a limited company

A company is created by registration under the Companies Act 1985. The process of registration is considered later in this chapter. Here it is enough to say that the promoters of the company must send certain documents to the Registrar of Companies. If the documents are in order the Registrar will issue a certificate of incorporation and the company will then exist as a corporate body.

Incorporation has several important consequences. To some extent these are interconnected, but they are easier to understand if considered separately.

The company is a separate legal entity

The most important consequence of incorporation is that a company is regarded as being a legal person in its own right. This means that a company has a legal identity of its own which is quite separate from the legal identity of its owners. If a wrong is done to a company, the company and not its owners must sue. Conversely, if a company injures a person that person must sue the company and cannot sue the owners. This well-established principle was laid down by the House of Lords in the following case.

Salomon v Salomon and Co Ltd [1897]

*For several years Salomon had carried on a business as a boot repairer and manufacture.
He formed a limited company and sold his business to the company for £39,000. Th*
company paid the purchase price by issuing Salomon with 20,000 £1 shares, l
regarding him as having loaned the company £10,000, and by making up the balance
cash. Salomon took all of the company's assets as security for the loan which had bee
made to him. Unsecured creditors lent the company a further £8,000. Shortly after .
incorporation the company got into financial difficulty and was wound up. The assets
the company amounted to about £6,000. Creditors who have been given security f
their loan are entitled to be repaid before unsecured creditors. Salomon therefore took ∢
of the £6,000. The unsecured creditors claimed that Salomon should repay their loa.
himself because he was the same person as the company.

Held *The company had been formed properly and without any fraud. Although Salomo*
owned all but 7 of the issued shares, he was one person and the company was anothe
Salomon therefore had no more obligation to pay the company's debts than he had
pay his next-door neighbour's debts.

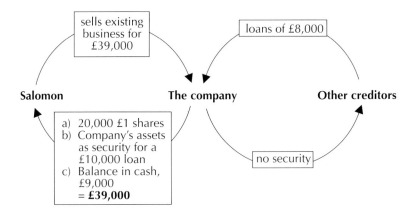

Figure 7.1 Salomon v Salomon and Co Ltd

Salomon's case is regarded as one of the most important in English law, mainly becau
of the protection which it offers to the owners of companies. However, the decision t▮
a company has a legal identity of its own has many other consequences, as the followi▮
two cases show.

Macaura v Northern Assurance Ltd [1925]

Macaura and his nominees owned all of the shares in a timber company. The compa
owed money to Macaura but not to anyone else. Macaura insured the company's tim.
in his own name. Two weeks later the timber was destroyed by fire and Macaura claim
on his insurance.

Held Macaura could not claim on the insurance policy because he did not own the timber. The company owned the timber, and it is a rule of insurance law that only the owner of goods can insure them.

Tunstall v Steigmann [1962]

Mrs Steigmann ran a pork butcher's shop and leased the shop next door to Mrs Tunstall. Mrs Steigmann wanted to end the lease. As the law stood at that time, Mrs Steigmann could order Mrs Tunstall to leave the shop only if she intended to occupy the building herself, to carry on a business there. Mrs Steigmann did intend to occupy the shop herself to carry on her butchery business. But before the case came to court she turned her business into a company. Mrs Steigmann claimed that as she owned all but two of the shares in the company it was still herself that wanted to take over the premises.

Held Mrs Steigmann lost. It was not her that wanted to take over the business, but her company.

Willmer LJ:

> 'There is no escape from the fact that a company is a legal entity entirely separate from its corporators–see Salomon v Salomon and Co. Here the landlord and her company are entirely separate entities. This is no matter of form; it is a matter of substance and reality. Each can sue and be sued in his own right; indeed, there is nothing to prevent the one suing the other. Even the holder of 100% of the shares in a company does not by such holding become so identified with the company that he or she can be said to carry on the business of the company.'

Student Activity Questions 7.1

1) If Salomon had not formed a company, but had carried on his business as a sole trader, would the unsecured creditors have been entitled to the £6,000 which the assets of the business generated?

2) In *Macaura v Northern Assurance*, did the shareholders in the company own the timber when it was destroyed?

Further Activity Questions 7.1

1) It is now possible for a person to own all of the shares in a company. If X owned all of the shares in X Co Ltd, and X Co Ltd owed no money to any creditors:

   a) Could X steal from the company?

   b) Could X sue the company?

   c) Could X be employed by the company?

2) In *Lee v Lee's Air Farming Ltd [1961]*, Mr Lee owned 2,999 of the 3,000 shares in a crop-spraying company. While at work Lee crashed his plane and was killed. His widow sued under a statute which required employers to pay compensation if an employee was killed at work. The company's insurers refused to pay, arguing that Lee was employed by himself, and could not therefore be an employee. Did the insurers have to pay up?

3) In *Firsteel Products Ltd v Anaco Ltd [1994]*, a High Court judge had to decide whether or not a company could sue for 'stress and aggravation,' which it claimed to have suffered as a result of a breach of contract. What do you think the judge decided? Can a company suffer stress?

Limited liability

In *Salomon's* case we saw that Salomon was not personally liable for the debts of the company. When people buy shares in a limited company the only commitment they make is that they agree to pay the price of the shares. Often they do not pay the full price immediately. When the public utilities were privatised, for example, investors generally paid half of the share price when subscribing for the shares and remained liable for the other half. If one of these privatised companies had gone into liquidation before shareholders had paid this second instalment the shareholders would have been liable to pay the amount outstanding. However, beyond this they would not have been liable contribute any more money. A shareholder who has already paid the full price of the shares held has no liability to pay any more.

It must of course be emphasised that it is the shareholders who have limited liability, and not the company. If a company has debts it must pay these debts, even if this means selling all of its assets and going into liquidation.

Perpetual succession

A company can be liquidated at any time if the members of the company pass a special resolution that it should be liquidated. If a company is liquidated then the company will cease to exist. However, companies can continue in existence indefinitely, and therefore it is said that they have perpetual succession.

Shareholders, of course, must die. But even if all the shareholders in a company die, their shares will be inherited by others and the company will continue in existence. For example, the Hudson Bay Company has been in existence since 2 May 1670. Generations of its shareholders have died, but the company still exists.

As we shall see, the death of a partner ends a partnership. The existing partners might agree to carry the partnership on but, technically at least, the firm will be dissolved when a partner dies.

Ownership of property

A company can own property, and this property will continue to be owned by the company regardless of who owns the shares in the company. This can be important when a company is trying to borrow money because the company can give its own property, both present and future assets, as security for a loan.

Contractual capacity

A company has the power to make contracts and can sue and be sued on these contracts. This power must be delegated to human agents, and it is the company directors who actually go through the process of forming the contracts. But the important point is that it is the company itself which assumes the rights and liabilities which the contract creates.

A company can also sue and be sued in tort. (A tort is a civil wrong other than a breach of contract, for example negligence, trespass or defamation.)

Criminal liability

To commit a crime a defendant must generally commit a guilty act while having a guilty mind. At first sight it would seem that companies cannot commit crimes because they have not got minds of their own. However, the courts are sometimes prepared to regard the controllers of the company as the minds of the company.

In *Tesco Supermarkets Ltd v Nattrass [1971]* the House of Lords held that a person who was sufficiently senior in a company could be regarded as the mind of the company. If a person senior enough to be regarded as the mind of a company had a guilty mind then the company could be regarded as having a guilty mind. Persons who were not senior enough could only be regarded as the hands of the company. If such a person had a guilty mind then this could not be regarded as the guilty mind of the company.

Student Activity Questions 7.2

1) Does the concept of limited liability mean that companies do not have to pay their debts?

2) Shabana buys shares in a limited company. What is the maximum amount she can be required to contribute towards the company's debts?

3) Companies are said to have perpetual succession. What does this mean?

4) Can a company:

   a) Own property?

   b) Make contracts in it's own name?

   c) Be found guilty of a crime?

Further Activity Questions 7.2

1) The decision in *Salomon's* case means that investors in a limited company do not have to pay the company's debts. They may lose the value of their shares, but they can lose no more. Why is this regarded as such an important rule in a capitalist society? In what way would society be different if members of companies did not enjoy limited liability?

2) In 1768 Lord Blackstone said. 'A corporation cannot commit treason, or felony or other crime, in its corporate capacity; though its members may in their distinc individual capacities.'

In the *Tesco* case, and in others, it has been recognised that nowadays, a company can commit a crime. Why do you think that this change in judicial attitudes has taken place? Is it only relatively trivial crimes which a company could commit, or could a company be found guilty of a crime such as murder or manslaughter?

3) The Race Relations Act 1976 makes discrimination on racial grounds unlawful Can a company commit such discrimination? Could a company be liable under the Sex Discrimination Act?

Classification of companies

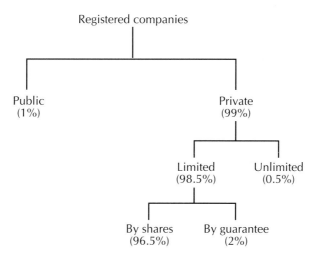

Figure 7.2 Classification of companies

Companies can be classified in several different ways, but from a business perspective only three classifications are useful.

Public companies and private companies

Public companies can offer shares and debentures for sale to the public. The articles of private companies usually restrict the sale of the company's shares. The most common restrictions are either that the shares must first be offered to other members of the company, or that the shares can only be sold to persons of whom the directors approve. No matter what the articles of association say, it is a criminal offence for a private company to offer its shares for sale to members of the public.

Although public companies make up only about one per cent of all companies they tend to be very much larger than most private companies. The assets of the one per cent of companies which are public would far outweigh the assets of the ninety-nine per cent of companies which are private. Although plcs can be listed on the London Stock Market, most are not. Only about 2,000 plcs are listed. The shares of many more plcs are traded on the Alternative Investment Market.

It is possible for a private company to re-register as a plc and vice versa. If this is done, a new certificate of incorporation is issued. Most plcs began as private companies and made the change after they had become very successful. A special resolution is needed to change from a private company to a plc or to change from a plc to a private company.

Public companies	Private companies
Must have at least 2 members	Need have only one member
Name must end with the words 'Public limited company' or 'plc'	Name must end with 'Limited' or 'Ltd' (unless the company is unlimited)
Must have £50,000 allotted share capital, one quarter of which must be paid up	No limit on share capital
Shares can be listed on Stock Exchange (No requirement that they should be)	Shares cannot be quoted on Stock Exchange nor advertised for sale
Must have at least 2 directors	Need have only one director
Shares must be paid for in cash (or independent expert must value assets given as payment)	Shares can be given away
Company secretary must be suitably qualified	Company secretary needs no qualifications
Must hold an AGM every calendar year	Can elect not to hold AGMs
Cannot pass written resolutions	Can pass written resolutions

Figure 7.3 Differences between public and private companies

Limited and unlimited companies

Slightly under half of one per cent of registered companies are unlimited companie These companies do have a legal personality distinct from that of the company membe but the members have agreed that they will have unlimited liability for the debts of th company.

Unlimited companies enjoy some advantages over limited companies. For example, the accounts need not be published or delivered to the Registrar of Companies. Howeve these advantages are generally considered to be far outweighed by the unlimited liabili of the members.

The names of unlimited companies must not contain the words 'limited' or 'Ltd.'

Public companies may not register as unlimited companies.

Companies limited by shares and companies limited by guarantee

Limited companies can themselves be classified into two types.

a) *Companies limited by shares*

The vast majority of companies are limited by shares. As we have seen, this mea that in the event of liquidation of the company a member's liability is limited paying off any amount unpaid on his or her shares. (When any reference to a company is made it should be assumed that the company is limited by shares.)

b) *Companies limited by guarantee*

The liability of members of companies limited by guarantee is limited to paying an amount which they have agreed to pay in the event of the company going into liquidation. This amount is usually small, typically £5, and is spelt out in the memorandum of association, which must be registered with the Registrar of Companies when the company is formed.

Before the Companies Act 1985 a company could be limited by shares and by guarantee, in which case the members were liable to pay both the amount guaranteed and the amount unpaid on their shares. Some such companies, formed before 1985, continue to exist. However, since the 1985 Act a company must either be limited by shares or be limited by guarantee.

Most companies limited by guarantee are educational or charitable. Guarantee companies are not a suitable medium for trading companies.

Public companies have never been allowed to be limited by guarantee. They must be limited by shares.

Method of creation

Companies are created by registration under the Companies Acts, a procedure which is examined later in this chapter. Some very few companies have been created by Royal Charter or by statute. However, these methods of creation are not significant in a business context. Almost all companies currently in existence were created by registration under the Companies Acts. The process is quick and cheap, and it is generally understood that when people speak of a company this is the type of company which they mean.

Student Activity Questions 7.3

1) A business is registered under the name Acme Trading Ltd. Which one of the following might the company be?

a) A Public Limited Company.

b) A partnership.

c) A private limited company.

d) Either a limited private company or an unlimited private company.

... continued

2) Arthur owns 100 shares in a private limited company which has gone into liqui-dation with heavy debts. Arthur has paid half the price of his shares. Which one of the following statements would be true?

   a) As the company is limited it need not pay its debts.

   b) Limited liability will mean that Arthur has to pay nothing towards the company's debts.

   c) Arthur must pay the amount unpaid on his shares. Beyond that he need pay no more.

   d) The amount of the company's debts must be paid by all shareholders in proportion to their share holding.

3) Which one of the following statements is true?

   a) A public company need only have 1 director.

   b) A public company cannot be unlimited.

   c) A public company's shares must be quoted on the stock exchange.

   d) A public company's shares must be offered for sale to the public.

4) Which one of the following statements is not true of a private limited company?

   a) The company will continue in existence indefinitely unless it is liquidated.

   b) The company can sue on contracts made in its name.

   c) The company can employ the person who owns all the shares in the company.

   d) A major shareholder in the company cannot hold shares in a rival company.

Characteristics of a partnership

Definition of a partnership

Partnerships, commonly known as firms, are defined by section 1(1) of the Partnership Act 1890, which states:

> *'Partnership is the relation which subsists between persons carrying on a business in common with a view of profit.'*

This definition is deceptively complex. It is best understood if broken down into smaller parts.

a) *'Partnership is the relation which subsists between persons'*

This opening phrase is revealing. A partnership is not a separate entity with a legal personality of its own. It is merely a relationship between persons. Such a relationship gives rise to legal rights and liabilities, but it does not create a new legal person.

b) *'Business'* is defined by section 45 of the Partnership Act as including 'every trade, occupation or profession.'

However, some professionals, such as barristers, have their own rules which prevent partnership between their members.

Mann v D'Arcy [1968] established that even if the business is only to make one deal (in this case to buy and sell 350 tons of potatoes) this can be enough to create a partnership.

c) *'In common'* means not only that all of the partners carry on the business, but that the business is carried on for the benefit of all of them. It is quite common for partnerships to employ workers. These employees are not partners. They may help to carry the business on, but it is not carried on for their benefit.

d) *'View of profit'* does not mean that the business must make a profit, but rather that the partners should intend to make a profit. This intention to make a profit distinguishes partnerships from non profit making members clubs, such as social clubs.

Despite the statutory definition provided by section 1(1) of the Partnership Act, it is often very difficult to tell whether or not a business is or is not a partnership. Some slight help is provided by Section 1(2) of the Partnership Act which states that a company can not be a partnership.

Agency

Partners can be the agents of their fellow partners and of the firm. This means that contracts made by individual partners can become binding on all of the partners. Furthermore, if an individual partner commits a tort other partners can become liable for this. To understand the way in which one partner can make fellow partners liable it is best to separate liability in contract from liability in tort. First, however, the following figure gives an outline of the position as regards both contract and tort.

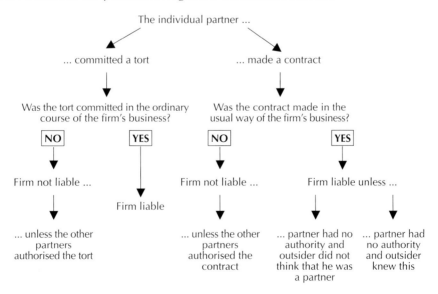

Figure 7.4 The firm's liability for the act of an individual partner

The firm's liability in contract

Section 5 of the Partnership Act explains the partnership's liability under contracts made by individual partners on behalf of the firm. This section takes the form of one very long sentence, and if it is is read as a whole it can be difficult to understand. But if the section is broken down into its component parts it becomes relatively straightforward. First though it is necessary to reproduce section 5 in its entirety.

Section 5:

> *'Every partner is an agent of the firm and his other partners for the purpose of the business of the partnership; and the acts of every partner who does any act for carrying on in the usual way business of the kind carried on by the firm of which he is a member bind the firm and his partners, unless the partner so acting has in fact no authority to act for the firm in the particular matter, and the person with whom he is dealing either knows that he has no authority, or does not know or believe him to be a partner.'*

Now we break section 5 down into its component parts.

> *'Every partner is an agent of the firm and his other partners for the purpose of the business of the partnership...'*

An agent has the power to make contracts on behalf of a third party, his or her principal.

Shop assistants, for example, are agents; they sell goods which belong not to themselves but to the shops for which they work. Once a contract with a customer has been made it is binding on the shop, not on the shop assistant. Similarly, purchasing clerks and salesmen are agents. It is not their own goods which they buy and sell.

So when the opening part of section 5 states that partners are agents of the firm and of their other partners this is of enormous significance.

It means that no matter how disastrous a contract a partner makes on behalf of the firm all fellow partners will be completely bound by the contract. If there are not enough partnership assets to honour the contract then this liability will extend to each partner personally.

This agency of the partner only applies to contracts made

> *'..for carrying on in the usual way business of the kind carried on by the firm of which he is a member...'*

This is a very important limitation. The firm will not be bound by all contracts made by a partner on behalf of the firm. It will only be bound if the contract was the type of contract which the firm would usually make in the course of its business, and if the contract was made in the usual way one would expect such a contract to be made.

For example, if a partner in a firm of accountants ordered office furniture or a new computer for the firm these contracts would be binding on the firm. But if the partner ordered a new sports car for the firm this contract would not; it is not in the usual way of business for a firm of accountants to order sports cars.

The final part of section 5 allows for situations where a partner will not be the agent of the firm even as regards goods which were ordered in the usual way of the firm's business.

> *'...unless the partner so acting has in fact no authority to act for the firm in the particular matter, and the person with whom he is dealing either knows that he has no authority, or does not know or believe him to be a partner.'*

It can be seen that there are two requirements here. First, the partner must have had no authority to act for the firm in the way that he did. Second, the person with whom the partner dealt must either have known this or must have thought that the partner was not in fact a partner in the firm.

For example, let us assume that the partnership deed of firm ABC say that partner C has no authority to buy supplies on the firm's behalf. If C does buy the type of goods which the firm usually needs, on the firm's behalf, the firm will be bound by the contract unless:

a)   The supplier knows that C has no authority to buy, or

b)   The supplier does not know or believe C to be a partner in the firm.

Section 7 deals with contracts which are *not* made in the ordinary course of the firm's business.

> *'Where one partner pledges the credit of the firm for a purpose apparently not connected with the firm's ordinary course of business, the firm is not bound, unless he is in fact specially authorised by the other partners; but this section does not affect any personal liability incurred by any individual partner.'*

Again, it might be helpful to break this section down.

Section 7 begins,

> *'Where one partner pledges the credit of the firm for a purpose apparently not connected with the firm's ordinary course, the firm is not bound....'*

For example, in a firm of accountants, DEF, partner D orders a new snooker table for the firm, saying that the firm will pay for it later. Under section 7 this contract would not be binding on the firm because it is not in the ordinary course of business for a firm of accountants to need a snooker table.

Section 7 continues,

> *'unless he is in fact specially authorised by the other partners.....'*

So the contract to buy the snooker table would be binding on the firm if E and F had authorised D to order it.

The final part of section 7 says,

> *'but this section does not affect any personal liability incurred by any individual partner.'*

This merely means that the one who made the contract, (in this case D who ordered the snooker table,) will be personally liable whether the other partners are liable or not.

Student Activity Questions 7.4

1) If one of the partners in a firm of dentists orders a new dental chair for the firm, without the knowledge or permission of his or her fellow partners, will the partnership be bound by the contract?

2) Would the partnership still be bound if one of the other partners had previously told the supplier of the chair that the partner who ordered the chair had no authority to order such goods on behalf of the partnership?

3) Would the partnership of dentists be bound if one of the partners, without authority of the other partners, orders a new fur coat for the partnership?

Further Activity Questions 7.4

Using sections 5 &7, decide whether or not the firm was bound in the following case. The actual decision is available on this book's Website.

Mercantile Credit Co v Garrod [1963]

Parkin and Garrod were partners in a firm which carried on the business of repairing cars and letting lock-up garages. The partnership deed stated that neither partner had authority to buy or sell cars. Parkin, without Garrod's permission, sold a car to Mercantile Credit for £700. Parkin did not in fact own the car and Mercantile Credit claimed their £700 back. Garrod was much wealthier than Parkin and so Mercantile Credit sued Garrod, arguing that the partnership, and all members of the firm, were liable on the contract to sell the car.

Held ... ?

The firm's liability for a partner's torts

Here we consider whether the partnership as a whole is liable if one partner commits tort. Let us assume for example, that partner G in the firm GHI accidentally crashes h car into a bus, injuring several passengers. Can the injured passengers sue H and I as par ners of G? Or are they restricted to suing G alone?

Section 10 provides the answer.

> 'Where, by any [tort]..of any partner acting in the ordinary course of the business of the firm, or with the authority of his co-partners, loss or injury is caused to any person not being a partner in the firm....the firm is liable therefor to the same extent as the partner [who committed the tort]...'

It can be seen that the partnership is only liable for another partner's torts if *either*:

a) The tort was committed *in the ordinary course of the firm's business, or*

b) The other partners *authorised the tort.*

So a firm of accountants would be liable for a partner who stole money which he or she had been given to invest for a client. (Investing money would be in the ordinary course of the firm's business, and stealing money would amount to the tort of conversion.) But the firm would not be liable for a partner who lost his or her temper and battered a client. (Unless the other partners had authorised the battery!)

Hamlyn v Houston & Co [1903]

Partners in Houston & Co were encouraged to get information on rival firms by all legal means. One of the partners went further and bribed a clerk in a rival firm into giving information. As a result the rival firm suffered loss and it sued Houston & Co for the tort of inducement to break a contract.

Held *The firm were liable under section 10. It was within the ordinary course of the firm's business to obtain information about rival firms.*

Collins MR

> 'If it was within the ordinary course of the business of the partnership to obtain this information by legitimate means, it was within the scope of Houston to obtain it, and the firm is liable if it is obtained by unlawful means.'

If we have another look at the case of partner G, who crashed into the bus, we can now decide whether or not the other partners are liable. They will be liable if G was driving on the firm's business, (if he or she was going to see one of the firm's clients or fetching goods for the firm), but they will not be liable if G was driving otherwise than on the firm's business, (if he or she was going home after work or driving to visit friends.)

iability by 'holding out'

A person 'holds himself out' to be a partner if he leads third parties to believe that he is a partner. If a third party gives credit to the firm as a consequence then the person who held himself out to be a partner will be liable as if he really was a partner.

Section 14 states that:

> 'Every one who by words spoken or written or by conduct represents himself, or who knowingly suffers himself to be represented, as a partner in a particular firm, is liable as a partner to anyone who has on the faith of any such representation given credit to the firm...'

Note that the person can hold himself out as a partner by

> 'words spoken or written or by conduct.'

If the representation is made by a third party, the person represented as a partner will not be liable unless he

> 'knowingly suffers himself to be represented as a partner.'

Tower Cabinet Co v Ingram [1949]

Christmas and Ingram were partners in a firm of furnishers called Merry's. After Ingram's retirement Christmas ordered goods using old partnership notepaper. This notepaper contained the names of both Ingram and Christmas. Ingram did not know that Christmas had used the notepaper and the supplier of the goods had never dealt with the firm when Ingram was a partner. The suppliers were not paid for their goods. Having sued the firm and won, they claimed the money from Ingram.

Held *Ingram was not liable under section 14 because he had not knowingly allowed himself to be represented as a partner. If he had known that Christmas had used the notepaper then Ingram would have been liable.*

Lynskey J

> 'Before the company can succeed in making Mr. Ingram liable under this section [section 14] they have to satisfy the court that Mr. Ingram, by words spoken or written or by conduct, represented himself as a partner. There is no evidence of that. Alternatively, they must prove that he knowingly suffered himself to be represented as a partner. ......it is impossible to say that Mr. Ingram knowingly suffered himself to be so represented.'

Student Activity Questions 7.5

1) While at work, a partner in a firm of dentists negligently performs a tooth extraction. This causes the patient to become seriously ill with an infected jaw. Is the partnership liable for the partner's negligence?

... continued

2) While on a skiing holiday, a partner in a firm of dentists negligently collides with a fellow skier, causing serious injury. Is the partnership liable for this?

3) What risk does a person run by allowing outsiders to believe that he or she is a partner?

Unlimited liability

Partners are not protected by limited liability because a partnership is not a legal person with a legal identity of its own. Every partner is liable for the firm's debts to the full extent of his or her personal wealth.

These concepts of agency and unlimited liability can have extremely serious consequences, as is demonstrated by the classic quotation from James LJ in *Baird's Case [1870]*.

> 'Ordinary partnerships are by the law assumed to be based on the mutual trust and confidence of each partner in the skill, knowledge and integrity of every other partner. As between the partners and the outside world (whatever may be their private arrangements between themselves), each partner is the unlimited agent of every other in every matter connected with the partnership business .... A partner who may not have a farthing of capital left may take money or assets of the partnership to the value of millions, may bind the partnership by contracts to any amount ..... and may even – as has been shewn in many painful instances in this court – involve his innocent partners in unlimited amounts for frauds which he has carefully concealed from them.'

Limited partners

It is not possible for all of the partners in a firm to have limited liability in the same way that all the shareholders in a limited company have limited liability (but see Limited Liability Partnerships below).

It is however possible for one or more of the partners to have limited liability under the *Limited Partnerships Act 1907*. However, there must always be at least one general partner who has unlimited liability.

Every limited partnership must register with the Registrar of Companies, giving the following information:

a) The firm name.

b) The general nature of the business.

c) The principal place of business.

d) The full name of each of the partners.

e) The date of commencement and the length of time for which the business is entered into.

f)   A statement that the partnership is limited, and the description of every limited partner.

g)   The sum contributed by every limited partner, and whether paid in cash or otherwise

There must then be two classes of partner in a limited partnership. General partners, who manage the business and have unlimited liability. Limited partners, who contribute a certain amount of capital and are not liable beyond this amount. They are not allowed to take part in the management of the business and are not agents of the firm. If a limited partner does take part in management he or she will lose his limited liability. In practice the Limited Partnerships Act is of very little significance.

Limited liability partnerships

When the Limited Liability Partnerships Act 2000 comes into force a new type of business organisation will be created - the Limited Liability Partnership (LLP). The Act should come into force early in 2001 and this book's Website will indicate when this ha happened.

An LLP must be regarded as a quite different thing from an ordinary partnership. Indeed in most ways an LLP is more similar to a company than to a partnership. LLPs will be regarded as corporate bodies with a legal personality of their own. The members of an LLP will not therefore usually be liable for the LLP's debts. One major difference between a company and an LLP is that an LLP will have no directors and so every member of an LLP will be an agent of the LLP in the same way that a partner is an agent of an ordinary partnership.

Sole traders

A person can be in business alone, without being in partnership or a member of company. Such a person, and there are a good number of them, is called a sole trader. A sole trader might well employ other people, but is not in business with them.

Sole traders have unlimited personal liability for the debts of their business. If necessary they must sell all of their possessions, and can even be made bankrupt, in order to pay the business debts.

When a sole trader dies the business comes to an end. Somebody else might buy the business as a going concern and take it over, but if this happens the purchaser will be regarded as a new business. The sole trader's estate will not be liable for any debts which the business incurs after it has been taken over.

No formalities are attached to the formation of a business carried on as a sole trader. The trader creates the business by beginning to trade.

Student Activity Questions 7.6

1) If Salomon had carried on his business as a partnership with his family:

   a) Would he have had to repay the unsecured creditors their £8,000?

   b) Would his fellow partners (who might have had nothing to do with the loans made by the unsecured creditors and known nothing of them) have had any liability to repay them?

2) a) Who makes business contracts on behalf of a partnership?

   b) When a person goes into partnership with another, what is the maximum liability that person can incur?

   c) A cleaner is employed by a partnership of doctors. Does this make the cleaner a partner?

Further Activity Questions 7.6

Alma, Billy and Claire go into business together to make a film, imagining that this will make them a lot of money. They do not form a company or give any thought as to what sort of business they might be. Alma and Billy, without Claire's knowledge or permission, make contracts to hire actors, sets and costumes. The project is abandoned when Claire discovers that the other two have no money. None of the money spent is recouped by the business. Which one of the following statements is true?

a) As a partner, Claire is liable for all of the debts incurred.

b) Claire has no liability. The business can not be a partnership because no profits were ever made.

c) Claire has no liability. She did not know of the contracts and gave no permission for them to be made.

d) Claire has no liability because she is protected by the corporate veil.

Formation of business organisations

Registered companies

A company is formed by promoters, who must register certain documents with the Registrar of Companies. If the Registrar is satisfied with the documents he will issue a certificate of incorporation, and the company will then exist as a corporate body.

The documents which must be sent to the Registrar are:

1) The company's memorandum of association.

2) The company's articles of association.

3) A statement giving the names and addresses of the company's first directors and of the company secretary. (Form 10.)

4) A statement that all the statutory requirements of registration have been complied with. (Form 12.)

These four documents must be sent to the Registrar of Companies, along with a £20 fee. Form 12 must be witnessed by a solicitor, a magistrate, or a Commissioner for Oaths, who must also sign to say that he or she has witnessed the signature. Form 10 must be signed by the proposed directors and the company secretary and by or on behalf of all those who are taking shares in the company.

The memorandum of association

A company's constitution is contained in its memorandum and articles of association. The memorandum regulates the company's external affairs. It is designed to provide information to outsiders.

Section 2 of the Companies Act 1985 states that the memorandum of a company limited by shares must contain five obligatory clauses.

The company name (Clause 1)

This clause states the name of the company. If a private company is limited then its name must end with the word 'limited' or the abbreviation 'Ltd'. If the company is a public company the name must end with the words 'public limited company' or the abbreviation 'plc'. If the company's registered office is to be in Wales, the Welsh equivalents of limited ('cyfyngedig') or 'Ltd.' ('cyf.') or 'public limited company' ('cwmni cyfyngedig cyhoeddus') or 'plc' ('c.c.c.') may be used instead.

The registered office (Clause 2)

This clause must state whether the company's registered office is in Wales, England and Wales (which are regarded as one area) or in Scotland. The address does not need to be given here. However the address will have to be declared in Form 10.

The objects (Clause 3)

The objects clause states the purposes for which the company is being formed. Until recently a company could not make valid contracts which were outside its objects clause. For this reason most companies tended to have extremely long objects clauses, often running to several pages. Such clauses are no longer necessary because companies may now state that their objects are to carry on business as a general commercial company. Such an objects clause would allow the company to make any type of contract. Even where an objects clause does limit the type of contracts which a company may make, persons dealing with a company in good faith are nowadays able to assume that a company has the power to make any contract which it does make.

Limited liability (Clause 4)

This clause merely states that the liability of the company is limited (if it is).

Share capital (Clause 5)

The company must state the amount of share capital with which it is to be registered and the way in which this capital is to be divided into shares. For example, a company might state that it has a share capital of £100, divided into 100 shares of £1 each.

The amount of share capital declared in clause 5 is known as the authorised share capital. This is the maximum number of shares, of a stated value, which the company is authorised to issue. Not all of this authorised capital needs to be issued as shares.

Every subscriber to the memorandum must take at least one share in the company and so the subscribers are the first members of the company. Since 1992 it has been possible to have single member companies. Such a company might have a share capital of £1, made up of a single £1 share.

Additional clauses

The memorandum may have additional clauses and if these are stated to be unalterable then they cannot be altered by the company members.

The articles of association

The articles are the internal rules of the company. They bind the members and the company as if signed and sealed by each member. The articles are therefore of the utmost importance. They deal with matters such as the transfer of shares, the powers of directors, the appointment and removal of directors and the remuneration of directors.

A company which does not wish to draw up its own articles can adopt a model set of articles contained in Table A of the 1985 Companies Regulations. Table A articles are not suitable for all companies, but many do adopt them.

Student Activity Questions 7.7

Blank copies of Forms 10 and 12 are reproduced in an Appendix at the back of this book. Complete both forms to register a fictitious company. Before starting you will need to decide upon the following information:

a)   The company name.

b)   The address of its registered office.

c)   The name and address of the solicitors or accountants who are to act as agents.

d)   The names of the company secretary and the first directors.

Contracts made before the company is formed

A company does not come into existence until the Registrar issues its certificate of incorporation. It follows that until the certificate is issued the company has no capacity to make contracts.

However, the promoters might want to make contracts on the company's behalf in advance of incorporation. For example, if a shop intended to begin trading as a company on 1 October then the promoters would need to buy stock in advance of that date.

Section 36 (c) of the 1985 Act provides that:

> *'A contract which purports to be made by or on behalf of a company when the company has not been formed has effect, subject to any agreement to the contrary, as one made with the person purporting to act for the company or as agent for it, and he is personally liable on the contract accordingly.'*

It will be noticed this section applies *'subject to any agreement to the contrary'*. It is therefore possible for the promoter to disclaim personal liability when making the contract on the company's behalf. However, it would be inadvisable for others to deal with the promoters on this basis. In effect they would be making contracts which could be enforced against themselves but which they might not be able to enforce against anyone.

Suppliers to the company might do well to insist that the company is actually formed before they make any contract. Another way around the problem would be for the supplier to make two contracts. The first draft contract would be with the company stating that it will pay as soon as it is formed. The second contract would be made with the promoters, who would agree that they would pay in the event that the company does not.

The company name

Limited or public limited company

The name of every public company must end with the words 'public limited company' or the abbreviation 'plc'. The name of every private limited company must end with the word 'limited' or the abbreviation 'Ltd'. (We have seen that if the company's registered office is in Wales then the Welsh equivalents of these names may be used.) So the word 'limited' must appear in the names of both types of companies, although of course it is not the company's liability which is limited, but the liability of its members.

Unlimited companies may not include the word 'limited' in their names.

The word 'company' is not often included in the names of companies. Strangely, the word appears in the names of partnerships more frequently than in the names of companies.

Prohibited names

The Companies Act 1985 prohibits the use of certain names.

1) The words 'limited' or 'unlimited' or 'public limited company' can only be used at the end of the name.

2) The Registrar will refuse to register a name which is identical to the name of another company already on the register.

3) The Registrar will refuse to register a name the use of which would, in the opinion of the Secretary of State, constitute a criminal offence or be offensive.

4) Regulations made by the Secretary of State prohibit the use of certain words without permission. These words suggest a connection with Government or with local authorities. Other Regulations prohibit the use of certain words without permission from the Secretary of State. The Secretary of State will only give permission for these words to be used in a company name if permission is granted by an appropriate body. Currently about 100 words are listed, including 'Building Society,' 'Chamber of Commerce,' 'English,' 'Insurance,' 'National,' 'Prince,' 'Queen,' 'Royal,' 'Trade Union,' 'Trust,' and 'Windsor'.

The Regulations explain from whom permission to use the words must be sought.For example, the words which suggest a Royal connection can only be used if the Home Office gives permission.

Passing off

If a company registers a name which is too similar to the name of an existing business, a passing off action might prevent the company from trading under its registered name. If such a passing off action is brought the court will grant an injunction to prevent use of that name if it is likely to divert customers away from the existing business or cause confusion between the two businesses.

This applies whether the name was deliberately made similar or was done so accidentally. But the fact that it was done deliberately is likely to influence the court's decision against the new name. The following case provides an example of a successful passing off action.

Ewing v Buttercup Margarine Co Ltd [1917]

The claimant carried on an unincorporated business under the name Buttercup Dairy Co. The business dealt in margarine, mainly in Scotland. The defendant company was later registered under the name the Buttercup Margarine Co Ltd. It also dealt in margarine, but in the South of England. The claimant brought a passing off action.

Held The claimant's action was successful. The defendant company was prohibited from continuing to trade under its registered name. The public might have thought that there was a connection between the two businesses.

Section 28 of the 1985 Act gives the Secretary of State the power to order a company to change its name within one year of registration if the name is too similar to one which is already on the register.

Publication of name and address

All companies must publish their names:

1) Outside the registered office and all places of business.

2) On all letters, invoices, notices, cheques and receipts.

3) On the company seal, if it has a seal.

If the company does not publish its name as required then every one of its officers is liable to be fined. Furthermore, a person who signs company letters or cheques which do not publish the company name will be personally liable to any creditor who relies on the document and loses money. This liability will also be imposed if the company name is incorrectly stated.

For example, in *Penrose v Martyr [1858]*, a company secretary signed a cheque on the company's behalf and was held personally liable because the word 'limited' was omitted from the company name.

Change of name

A private limited company may change its name by special resolution or by written resolution. A plc can change its name only by special resolution.

The same prohibitions will apply to a change of name as applied to the use of a name on formation of a company. The Registrar must register the changed name and has the same powers to refuse.

Business names

Sometimes companies trade under a name other than their registered corporate name. A company which does trade under another name will have to comply with the Business

Names Act 1985. The effects of this Act are considered later in this chapter as the Act applies more often to partnerships than to companies.

Even if the company does trade under another name it must continue to print its proper corporate name on all letters and cheques.

Student Activity Questions 7.8

In which of the documents sent to the Registrar of Companies will the following information be found?

a)   The company name and address.

b)   The company's capacity to make contracts.

c)   The rules on the transfer of shares.

d)   The name of the company secretary.

e)   A declaration that all the necessary formalities relating to formation of the company have been complied with.

f)   The previous names of the directors.

g)   The authorised share capital of the company.

Partnerships

Earlier in this chapter we saw that a partnership is formed merely by the fact of people carrying on a business in common with the intention of making a profit. Partners might or might not enter into a written partnership agreement, usually called a partnership deed.

If a partnership deed is signed by the partners then this will govern the partners' relationship with each other. The deed will also state the date at which the partnership commenced. Firms carrying on a professional business, such as firms of accountants or solicitors, would almost certainly regulate their relations with a detailed partnership deed. Other firms, such as firms of window cleaners or market traders, might not have a written agreement. This would not prevent them from being partnerships.

The Partnership deed

A very simple partnership deed is reproduced on the following 2 pages.

Model Partnership Deed (Page 1)

This partnership agreement is made on <u>Date</u>

between <u>Name</u> of <u>Address 1</u>

and <u>Name</u> of <u>Address 1</u>

and <u>Name</u> of <u>Address 1</u>

It is agreed as follows:

1. The partners shall carry on business in partnership as:
   <u>Type of business</u>

   under the firm name of:
   <u>Partnership name</u>

   of: <u>Partnership address</u>

2. The partnership will commence on the date of this agreement and shall continue in existence for five years.

3. The partners shall be entitled to the profits arising from the partnership in equal shares.

4. The bankers of the firm shall be:
   <u>Name</u>

   of: <u>Address</u>

   Cheques drawn in the name of the firm must be signed by all the partners.

5. Each partner shall devote his or her whole time to the business of the partnership

---

Model Partnership Deed (Page 2)

6. Each partner shall be entitled to ___Number___ weeks holiday each year.

7. None of the partners shall, without the consent of the other(s), engage in any business other than partnership business or employ or dismiss any partnership employee.

8. Each partner shall be entitled to draw ___Amount___ as salary from the partnership bank account each month.

9. All matters relating to the management of the affairs of the partnership shall be decided by votes taken at a meeting of the partners. At such meetings, each partner shall be entitled to one vote and resolutions shall be passed by a simple majority vote.

10. If any disputes should arise as to the meaning of this partnership deed or as to the rights and liabilities of the partners under it, such disputes shall be referred to an arbitrator to be appointed by the President of the Chartered Institute of Arbitrators. The decision of the arbitrator shall be binding on all the partners.

Signed as a deed by ___Name 1___ in the presence of ___Witness___

Signed as a deed by ___Name 2___ in the presence of ___Witness___

Signed as a deed by ___Name 3___ in the presence of ___Witness___

It should be stressed that such a deed is very brief and is only a model. In its current form it is unlikely to be ideal for many firms. The partners should ensure that changes are made to suit their particular circumstances.

More complicated partnership deeds can run to several thousand words. These deeds cover the same matters as the simple deed in very much more detail. In addition, they might contain articles dealing with matters such as leasing premises, payment of private debts, negative covenants, banking arrangements, retirement provisions, expulsion of partners, provisions for retiring partners, options to purchase the share of outgoing partners, income tax and retirement annuities.

The partnership deed can be altered by unanimous consent of the partners and this consent can be inferred from the conduct of the partners. In *Const v Harris [1824]* Lord Eldon gave the following example of how this might happen:

> 'If in a common partnership, the parties agree that no one of them shall draw or accept a bill of exchange in his own name, without the concurrence of all the others, yet, if they afterwards slide into a habit of permitting one of them to draw or accept bills, without the concurrence of the others, this Court will hold that they have varied the terms of the original agreement in that respect.'

Further Activity Questions 7.9

Andy and Brendan are intending to go into partnership as market traders. Andy is to work full-time in the business, actually standing behind the market stall, and take 75% of the profits. Brendan, who has a full-time job as a sales representative, is to work 10 hours a week and receive 25% of the profits. Brendan is also to act as the firm's buyer and look after the paperwork. Andy's father, an accountant, is prepared to check the books free of charge on a regular basis.

If Brendan spots a bargain he often has to buy it immediately. Andy is happy to let Brendan write cheques for up to £100 on the firm's behalf. Brendan has an ambition to work in Australia but would not travel there without a definite job offer. Occasionally he writes to Australian firms, asking for jobs. He realises that he has very little chance of getting a job in this way, but if he was offered one he would want to leave for Australia immediately.

Andy and Brendan want a partnership deed. They think that the model partnership deed on pages 206 and 207 is a suitable model but realise that changes would have to be made if the deed was to suit their needs.

a) List the articles which you think should be changed.

b) Write alternative articles to replace those which you consider unsuitable

Absence of written partnership agreement

If there is no written partnership agreement then it may be very difficult to state whether or not there is a partnership. Many people who are partners do not realise that they are.

The decision as to whether or not a partnership exists is based on sections 1 and 2 of the Partnership Act 1890.

As we have seen, section 1 provides the classic definition of a partnership as *'the relation which subsists between persons carrying on a business in common with a view of profit'*.

Section 2 states that joint ownership of property does not by itself create a partnership; that the sharing of gross takings does not necessarily indicate that a partnership exists; and that sharing gross profits is a strong indication of partnership.

Partnership is a contractual relationship. Ultimately the question is whether those who carried on the business made a contract with each other (expressly or impliedly) that they should carry on a business with each other to try and make a profit. (It should be noticed that the question is not whether they made a contract with each other agreeing that they would be partners.)

Student Activity Questions 7.10

1) Can people become partners without signing a written partnership agreement?

2) Two authors jointly write a book. The publisher pays the authors a percentage of the price of each book sold.

   a) Are the authors in partnership with each other?

   b) Are they in partnership with the publisher?

3) Mr and Mrs Smith sell their existing house to buy a dilapidated mansion. They intend to live in the mansion for five years during which time they will completely renovate it. At the end of the five years they hope to sell at a much higher price than the one they paid. Are Mr and Mrs Smith in partnership? Would your answer be different if:

   a) They were not married but were cohabiting?

   b) They were strangers to each other, each selling their own house in order to buy the mansion?

   c) They continued to live in their own houses, working on the mansion whenever they could?

   d) The mansion was not the only property which they were renovating together?

Numbers of partners

In general, no firm may have more than 20 members. If more than 20 people want to go into business together they must do so as a company. However, firms of solicitors, accountants and various other professional people are allowed to have more than 20 members

Barristers are not allowed to practice as partners. (The firm might be representing both sides in the same case, or the judge might be hearing a case presented by an ex-partner.)

Illegal partnerships

A partnership formed for an illegal purpose will be void. The purpose will be illegal if either statute or the common law prohibits it. So many statutes prohibit so many types of behaviour that it would be pointless to try to list them all. As we saw in Chapter 3, the common law makes several different types of contract illegal, including contracts to commit a crime, tort or fraud.

Everet v Williams [1725]

Two highwayman robbed a coach intending to share the proceeds. One highwayman sued the other for his share, claiming that he was entitled to this as a partner.

Held *No partnership existed as the business carried on was illegal. (Both highwaymen were hanged and the claimant's lawyer was fined for bringing the case!)*

If a partnership is declared illegal the courts will refuse to recognise its existence and will not order one partner to pay towards losses suffered by another.

The partnership name

Partnerships do not need to register the names under which they trade. Apart from the prohibition as to using the word 'limited' or 'Ltd.' partners can trade under any name they like, as long as they comply with the Business Names Act 1985, and as long as the name is not designed to confuse the public.

The Business Names Act 1985

This Act applies to partnerships if they carry on business in a name other than the surnames of all the partners. If the partners merely add their forenames or their initials to their surnames they will not be subject to the Act. But if anything else is added, even the words '& Co.' the name must comply with the Act

Section 2 makes it a criminal offence to use names which would suggest a connection with Government or local authorities. The Secretary of State can grant permission for such names to be used.

Section 4 states that a notice containing the names of all the partners must be prominently displayed by a notice at any business premises to which customers or suppliers have access. An address at which documents can be served on each named partner must also be displayed. Further, partnerships with fewer than 20 members must include the name of each partner (and an address at which documents can be served on them) on all business letters, written orders for goods or services, invoices and receipts. Firms with 20 or fewer partners do not have to give the names of all the partners on business documents. However, they have to keep a list of the names and addresses of all the partners at the firm's main place of business. A statement on the firm's stationery must state where this list is kept and the times when it is available for inspection. (The list must be available for inspection during office hours.)

Section 5 states that if section 4 is not complied with then in some circumstances contracts made by the firm may be unenforceable by the partners.

Confusion with other names

A passing off action can be brought to prevent partners from trading under a name which is likely to cause confusion with another business.

In *Levy v Walker [1879]*, James LJ explained the nature of a passing off action:

> *'it should never be forgotten in these cases that the sole right to restrain anybody from using any name that he likes in the course of any business that he chooses to carry on is a right in the nature of a trade mark, that is to say, a man has a right to say 'you must not use a name whether fictitious or real, you must not use a description, whether true or not, which is intended to represent, or is calculated to represent to the world that your business is my business, and so by a fraudulent misstatement deprive me of the profits of the business which would otherwise come to me."*

Croft v Day [1843]

A well-known firm of boot polish manufacturers, Day and Martin, carried on business in Holborn. Two people called 'Day' and 'Martin' set up as partners making boot polish with the intention of diverting business from the well-known firm. The established firm applied for an injunction to prevent Day and Martin from trading in boot polish in their real names.

Held *The injunction was granted. Although 'Day' and 'Martin' were the real names of the defendants, the intention of the partnership was to deceive the public.*

Formation of limited liability partnerships

To form an LLP the members of the LLP must subscribe their names to an incorporation document and send this to the Registrar of Companies, along with a statement that all the formalities required to form an LLP have been complied with. The incorporation document will require the name of the LLP, the jurisdiction of the registered office, and the names and addresses of all the members of the LLP. The name must end with the words 'limited liability partnership' or the Welsh equivalent 'partneriaeth atebolrwydd cyfyngedig' or the abbreviations 'llp', 'LLP' 'pac' or 'PAC'. When the membership of an LLP changes the Registrar of Companies must be informed of this.

Student Activity Questions 7.11

1) Can a partnership include the word 'limited' in it's name?

2) Do partners have to include their own surnames in their trading name?

3) Are partners always entitled to trade under their own surnames?

Essential points

Characteristics of a limited company

■ A company is a legal person, with a legal identity of its own.

■ The members of a limited company have limited liability for the debts of the company.

■ A company has perpetual succession and may therefore continue in existenc indefinitely.

■ Companies can own property and can make contracts in their own names.

■ It is possible for a company to be convicted of a crime.

Public and private companies

■ Public limited companies (plcs) can offer their shares for sale to members of th public. It is a criminal offence for a private company to offer its shares for sale the public.

■ Plcs must have at least 2 members and 2 directors. Private companies need hav only 1 director and 1 member.

■ Plcs must have at least £50,000 share capital, at least one quarter of which mu be fully paid up. Private companies have no such requirements.

■ Private companies can pass written resolutions and elect to dispense with holdi Annual General Meetings. Plcs cannot do either of these things.

Characteristics of a partnership

- Partnership is the relationship which exists between persons who carry on a business with each other with the intention of making a profit.

- A partnership does not have a separate legal identity of its own. It is merely a relationship between the partners.

- Every partner has the power to make contracts in the firm's name which will be binding on the firm and all the partners in the firm. These contracts can be binding upon all of the partners even if all the partners have agreed that the individual partner should not have such power. However, this is only the case if the contract made was for carrying on in the usual way business of the kind carried on by the firm in question.

- All the partners in a firm will be liable for a tort committed by one partner if either the tort was committed in the ordinary course of the firm's business or if the other partners authorised the commission of the tort.

- A person who is not a partner but who allows outsiders to believe that he or she is a partner can become liable to those outsiders as if he or she really was a partner.

- A person who registers as a limited partner, under the Limited Partnerships Act 1907, will not be liable for the firm's debts.

- A limited partner may not take part in the management of the firm and will lose his or her limited liability if he or she does take part in the firm's management.

Limited liability partnerships

- Limited liability partnerships (LLPs) are not the same as ordinary partnerships.

- LLPs are corporate bodies with a legal personality of their own.

- Every member of an LLP will be able to make contracts which bind the LLP and the other members of it.

Formation of registered companies

- Companies are created by registration with the Registrar of Companies. Once registered, a company will be given a certificate of incorporation and will exist as a legal person.

- In order to register a company, the promoters of the company must send to the Registrar the company's memorandum of association, its articles of association, a form giving the names and addresses of the first directors and the company secretary, and a form stating that all the requirements of registration have been complied with.

■ The memorandum of association must contain five obligatory clauses, whic state: the company name; the jurisdiction of the registered office; the purposes fc which the company is formed; whether the liability of the company members limited; and the amount of authorised share capital and how this is divided in shares.

■ The articles of association are the internal rules of the company. They bind th company and all of the members as if they had been signed by all of th members.

■ Companies cannot validly make contracts until they have been given a certifica of incorporation.

Company names

■ The names of public companies must end with 'public limited company' or 'plc

■ The names of private limited companies must end with the word 'limited' or th abbreviation 'Ltd.'

■ The Registrar of Companies will refuse to register a company in a name which identical to the name of an existing company.

■ A company can be prevented by a passing off action from trading under a nan which is too similar to the name of an existing business.

■ Companies must publish their names outside the registered office and all plac of business; on all letters, invoices, notices, cheques and receipts; and on t company seal if the company has a seal.

Formation of partnerships

■ A partnership can be created without any formalities, merely by carrying on business in common with others with the intention of making a profit.

■ Most large partnerships will draw up a partnership agreement, known as a pa nership deed.

■ A partnership deed can be altered by unanimous agreement of the partne which may be inferred from their conduct.

■ Generally, there may not be more than 20 partners in a firm. (However, m firms of professional people are exempted from this rule.)

The partnership name

■ Partners who trade under a name other than the surnames of all the partners subject to the Business Names Act 1985.

■ The Business Names Act requires the names of all partners to be prominer displayed by a notice at any business premises to which customers or suppli have access. An address at which documents can be served on each named partner must also be displayed.

■ The Act also requires the names of all partners in firms with 20 or fewer partners to be included on all business letters, invoices, receipts and orders for goods or services. An address at which documents can be served on each named partner must also be displayed.

■ Firms with more than 20 partners must keep a list of the names and addresses of all the partners at the firm's main place of business. The firm's stationery must state where this list is kept and the times at which it is available for inspection.

End of chapter questions

Question 1

Alice, Belinda and Cherry run a shop as partners. The partnership deed states that only Alice can buy goods on behalf of the firm. Yesterday, in contradiction of this, Belinda bought a large quantity of new stock from Duncan. Alice and Cherry think that Belinda paid far too much for the stock and that it will be very difficult to sell. Two days ago Alice negligently spilt some oil on the shop floor and failed to clean it up. A customer slipped on the oil and badly injured herself. The partnership had failed to renew its insurance policy and so there was no insurance in place at the time of the accident. It seems likely that the firm has not got enough money to pay the likely damages to the injured customer and to pay Duncan's bill. Advise the three partners of their legal position in respect of the above facts.

Question 2

Eddy, Frank and Gerry are equal partners in a firm of market traders. They are thinking of running the business as a limited company or as a limited liability partnership. Explain the ways in which the characteristics of the business would change if the business was turned into:

a) a company; and

b) a limited liability partnership.

Question 3

a) Find the full names of 5 plcs. Where must these names be displayed?

b) Find the names of 5 private limited companies. Where must these names be displayed?

c) Find the names of 5 partnerships. Where must these names be displayed?

Task 7

A friend of yours from France is considering setting up a business in England. Your frien
has asked you to draw up a report briefly explaining the following matters.

a) The characteristics of a company.

b) The distinction between a public company and a private company.

c) The names which a company may use and the places in which the company nam
must be displayed.

d) The characteristics of a partnership.

e) How a partnership is formed.

f) The matters with which a partnership deed should deal.

g) The names which a partnership may use and the places in which the name must b
displayed.

h) The characteristics of a limited liability partnership.

8 Business organisations 2

In the previous chapter we examined the characteristics of business organisations and the way in which different types of business organisations are formed. We begin this chapter by considering the management and control of business organisations. We then consider the ways in which business organisations can be wound up. This chapter is concluded with a comparison of the relative advantages and disadvantages of trading as either a company or as a partnership.

Management and control of companies

In the previous chapter we saw that a company limited by shares must have shareholders, and that these shareholders are known as the company's members. We also saw that a company's articles of association lay down the internal rules of the company, and that the articles are contractually binding between every member of a company and every other member. A company's articles will provide that directors should manage the company and will set out the rules relating to the appointment and removal of directors.

Appointment and removal of directors

The first directors of a company agree to become directors when the company is incorporated. In the previous chapter we saw that they give their consent by signing Form 10, which is sent to the Registrar of Companies. Unless the articles provide otherwise, directors are subsequently appointed by the company members passing an ordinary resolution at a company meeting. Articles often provide that directors may be appointed in other ways. For example, the articles of many large companies allow the board of directors to appoint directors to fill casual vacancies which have arisen.

Public companies must have two directors but private companies need only have one. Usually the directors of a company also own shares in the company. (In small companies they often own a majority of the shares.) However, there is no requirement that a director should also be a member of the company.

No matter what the articles might say, section 303 of the Companies Act 1985 provides that a director can always be removed by an ordinary resolution of which the members have been given special notice. (This means that the company has been given 28 days notice of the resolution and the members must be given 21 days notice.) When a director is removed in this way, the director has a right to speak at the meeting at which his or her removal is proposed. For this reason the written resolution procedure cannot be used to remove a director by means of section 303.

On a resolution to remove a director the shares of the director who's removal is proposed might have enhanced voting power.

Bushell v Faith [1970]

The 300 shares in a company were owned equally by a brother and two sisters. All three shareholders were also directors. The articles provided that on any resolution to remove a director that director's shares should carry three votes per share. The two sisters wanted to remove their brother as a director. At a general meeting the sisters voted for removal, the brother voted against. The sisters claimed that the resolution had been passed by 200 votes to 100. The brother claimed that it had been defeated by 200 votes to 300.

Held *The article giving the enhanced voting rights was perfectly valid. Therefore the resolution to remove the brother from the board of directors had been defeated by 200 votes to 300.*

The powers of directors

The powers of the directors will be contained in the articles of association. Article 70 of Table A is fairly typical, and provides that:

> 'Subject to the provisions of the Acts, the memorandum and the articles and to any directions given by special resolution, the business of the company shall be managed by the directors who may exercise all the powers of the company......'

The directors then are usually given very wide powers to manage the company. They might exercise these powers to employ people to work for the company and might delegate some powers of management to these employees. As long as they stay within these powers, the directors need not obey resolutions passed by the members.

ASCFS Co Ltd v Cuninghame [1906]

One of the company's articles gave the directors the power to sell the company property on whatever terms they thought fit. At a general meeting of the company an ordinary resolution was passed, ordering the directors to sell company property to a new company. The directors did not approve of the terms of the contract and refused to sell.

Held *The directors were within their rights. Whether or not to sell was a question for them and not for the shareholders.*

However, it must be remembered that a majority of the shareholders have very considerable powers. Subject to a *Bushell v Faith* clause in the articles, they can always vote to directors out of office. Furthermore, if three-quarters of the shareholders decide to do so, they can pass a special resolution to change the articles. Such a change could either alter the powers of the directors or remove any *Bushell v Faith* clause. But these changes would only apply in the future. The articles can not be changed retrospectively.

Directors as agents

The directors are the agents of the company, and a company can only act through its directors. Sometimes those who manage a company call themselves something other than directors. Section 741(1) of the 1985 Act provides that anyone who occupies the position of a director is to be regarded as a director, whatever name they give to their position.

A director acting within the authority laid down in the articles of association will incur no personal liability. When the directors act collectively they act as the board of directors. Directors must attend board meetings (which are quite different from general meetings of the company members). Generally, most company's articles provide that any director may call a board meeting. The articles of some companies allow a managing director to be appointed. Such a managing director is usually given the power to exercise the powers of the board of directors without calling a board meeting.

Section 35 of the 1985 Act says that if a contract is made between the board of directors and a person acting in good faith, then the contract will always be binding on the company. This is so even if the board exceeded the powers which the company articles or memorandum conferred, or even if they had used these powers improperly. The company will similarly be bound if the board of directors authorised someone else to make a contract on the company's behalf.

TCB Ltd v Gray [1987]

A company borrowed money from TCB Ltd and issued a debenture as security for the loan. The debenture was approved by the company's board of directors, and following the board's instructions it was signed by a solicitor who was not a director. The company's articles stated that debentures would only be valid if they had been signed by a director. The company therefore argued that the debenture was invalid.

Held *The debenture was valid. The board had failed to follow the correct procedures, but section 35 gave protection to TCB Ltd because they had dealt with the company in good faith.*

Holding Out

If a company gives the impression that a person has the authority to make a transaction on the company's behalf then the company will be bound by such a transaction, whether or not the person who made it really did have such authority. This is known as holding out. The company is said to have held out that the person had authority.

Freeman & Lockyer v Buckhurst Park Properties Ltd [1964]

A company was formed to buy and resell an estate. The directors had the power to appoint a managing director but they never did so. One of the directors, Mr Kapoor, acted as if he had been appointed managing director. The other directors knew this but did nothing about it. Kapoor asked architects to do work on behalf of the company. When the architects sued the company for their fees the company argued that Kapoor had no authority to employ architects and therefore the contract was not binding on the company.

Held *A managing director would usually have authority to employ architects. The company had given the impression that Kapoor was managing director. Therefore, as regards people dealing with the company in good faith, Kapoor had the authority to bind the company as if he really was managing director. The company had held him out to have such powers to bind the company, so he did have such powers.*

Remuneration

Directors are not automatically entitled to any salary. But if, as is usual, they have contract which gives them a salary then they will be able to sue for compensation if the contract is breached. The directors can be paid even if the company does not make any profit.

Director's duties

Directors have duties towards the company and towards the members of the company as a whole. These duties can be either fiduciary duties or ordinary duties.

A director stands in a fiduciary position to the company, and is therefore in a position of great trust.

There are two separate aspects of the fiduciary duty owed by directors:

1) The directors must exercise their powers for the benefit of the company as a whole

2) There must be no conflict between the directors' interests and the interests of the company.

Regal (Hastings) Ltd v Gulliver [1942]

Regal Ltd owned a cinema. It wanted to acquire two more cinemas so that it could sell all three as a going concern. A subsidiary company was formed to make the purchase. The sellers of the cinemas would not go ahead with the deal unless the subsidiary company had at least £5,000 paid up share capital. Regal could only provide £2,000 the money which the subsidiary needed. The directors of Regal therefore personally subscribed for a further 3,000 £1 shares in the subsidiary. At the conclusion of the whole business the shares in the subsidiary were sold for £3.80 each. Both Regal and its direc-tors had therefore made a handsome profit.

Held *The directors had to account to Regal for the profit they had made. It was only because they were directors of Regal that they gained the opportunity to make the profit.*

The main non-fiduciary duty of directors is to show an appropriate amount of care and skill to the company. The standard expected is that of a reasonable man looking after his own affairs. Generally this standard is not very high. However, if a director is employed in a professional capacity then a higher standard will be expected. Directors should also have regard to the interests of the company's employees.

Effects of breach of duty

A director will not be liable to the company for the act of other co-directors if he or she did not know of the act and should not have suspected it. This is because directors do not employ each other and are not each other's agents.

If directors are liable together they are jointly and severally liable. This means that a director who is sued and ordered to pay damages will be entitled to a contribution from the other directors.

Even if the directors do exceed their powers, or do use them irregularly, the shareholders may still ratify their acts at a general meeting.

Bamford v Bamford [1970]

The company was in danger of being taken over. To avoid this the directors issued an extra 500,000 shares to a business which distributed the company's products. This might have been contrary to the company's articles. (This point was never decided.) The share-holders approved the issue of the shares by passing an ordinary resolution at a general meeting.

Held *Even if the directors had irregularly exercised their powers, the ratification by the shareholders made the contract a good one, and absolved the directors from all liability.*

Harman LJ:

> 'Directors can, by making a full and frank disclosure and calling together the general body of the shareholders, obtain......forgiveness of their sins; and...everything will go on as if it had been done right from the beginning. I cannot believe that this is not a commonplace of company law. It is done every day. Of course, if the majority of the general meeting will not forgive and approve, the directors must pay for it.'

Section 727 of the 1985 Act allows the court to grant relief to a director in breach of his duty if the director 'acted honestly and reasonably and ought fairly to be excused.'

Business Law

Student Activity Questions 8.1

1) Assuming that a company's articles give no power to do so, how can directors be prematurely removed from office?

2) Are directors automatically entitled to a salary?

3) How can a person be 'held out' to be a director. What consequences could follow from this?

4) What are the two aspects of the fiduciary duty which directors owe to the company?

5) In what two ways can directors who have breached their duties be excused from liability?

Further Activity Questions 8.1

Old Joe Bloggs owns all the shares in a company. He wants to leave his shares equally to his three children. Joe wants all of his children to be directors and he wants to ensure that they all remain directors for as long as they want.

a) Will it be possible for Joe to ensure that his three children all have the right to remain as directors?

b) If Joe had five children, could he still ensure that any group of four could not remove any one director against his or her will?

Control of the company

The directors have the power to manage the company while they hold office. However the long term control of the company lies in the hands of the company members. The members exercise this power by passing resolutions at company meetings. As we have seen, a company's directors can always be removed by an ordinary resolution of which special notice has been given.

Types of shares

A company's articles may allow for the creation of different types of shares, with each class enjoying different rights. If there is only one class of share then each share will carry the same right to vote. However, different classes of shares might carry different voting

222

rights. For example, in *Holt v Holt [1990]* a company had 999 class B shares, which carried one vote per share, and one class A share, which carried 10,000 votes.

Generally, ordinary shares will carry the right to vote at company meetings, the right to a dividend if one is declared and the right to share in the company's surplus assets if the company is wound up. Members with these ordinary shares are known as ordinary members. The dividend paid to any ordinary member is paid as a certain amount per share held.

The most common type of shares which are not ordinary shares are preference shares. The term preference share is not strictly defined and any rights might possibly attach to preference shares. (The articles of association will spell out the rights attaching.) However, in general preference shares have the following characteristics. The dividend paid to preference shareholders is usually expressed as a certain rate per annum. For example, the articles might state that the preference shares are to receive interest at 8% per annum. A shareholder with 1,000 £1 preference shares would therefore receive a yearly dividend of £80, if a dividend is declared. Preference shareholders, like ordinary shareholders, have no right to a dividend. However, if a dividend is not paid to preference shareholders in any particular year then all dividends not paid must be paid before ordinary shareholders can receive any dividend. Unless it is agreed otherwise, preference shares will carry the same right to vote as ordinary shares. However, it is often agreed in the articles that preference shares carry no right to vote. When a company is wound up the preference shares are usually repaid in full before the ordinary shares are repaid. This is an advantage where the company is insolvent, as preference shareholders are more likely to get their capital returned. However, it is a disadvantage where a company is wound up with large surplus assets. As the preference shares are repaid at face value, the preference shareholders will have no right to share in these assets.

Example

X Co Ltd has two classes of shares: 1,000 £1 preference shares and 1,000 £1 ordinary shares. X Co Ltd is wound up. After all costs of winding up and outside creditors have been repaid, the realised assets amount to £800. Each preference share will be repaid at 80p in the pound. The ordinary shareholders will not be repaid any of their capital. If the surplus assets had amounted to £101,000, the preference shareholders would have had their capital repaid and would therefore have received £1 per share. The ordinary shareholders would have shared in the surplus assets, each ordinary shareholder receiving £1,000 per share.

Some companies issue non voting shares. These shares carry no right to vote at company meetings, but do allow the shareholders to receive a dividend if one is declared and to share in surplus assets when the company is wound up.

Company meetings

There are two types of company meetings; annual general meetings and extraordinary general meetings.

Annual general meeting (AGM)

A company which has not elected to do away with the need to hold AGMs must hold an AGM once every calendar year and within fifteen months of the last one. For example, if X Co Ltd held its 2000 AGM on June 1st, it would have to hold its 2001 AGM before September 1st.

Since the 1985 Companies Act a private company can elect to dispense with the requirement to hold an AGM. Such an election must be made by all the members of the company. Even after such an election has been made, any member of the company has the right to insist that an AGM is held.

The AGM gives the company members the chance to question the way in which the company is being run. The directors would set the agenda for the AGM and typically this would include laying the accounts before the members, the appointment of the auditors and the presentation of the directors' report. The directors' report is important because it reports upon the general position of the company and because it sets out what dividend, if any, the directors are recommending. Shareholders invest money in a commercial company because they expect a dividend to be paid. This dividend can only be paid out of company profits. It can also be paid only if the directors recommend that it should be paid. (The directors might instead recommend that profits be retained in the company.) Generally, the articles of most companies provide that the members would have no power to increase the dividend which the directors recommend. (They can approve the dividend recommended or reduce it.) If the members are unhappy with the dividend recommended they might consider removing the directors at a future meeting.

Section 376 of the Companies Act 1985 provides that if 5% of the members with voting rights give the company six weeks written notice of a resolution which they propose to move at the AGM, then the company must put the resolution on the agenda of the AGM and give notice of the resolution to all members. The members proposing the resolution must pay the costs of this.

Extraordinary general meeting (EGM)

All meetings of the members other than the AGM are extraordinary general meetings. Most articles provide that the directors have the right to call an EGM. (For example article 37 of Table A provides this.)

Section 368 of the 1985 Act provides that, no matter what the articles say, 10% of voting members with fully paid up shares can compel the directors to call an EGM. They do this by depositing a signed requisition, which states the object of the meeting, at the company's registered office. The directors then have 21 days in which to call a meeting. If they do not do this then the members who presented the requisition can call the meeting themselves.

EXTRA-ORDINARY GENERAL MEETINGS—
NOT LIKELY TO BE THIS INTERESTING

Conduct of meetings

A meeting must have a quorum (set minimum number) of members. In all but single member companies the quorum will be set at two members, unless the articles provide otherwise. This means that if only one member turns up to the meeting it will be inquorate and therefore invalid. Proxies do not count towards a quorum, only members are counted.

A meeting only needs to be quorate at its commencement. Once the meeting has begun the number present may fall below the quorum.

There must be a chairman to preside over the meeting. The chairman's job is to ensure that the meeting follows the procedure set out in the agenda.

Voting

Usually a vote is taken by a show of hands. Each member has one vote, regardless of how many shares he or she holds. However, any member has the right to demand a poll. If this is done each voting share will carry the voting rights conferred on it by the articles. Generally, matters which are not contentious are voted on by a show of hands. When a matter is contentious some members are likely to insist on a poll. A member can insist on a poll either before the vote on a show of hands or when the outcome of the vote on a show of hands is declared.

Example

Ace Ltd has one class of shares, each share carrying one vote. X holds 55 of these shares, Y holds 30 and Z holds 15. An ordinary resolution is proposed at the AGM of Ace Ltd. On a show of hands X votes in favour of the resolution. Y and Z vote against it. X was outvoted on the show of hands, but can demand a poll where all of the shares will carry one vote each. X then outvotes Y and Z by 55 votes to 45 and so the resolution is passed.

Proxies

A member who does not attend the meeting can ask a proxy to attend and vote instead. The proxy does not need to be a company member. A general proxy is given a discretionary power to vote. A special proxy must vote as instructed.

Notice of meetings

All members must be given 21 days written notice of an AGM. (This period can be reduced if all the members entitled to attend and vote agree to the reduction.)

Only 14 days notice of an EGM is required, but the period remains 21 days if a special resolution is to be proposed.

The written notice must explain the nature of any business which is not ordinary business, as well as the date, the place and the time of the meeting. If a special, elective or extraordinary resolution is proposed the text of the resolution must be specified in full. Minutes of company meetings must be kept and must be available for inspection by members. A fictitious notice of a company's AGM is reproduced on the opposite page.

Resolutions

As we have seen, it is the directors who manage a company. But to appoint directors, or remove them, or to do other acts which can only be done by the members themselves, a resolution must be passed at a company meeting.

The following table shows the different types of resolutions and the kinds of business for which they are required.

	Ordinary	**Extraordinary**	**Special**
Proposed by	Board of directors or 5% of members under S.376	Board of directors or 5% of members under S.376	Board of directors or 5% of members under S.376
Majority needed	Over 50% of members present and voting	75% of members present and voting	75% of members present and voting
Proxies allowed?	Yes	Yes	Yes
Notice of meeting	21 days at AGM 14 days at EGM	21 days at AGM 14 days at EGM	21 days at AGM or EGM
Formalities	Minutes kept No need to register	Minutes kept. Must be registered with Registrar within 14 days	Minutes kept. Must be registered with Registrar within 14 days
Type of business	To remove directors To resolve not to sue directors for breach of duty	To initiate a creditor's voluntary winding up when the company is insolvent	To initiate a member's voluntary winding up To change the company's articles or memorandum

Table 8.2 Company resolutions

NOTICE OF GENERAL MEETING OF ACME LTD

Notice is hereby given that the Annual General Meeting of the company will be held at 2.00 p.m. on 16th July 2001 at 1 Acme Street, Anytown, Anywhere.

ORDINARY BUSINESS

1) To receive and consider the balance sheet as at 31st December 2000, with the profit and loss account for the year ended on that date, together with the reports of the directors and auditors thereon.

2) To declare a dividend of £2.50 per ordinary share for the year ended 31st December 2000.

3) To re-elect Anne Cherie Mee as a director of the company.

4) To re-elect the company's auditors until the 2002 Annual General Meeting and to fix their remuneration.

5) To transact any other ordinary business of the company.

SPECIAL BUSINESS

To consider and, if thought fit, pass the following resolution, which will be proposed as a special resolution:

6) That the memorandum of association should be changed so that the existing objects clause is removed and is replaced with the following objects clause: "The company's objects are to carry on business as a general commercial company."

ON BEHALF OF THE BOARD

Arthur Charles Mee

ARTHUR CHARLES MEE (Secretary)

1 Acme Street

Anytown

Anywhere

18th May 2001

Table 8.1 Notice of a general meeting

Written resolution procedure

The written resolution procedure may be used only by private companies. Any type of resolution (ordinary, special or extraordinary) can be passed by written resolution if all the members of the company sign the resolution. The resolution is regarded as passed from the moment when the last member signed.

Elective resolutions

Elective resolutions may be passed if all the members of a private company vote in favour. By elective resolution the members may agree to do the following things: not to hold an AGM each year; leave the current auditors in place indefinitely; and dispense with the laying of accounts before a general meeting of the company members. (The members would still be entitled to receive full accounts.) An elective resolution can be revoked by an ordinary resolution of the members. Even if an elective resolution has been passed to dispense with the holding of an AGM or the laying of accounts before the company members, any member can insist that these things are done. Often elective resolutions are passed by the written resolution procedure.

The company secretary

Every company must have a company secretary. The secretary may also be a director, bu may not be the only director. The company secretary of a plc must be suitably qualifiec (generally, as a lawyer or an accountant). The company secretary of a private company does not need to hold any qualifications.

The secretary's duties are to look after the administration of the company. This woulc include matters such as keeping the company register up to date, sending information tc the Registrar of Companies, arranging meetings, sending notice of meetings and resolu tions to members and keeping up to date with legislation which affects the company.

The company secretary has a limited power to make contracts which bind the company but only as regards the type of administrative contracts which a company secretary coulc be expected to make.

Student Activity Questions 8.2

1   What percentage of a company's voting shares must a person hold:

   a)   To be able to pass an ordinary resolution without the votes of other share-holders?

   b)   To be able to pass a special resolution without the help of other share-holders?

   c)   To make sure that any special resolution can be defeated?

2)   What is the function of a company secretary?

Further Activity Questions 8.2

1) Green Ltd has five shareholders (V, W, X,Y and Z) all of whom own 20% of the shares. V, W and Z are the only three directors. X wants to see the articles altered so that the directors must buy the shares of any member wishing to sell them at a fair price. Y is very much opposed to this. V, W and Z are open to persuasion on the matter.

    a) What type of resolution will be needed to change the articles?

    b) What support will X need in order to achieve the change?

    c) Assuming that the resolution is proposed, how much notice of the resolution must be given, and how the voting will take place?

    d) Can X insist that an EGM is called to propose the resolution?

    e) Can X insist that a resolution proposing the change is put forward at the next AGM?

2) What percentage of votes is required to pass a resolution to remove a director under s.303 of the Companies Act 1985?

    a) Over 50% of all the members of the company.

    b) Over 50% of those members who vote.

    c) 75% of all the members of the company

    d) 75% of those members present and voting.

Protection of minority shareholders

The voting shareholders control the company. A shareholder with more than 50% of the voting shares can pass any ordinary resolution. A shareholder with 75% of the shares can pass any extraordinary or special resolution. Similarly, shareholders who between them can muster over 50% or 75% can exercise the different types of control.

These percentages can be vitally important when a person is considering investing in a company. Let us look at an example. If Bill invites Alan to form a company with him, and suggests that Alan take 49% of the shares while Bill takes 51%, then their ownership of the company is almost equal. However, their control of the company is very far from equal, and Alan should be very wary about accepting such a proposition. However, Alan would at least have some degree of 'negative control,' in the sense that he could block a special resolution. If Alan was offered only 25% of the shares he would in effect have no control at all.

If two shareholders each have 50% of the shares then they will both have negative control. Neither will be able to force through any resolution without the consent of the other. This might sound an ideal way to run a company owned by two people, and while the shareholders get on with each other it probably is. But if complete deadlock is reached then the court may well wind the company up (if either party so requests) on the grounds that this is just and equitable.

The position of the minority shareholder is not improved by the rule in *Foss v Harbottle* which states that if a wrong is done to a company then only the company has the right to take action.

The case itself illustrates the problems which this can cause for minority shareholders.

Foss v Harbottle [1843]

Two members of a company sued five directors who had sold land to the company for more than it was worth.

Held *The shareholders had no right to sue. If the directors had wronged the company then only the company could sue in respect of that wrong. (The company was most unlikely to do this because it was controlled by the very directors who had cheated it!)*

The rule in *Foss v Harbottle* is a logical extension of *Salomon v Salomon and Co Ltd*. That case decided that a company is a separate legal person. It follows that if a company is wronged it alone has the power to sue.

The rule has the advantage of preventing multiple actions; if every shareholder in every company was able to sue for any perceived wrong to the company then there would be an enormous number of potential court cases. However, the rule could obviously be very unfair to minority shareholders, and now both the courts and statute offer protection to the minority.

The courts will protect a minority shareholder where the majority commit a fraud on the minority, or where the personal rights of a member have been infringed. In addition section 122 of the Insolvency Act 1986 allows any shareholder to petition the court to wind the company up on the grounds that it is just and equitable to do so. Section 459-61 of the Companies Act 1985 allows any member to petition the court on the ground that the affairs of the company are being, or have been, or will be, conducted in a manner which is unfairly prejudicial to the members generally or to particular members.

If the court agrees that the conduct is unfairly prejudicial it can:

a) order the company to behave in a certain way in the future;

b) prevent the company from doing certain acts;

c) order the company to sue for a wrong done to it;

d) order the majority or the company to buy the shares of the minority; or

e) make any order which it sees fit.

Student Activity Questions 8.3

1) If directors abuse or exceed their powers, can the shareholders absolve the directors from liability?

2) What is the rule in *Foss v Harbottle*?

3) Why do minority shareholders need protection from the courts and from statute?

Further Activity Questions 8.3

Bilco has two shareholders. Bill owns 750 shares and Connie, his wife, owns 250. Bill and Connie are not getting on too well and there is talk of a separation. Connie's brother Jim, who feels that pressures of company business are contributing to Bill's problems, has offered to buy 500 of Bill's shares. The company could be sold as a going concern for £50,000 and Jim has offered to pay £25,000. He is only prepared to buy the shares if he is made a director. Is Jim's offer reasonable in financial terms?

Management of partnerships

In Chapter 7 we considered a model partnership deed and the types of matters which would usually be found in such a deed. We also saw that partnership is a contractual relationship, created by a contract between the partners.

Usually a partnership agreement will state that most disputes between partners can be resolved by a simple vote. If this is the case then each partner will have one vote and the majority will get their way. (Of course many partnership agreements do not say this; they might state that one partner's vote is to count more than another's, or that certain partners are to have a veto.)

A partnership deed can be altered by the express or implied consent of all of the partners. (In contract terms, the contract which the partners have created can be discharged by agreement and a new agreement then be substituted.) Unanimous agreement is needed to admit a new partner. However, the partners might give this consent in advance when signing the partnership deed. It is not unusual for a partnership deed to state that a relative of one of the partners may later be introduced as a partner.

Implied rules of partnerships

In the previous chapter we saw that partners do not need to make any formal agreement. Indeed, those trading as partners may not agree at all about important matters. Section 24 of the Partnership Act 1890 therefore lays down a number of rules about the management of a partnership. These rules will apply if no agreement has been made, or if the agreement made does not cover the situation in question. The rules contained in section 24 are as follows.

Capital and profits

Section 24(1) states that all partners are entitled to share equally in the firm's capital and profits and all must contribute equally to losses of capital.

So if A and B go into partnership together and do not agree anything about profits and losses then they will share these equally, even if they are doing different amounts of work for the firm. (In most partnerships profits and losses will not be shared equally - there will be an agreement to the contrary.)

Indemnity

Section 24(2) states that if a partner incurs any expense in the ordinary and proper conduct of the firm's business, the firm must indemnify that partner in respect of the liability incurred.

For example, if partner A in firm ABC suddenly has to travel abroad on the firm's business then the firm must pay the expenses which A incurs.

Interest on capital and advances

Section 24(4) tells us that a partner is not entitled to any interest on capital contributed to the partnership.

But if a partner advances any money beyond the amount of capital he or she agreed to contribute this is treated as a loan to the partnership. Section 24(3) provides that interest on such loans should be paid at a rate of 5% per annum. (It is of course quite likely that partnership agreements will make other rules, particularly about the rate of interest.)

Management

Section 24(5) provides that every partner may take part in the management of the firm. The partnership deed might however state that partners do not have an equal right to manage.

If the deed went further and excluded one partner from management altogether that partner could apply to have the firm wound up on the just and equitable ground. Such an exclusion of the right to manage would run contrary to the very definition of a partner as a person who 'carries on a business in common.....' We have seen that partners will be liable for the firm's debts. It would not be fair to make them liable if they did not have a right to manage the firm.

Remuneration

Section 24(6) says that no partner is entitled to any salary for taking part in the business of the partnership.

(Again, it is very common for partnership agreements to provide that partners should be paid salaries. If salaries are paid this is really just a way of distributing the profits. Salary paid to one partner will obviously reduce the amount of profit available to be shared by the partners.)

Disputes about ordinary matters

Section 24(8) makes two provisions. First, it states that the nature of the partnership business may not be changed without the consent of all of the partners. Second, it states that differences about ordinary matters connected with the partnership business can be resolved by a simple majority.

So a majority of the partners in a firm of car dealers could take the decision to move to new premises. The decision to move into a new type of business, such as selling videos, would have to be unanimous.

Partnership books

Section 24(9) says that the partnership books are to be kept at the firm's place of business, and that every partner may have access to them, when he or she thinks fit, and inspect and copy any of them. A partner may also appoint an agent to inspect the books on his or her behalf.

Expulsion of partners

Section 25 provides that: 'No majority of the partners can expel any partner unless a power to do so has been conferred by express agreement between the partners.'

This express agreement may well be contained in the partnership agreement. It is fairly common for an article in a partnership deed to lay down that a partner can be expelled for breaking the partnership rules. Even if this is the case, the expelling partners must exercise the article in good faith. They cannot use the article to unjustifiably expel a partner.

The duty of good faith

Partners owe each other a duty of the utmost good faith. Sections 28-30 spell out three important consequences of this; that partners must render true accounts and information, that they must account for profits, and that they must not compete with the firm.

Rendering true accounts and information

Section 28:

> 'Partners are bound to render true accounts and full information of all things affecting the partnership to any partner or his legal representatives.'

Law v Law [1905]

Two brothers, W and J, were partners in a manufacturing business in Halifax. J ran the firm while W lived in London and took little part in the firm's affairs. J bought W out for £21,000, but later W discovered that the business was worth far more than J had led him to believe.

Held The court set aside W's agreement to sell his share of the partnership. J had not put W in possession of all material facts relating to the partnership's assets.

Accounting for profits

Section 29:

> 'Every partner must account to the firm for any benefit derived by him without the consent of the other partners from any transaction concerning the partnership, or from any use by him of the partnership property name or business connection.'

If a partner makes any personal profit as a consequence of his being a partner he must hand this profit over to the firm.

Bentley v Craven [1853]

Bentley and Craven were in partnership together in a firm which bought and sold sugar. Craven was the firm's buyer and on account of his business skill was occasionally able to buy sugar at a greatly reduced price. On one occasion he was offered a consignment of sugar at well below the wholesale price. He bought this sugar himself and then sold it to the firm at the going wholesale rate.

Held Craven had to account to the firm for this secret profit. That is to say he had to pay the profit he had made to the firm. He had used a partnership asset (his position in the firm) to make the profit.

Competing with the firm

Section 30:

> 'If a partner, without the consent of the other partners, carries on any business of the same nature as and competing with that of the firm, he must account for and pay over to the firm all profits made by him in that business.'

This section is similar to section 29. The difference is that under section 30 the partner is liable merely as a result of competing with the firm. He or she does not need to use partnership property or assets. Under section 29 a partner is liable for misusing partnership property or assets. He or she does not need to be competing with the firm.

Note that it is permissible for partners to compete with the firm or use the firm's assets to make a profit as long as the other partners consent to this. In *Bentley v Craven*, Craven also carried on a business as a sugar buyer in his own right. This did not break his duty not to compete with the firm because the other partners knew about it and agreed that he should be able to do this.

Student Activity Questions 8.4

1) In a firm of 6 partners, 5 partners want the partnership agreement to be changed and 1 partner does not. Can the 5 insist that the agreement is changed?

2) How will the profits of a partnership be shared if there is no express agreement about the matter?

3) If a partner incurs expenses while at work on partnership business, will the firm have to reimburse him?

4) Are partners automatically entitled to a salary?

5) A partner competes with the firm without telling fellow partners. What will happen to profits made by the competing partner?

Winding up of business organisations

Winding up of companies

The legal personality of a company is ended by a process known as liquidation or winding up. (The terms mean the same thing.) After the company is wound up it will cease to exist. A liquidation may be either ordered by the court or it may be brought about by the members of the company. A liquidation ordered by the court is called a compulsory liquidation. A liquidation brought about by the members is known as a voluntary liquidation.

A court will order the compulsory liquidation of a company if the company cannot pay its debts. A company will be regarded as unable to pay its debts if it does not satisfy a court judgement in favour of a creditor. For example, if X Ltd is sued by Alec and Alec is awarded damages of £2,000, the company will be regarded as unable to pay its debts if it does not pay the £2,000 damages to Alec. A company is also regarded as unable to pay its debts if a creditor who is owed more than £750 serves a written demand for payment at the company's registered office and is not paid within three weeks. For example, if X Ltd owed Billy £800 and Billy served a written demand for payment at X Ltd's registered office, X Ltd would be regarded as unable to pay its debts if it did not pay Billy within three weeks.

Even if a court is satisfied that a company cannot pay its debts it does not have to wind the company up. If the majority of the company's creditors think that the best thing would be to let the company keep trading then the court can allow this. Such a situation might arise where the company was about to complete a large profitable order for the Government, and the profit made from this order would mean that the company's inability to pay its debts was only likely to be temporary. Once a court makes a winding up order the liquidator takes over the directors' powers. The employees of the company are regarded as dismissed unless the liquidator decides to re-employ them until the winding up is finished.

A voluntary liquidation takes place without a court order. A members' voluntary liquidation can be made while the company is solvent. The members of the company might decide that they would like to end the company and share out any assets which remain after all creditors have been paid. In order to start a member's voluntary liquidation the members must pass a special resolution that the company be wound up. A liquidator will be needed to wind the company up, but the company members choose who the liquidator should be. A member's voluntary liquidation is only possible if the directors of the company can make a declaration of solvency. This declaration states that the company will be able to pay all of its debts within a period which may not be longer than 12 months.

If no declaration of solvency can be made, the company members might start a creditors voluntary winding up. In order to do this the members would need to pass an extraordinary resolution. A meeting of all creditors would then be called and the creditors would have the choice of who the liquidator should be.

When either type of voluntary winding up is made the company must cease trading as soon as the special or extraordinary resolution is passed. The liquidator would take over the directors' powers. Employees would be dismissed unless the liquidator decided to re-employ them.

As regards any type of winding up, the order in which the company's creditors are paid is the same. First, those with a mortgage over the company's property can sell that property and take what they are owed. Any remaining money goes into the pool of assets. Then the liquidator sells all the company assets for as much as possible and gathers in any money owing to the company. The assets gained in this way are distributed in the following order.

1) The costs of the winding up are paid.

2) Preferential creditors are paid. There are several types of preferential creditors. The two most important categories are the Revenue, who can claim back taxes for defined periods, and company employees who can claim their holiday pay and up to £800 worth of unpaid wages. As regards taxes or wages which are not regarded as preferential debts, employees and the Revenue must claim as unsecured creditors. For

example, an employee owed wages of £1,000 could claim £800 as a preferential creditor and £200 as an unsecured creditor.

3) Creditors who have taken a floating charge over the company assets. (A floating charge will be created if a creditor takes the company's assets as security for a loan, while leaving the company free to deal with the assets. Any charge must be registered with the Registrar of Companies. If it is not, the charge is invalid and the creditor is merely another unsecured creditor.) The assets over which the charge was taken will be sold. The chargeholders will be paid what they are owed, if enough money is generated. If the assets are sold for more than the amount of the charge, any surplus goes into the general pool of assets.

4) Unsecured creditors are paid next. Unsecured creditors are people to whom the company owes money, who are not preferential creditors and who have not taken a charge over the company's assets.

5) Company members are paid any amount which they are owed (such as dividends which have been declared but not paid).

6) Anything left over is divided amongst the company members according to their rights in the articles of association.

If there are not enough assets to pay each class of creditors then each member of the relevant class is paid the same percentage of the money owing to them.

Example

> X Ltd is wound up. The costs of Liquidation are £10,000. 10 employees are each owed £200 wages (total £2,000). The government is owed £3,000 VAT. Jim is owed £5,000 which he lent to the company. This loan is secured by a floating charge over all of the company's assets. Two suppliers of materials are owed £5,000 and £10,000 respectively.
>
> 1) If the pool of assets came to £12,500: (a) the costs of liquidation would be paid in full; (b) the remaining £2,500 would be enough to pay the preferential creditors (the VAT and the wages) half of what they were owed. Each employee would therefore receive £100 and the Revenue would receive £1,500.
>
> 2) If the pool of assets had come to £29,000: (a) the costs of liquidation would be paid in full (£10,000); (b) the preferential creditors would be paid in full (£5,000); (c) Jim would be paid in full (5,000); (d) the £9,000 left over would be used to pay the unsecured creditors the same percentage of what they were owed. The creditor owed £5,000 would receive £3,000 and the creditor owed £10,000 would be paid £6,000.
>
> 3) If the company assets had amounted to £135,000 then all the creditors would be paid in full. The remaining £100,000 would be divided amongst the members according to their rights under the articles of association. (For example, if there were 100 shares in the company, each shareholder would be paid £1,000 for each share held.)

Winding up of partnerships

A partnership may be dissolved either by the partners themselves or by the court. A dissolution by the partners themselves might be allowed for by the partnership deed. For example, the deed might state that the firm is to run for a fixed period. If this is the case the partnership will be dissolved when that period expires or if all the partners agree to dissolve it before the fixed time has expired. If a partnership is not for a fixed time any partner may dissolve it by giving reasonable notice of an intention to leave the firm. The death or bankruptcy of a partner will also cause the firm to be dissolved. A partnership will be dissolved by the court in several circumstances, the most important of which is that the firm can only be carried on at a loss.

Sometimes a dissolution of a partnership is little more than a technicality and does not lead to a full scale winding up. For example, when a partner leaves a large firm of solicitors, the firm is technically dissolved and a set of accounts will need to be drawn up. However, the other partners will generally then carry the business on much as before. When a firm is wound up it is permanently finished. After a winding up the authority of the partners to bind the firm remains only in so far as this is necessary to effect the most beneficial winding up. The firm's assets will be gathered in, and the goodwill of the firm may well be a valuable asset.

If the firm is solvent when it is liquidated payments are made in the following order. First, all outsiders will be fully paid what they are owed. Second, loans made by partners will be repaid. Third, the partners will be repaid the capital which they contributed to the firm. If there is not enough capital to repay all of the partners, the partners must contribute to the lost capital in the same proportion as they were to share profits (unless they had agreed otherwise). Finally, any surplus will be paid to the partners in the ratio in which they were to share profits.

Example

Firm RST is wound up. The three partners, R, S and T were to share profits equally. R contributed £30,000 capital, S contributed £20,000 and T contributed £10,000. (Total £60,000.) The partners made no loans to the firm. If after all the creditors had been paid there was a loss of capital of £12,000, each partner would have to contribute to this equally. They would all therefore contribute £4,000. R would therefore receive £26,000 (£30,000 - £4,000); S would receive £16,000 (£20,000 - £4,000); T would receive £6,000 (£10,000 - £4,000.) If after all the creditors had been paid there was enough to repay all of the capital and £66,000 was left over, each partner would receive £22,000 and full repayment of their capital.

If the firm does not have enough assets to pay all the outside creditors in full then all of the partners will become personally liable to pay the firm's debts. The partners will become liable in the same proportion as they were to share profits, unless there was an agreement to the contrary. If some partners are insolvent and cannot pay their share, the other partners will take over liability to pay the insolvent partner's share. Insolvent partners may be made bankrupt.

Partnership property

When a firm is wound up the partnership property will be used to pay the debts and liabilities of the firm. Partnership property does not belong to individual partners, it belongs to all of the partners, who hold it on trust for each other. Property is partnership property if it was brought into the firm as partnership property, if it was bought with the firm's money as partnership property, or if it was acquired for the purposes of the firm and in the usual course of the firm's business. Partnership property must only be used for the purposes of the partnership.

Suing a partnership

It is possible to sue a partnership in the firm's name. (This is merely a rule of convenience and does not detract from the principle that a partnership has no legal personality of its own.) A writ can be served on any of the partners or it can be sent to the firm's principal place of business.

Sole traders

A sole trader has unlimited liability for the debts of the business. If there is not enough money to pay all outside creditors then the trader can be made bankrupt.

Student Activity Questions 8.5

1) In what circumstances will a court regard a company as unable to pay its debts?

2) What are the differences between a members' voluntary winding up and a creditors' voluntary winding up?

3) When a company is wound up, in what order are the company's assets distributed?

Further Activity Questions 8.5

1) Y Ltd has been wound up. The costs of liquidation were £15,000. Y Ltd owed Jane £10,000 and this loan was secured by a floating charge over all of the company's assets. 20 employees of Y Ltd were each owed £500 (total £10,000). The Revenue was owed £5,000. X, an unsecured creditor, was owed £5,000. Y, another unsecured creditor was owed £10,000. The two shareholders in Y Ltd each own half of the company's shares. How much money will the various parties receive if the company's assets amounted to:

   a) £24,000?

   b) £49,000?

   c) £255,000?

2) Firm XYZ has been wound up. The assets of the firm amounted to £100,000. Partner X contributed capital of £20,000, Y contributed £10,000 and Z contributed £5,000. The three partners were to share profits equally.

   a) How would the loss of capital be borne if, after all outside creditors had been fully paid the capital had been reduced from £35,000 to £18,000?

   b) What would be the position if outside creditors were owed £200,000?

Company or partnership? Choice of legal status

A person wishing to go into business with other people must trade either as a company or as a partnership. (As we have seen, it may soon also be possible to trade as a Limited Liability Partnership.) People going into business together must therefore choose what sort of business organisation they wish to form. Often they might have very clear views. They might be quite sure that they want to trade either as a company or a partnership. In many other cases, however, the choice may not be so clear cut.

When a business is being set up there are often many matters requiring urgent attention. Perhaps staff must be employed, money borrowed or premises leased. It is easy to regard the decision as to whether to form a company or a partnership as less pressing. However, the choice of business status is a very important one. Prospective business people should consider the advantages and disadvantages of both companies and partnerships in some detail.

imited liability

In Chapter 7 we examined *Salomon v Salomon and Co Ltd* and saw that shareholders in a limited company cannot be required to pay the debts of a limited company. Partners on the other hand are completely liable for the firm's debts to the full extent of their personal fortune. This is, perhaps, the principal advantage of a company over a partnership.

There is another side to limited liability though, and that is that creditors may be much less willing to extend credit to a small company that they would be to a partnership.

Suppliers dealing with a partnership need not have any worries about getting paid as long as they know that some or all of the partners are financially sound. But suppliers dealing with a small company should be very careful. If the company fails, as very many have over the past few years, then suppliers who are owed money are likely to be unsecured creditors and to find themselves at the back of the queue. When a company is insolvent then the unsecured creditors will not receive full payment of their debts and may well be paid nothing.

he right to manage

As we have seen in this chapter, all partners have a right to manage the partnership's affairs, and all partners are agents of the firm as regards contracts made in the ordinary course of the firm's business.

Shareholders, no matter how large their percentage holding, do not have a right to manage a company. This right is vested in the board of directors, the directors being elected by a simple majority vote of the shareholders at a general meeting. Therefore a shareholder with over fifty per cent of the shares has the power to change the directors. But it must be emphasised that until the shareholder exercises this right the directors in place have the right to manage the company's affairs.

A shareholder with less than fifty per cent of the votes can be outvoted on a resolution to appoint or change the directors. So minority shareholders are in the unfortunate position of having no right to manage the company's affairs, and no power to change this situation.

A person going into business with one other might therefore be very unwilling to form a company unless he or she was to own fifty per cent of the shares. Similar problems arise when there are several shareholders. If a group of majority shareholders have a closer relationship with each other than they have with the minority shareholder then a minority shareholding can again be a very precarious position.

gency

The Board of Directors are the agents of a company, and this means that they can make binding contracts on the company's behalf. The shareholders, no matter how large their shareholding, are not the company's agents and cannot make contracts on its behalf.

Every partner is an agent of the firm in respect of contracts made in the ordinary cour of the firm's business. It is therefore absolutely vital that partners trust each other impl itly. A dishonest partner can bankrupt fellow partners and there have been countless cas where this has happened. A dishonest partner can order goods in the firm's name ar take possession of the goods. If he or she then steals the goods the other partners a absolutely liable to the suppliers for the price of the goods.

It is possible to have some safeguards over matters such as signing cheques, but liabil to outsiders dealing with the partner in good faith cannot be excluded. Of course, it not a good idea to form a company with a rogue but at least limited liability restricts t amount which can be lost.

Nor is it only a dishonest partner who can bankrupt fellow partners. An incompete partner may be just as bad. If he or she makes disastrous contracts on the firm's beh the firm will be bound to honour them.

Withdrawal from the business

Partnerships may be entered into for a fixed period of time, in which case the partne cannot leave before that time has expired (unless all of the partners agree). If partnershi are not entered into for a fixed time they are partnerships at will. Any partner can lea a partnership at will by giving reasonable notice of an intention to do so. If a partner do withdraw, the firm will then be dissolved, and each partner will recover a share of a surplus assets. If a partnership is for a fixed term a partner wishing to withdraw must w until the end of that term. Even so, an end is in sight.

In the case of companies shareholders may or may not have a right to transfer their shar to whoever they wish. It all depends on the articles of association, and these might w say that the board of directors can refuse a transfer to persons of whom they disapprov It is even possible for the articles to say that the board of directors has an absolute ve over any transfer of shares. If this is the case then the shareholders will be locked into t company. No matter how much they dislike the way the company is run they cann short of there being a fraud on the minority, sell their shares.

Shareholders who are worried about this happening might do well to insist that they w not buy the shares unless the articles do allow them to be freely transferred. Whether not the controllers of the company would agree to such an article might well depend how badly they wanted the shareholder's investment.

Business property

Company property belongs to the company and not to the shareholders. An importa consequence of this can be that a company is able to give its assets as security on floating charge and yet remain free to deal with the assets as it sees fit. (We have alrea seen that a floating charge will be created if a creditor takes the company's assets as sec rity for a loan, while leaving the company free to deal with the assets.)

Partnership property cannot belong to the partnership because a partnership has no separate legal existence of its own. Despite its name, partnership property belongs to all the partners jointly. A partnership is not allowed to offer a floating charge over partnership property. The partners can of course offer a mortgage but, this would restrict the use of the property over which the charge is granted.

orrowing power

If sole traders want to borrow money from a commercial lender then they will need to provide security for the loan. There are several ways in which they might do this, but generally they will either need to find a guarantor (who agrees to repay the loan if the trader defaults) or they will need to mortgage their property. Because of the current high level of business failures banks are demanding very solid security for any money advanced.

Partners are in the same position as sole traders, except that since there are more of them they might well find it easier to find guarantors, or might have more property to mortgage. Creditors who are to be repaid out of partnership profits should make it very clear that they do not intend that this should make them partners.

Members of a company can raise money in the same way as partners or sole traders. But companies also have additional options.

First, companies can sell shares to people who wish to invest in the company but who have no desire to manage it. Shares in a private limited company cannot be offered to the general public but, subject to the articles of association, they can be offered to individuals.

An investor who is convinced that the company will be a commercial success might be more than willing to pay for shares. Some small companies achieve spectacular success and eventually change into PLCs with enormous assets. If an investor had contributed capital into a company such as Body Shop International plc when it was first formed as a private company for, say, ten per cent of the shares this would have been an outstandingly good bargain. The converse of course is that very many small companies go to the wall, in which case the shares become worthless.

Second, companies can raise capital by granting floating charges over their assets. This means that the company gives its assets as security for a loan while still maintaining the right to use those assets. As long as the sale of the assets would be guaranteed to raise more than the amount loaned then the creditor has cast-iron security. Many lenders though take a particularly jaundiced view of the value of a company's assets. They value them on the basis that everything which could possibly reduce their value will in fact do so. This can make it difficult for companies without substantial assets to raise much money by means of floating charges.

Partnerships are generally limited to 20 partners. But there is no restriction on the number of shareholders in a company. This can give a company an advantage in raising capital in that there may simply be more people willing to contribute to the business than is allowable in the case of a partnership.

Formation

A business which wants to trade immediately will have to do so as a partnership rather than as a company. A partnership can be created without any formalities. As soon as two people carry on a business in common with a view to profit they will be a partnership whether they realise this or not. It is however quite likely that partners will want to have a deed of partnership drawn up by a lawyer. If so then this too is bound to involve some expense and delay.

A company is formed by registration, as we saw in Chapter 7. This process generally takes about one week. However, if a fee of £100 is paid a company will be registered within one day. This means that any advantage partnerships once had in respect of speed of formation is very much diminished.

Formalities

Partners do not need to adhere to any formalities. There is no need for them to hold formal meetings. This used to represent a significant advantage over companies. However, companies have been considerably de-regulated in recent years. Private companies with a turnover of less than £1,000,000 do not have to have their accounts audited. Furthermore, if all the members of a private company elect to dispense with the requirement to hold an Annual General Meeting there are no meetings which a company is compelled to hold.

Publicity

The affairs of a partnership are completely private. Like anyone else, the partners will of course need to declare their earnings to the Revenue. Beyond this there is no need to reveal their accounts to anyone.

Until relatively recently all companies had to publish full accounts. This is no longer true of small companies which may now publish abbreviated accounts. (The members of the company are still entitled to full accounts.) These abbreviated accounts would deliver very little meaningful information to an outsider and so the advantage which partnership used to enjoy in respect of keeping their financial affairs private has been considerably diminished.

Small companies are defined as having two out of three of the following qualifications

a) turnover of less than £2.8 million;

b) assets of less than £1.4 million;

c) fewer than fifty employees.

As can be seen these qualifications are fairly generous. A business which was too large to start trading as a small company would be unlikely to want to trade as a partnership

Tax

There can be tax advantages in trading as a company and taking dividends from the company, rather than taking a salary as a director or as a partner. It is beyond the scope of this book to consider these advantages in any detail. In recent years the Revenue have very often argued that persons who supply services through a company to one other person are in fact employees and should be taxed accordingly. The fact that the Revenue takes this line (and that the taxpayers vigorously oppose it) indicates that tax advantages can be enjoyed by trading as a company.

Perpetual succession

As we saw in Chapter 7, companies continue in existence until they are wound up. The death of a shareholder or even of all the shareholders will not end the company. This can be useful when a family company is passed down from one generation to the next.

In contrast, the death of a partner will end the partnership. However, the partnership deed might well provide that the surviving partners should carry on the business. (In which case they must pay an appropriate amount to the estate of the deceased partner.) If the surviving partners do carry the business on, then the dissolution of the partnership will only amount to a technical dissolution.

Numbers

We have seen that partnerships of twenty or more people are not usually allowed. (There are exceptions for several types of professional partnerships.) If twenty or more people want to go into business together they will generally need to do so as a company.

Limited liability partnerships

At the moment it is too early to say whether or not trading as a limited liability partnership will present any advantages over trading as a limited company. It seems unlikely that general trading businesses will register as LLPs. It is envisaged that the LLP option will prove most attractive to the very large firms of accountants. It seems that the following rules will apply to LLPs: members of LLPs will have limited liability for the LLP's debts; the LLP will be regarded as a separate legal entity; all members will have the right to manage the LLP and will be the agents of it; an LLP will be formed by registration with the Registrar of Companies and the members of an LLP will be taxed as partners.

Sole traders

By definition a sole trader is in business alone. However, a sole trader should consider the benefits of forming a company. In effect he or she can trade as a company and still be in business on his or her own. This is especially true now that it is possible to have private limited companies with only one shareholder and one director. (A different person would need to act as company secretary.)

We have considered whether groups of people forming a business should trade as companies or partnerships. Sole traders should consider the same advantages and disadvantages of incorporation.

Student Activity Questions 8.6

1) Jane buys 500 £1 shares in a company which she and her friends have formed. What is her maximum potential loss if the company should fail?

2) John goes into partnership with his friends and invests £500 in the business. What is his maximum potential loss?

3) Edward owns 40% of a business. The other 60% is owned by Edwina, his sister. Edward regards Edwina as very autocratic, wanting to make every decision herself. Which type of business organisation would give Edward more power to manage the affairs of the business?

4) Xavier, who is not a director, owns 75% of a company's shares. Can he buy a car on the company's behalf?

5) Helen is very much the junior partner in a market gardening partnership. She has contributed no capital and receives 10% of the profits. Her father has contributed all the capital and receives 90% of the profits. Can Helen buy a new tractor for the firm?

6) If your business was asked to supply goods on credit to another business, would your business be more willing to do this if the other business was a company or a partnership?

7) What methods of raising capital are open to a company but not to a partnership?

Essential points

Management and control of companies

- The directors of a company have all the power to manage the company.

- The members of a company have the power to elect the directors, but do not have the power to manage the company.

- A director of a company can always be removed by an ordinary resolution of the members, of which special notice has been given.

- Public companies must have at least two directors.

- Private companies need only one director, who may also be the only shareholder.

- Directors must exercise their powers for the benefit of the company as a whole and must not allow their own interests to conflict with the interests of the company.

- Directors must show an appropriate amount of care and skill.

- Directors in breach of their duties may be relieved from liability by an ordinary resolution of the company members.

- Directors in breach of their duties may be relieved from liability by the court, under the Companies Act 1985, if they acted honestly and reasonably and ought fairly to be excused.

- Every company must have a company secretary. The secretary may also be a director of the company but may not be the only director.

- The company secretary deals with the administration of the company and can make contracts which bind the company, as long as the contracts were concerned with the administration of the company.

- Companies may issue different classes of shares, with different rights attaching to the various classes.

- Ordinary shares usually carry the right to vote at company meetings, the right to receive a dividend if one is declared and the right to share in the surplus assets of the company if it is dissolved.

- The dividend on preference shares is usually expressed as a rate of interest per annum. If preference shareholders are not paid a dividend in one year they usually have a cumulative right to receive this dividend before the ordinary shareholders are paid any dividend.

- Preference shares might or might not have a right to vote at company meetings. On dissolution of the company preference shares are usually repaid at face value. Preference shareholders do not therefore usually have a right to share in the surplus assets of the company when the company is dissolved.

- Companies must hold an Annual General Meeting (AGM) of the members once every calendar year. (Private companies can dispense with this requirement if all the company members elect to do so.)

- Any meeting of the company members other than an AGM is an Extraordinary General Meeting (an EGM).

- At company meetings, ordinary resolutions are passed by a simple majority of members who vote, special and extraordinary resolutions are passed by a 75% majority of those who vote, elective resolutions must be passed by all the company members. (Company members who do not vote in person may vote by proxy.)

- Elective resolutions can be passed only by private companies. They allow the company to dispense with the requirements to: hold AGMs; elect auditors annually; and lay the company's accounts before the members at a company meeting.

- A private company may pass any type of resolution by the written resolution procedure, without the need to hold a company meeting.

- A written resolution must be signed by all the company members and is passed when the last member signs it.

Management of partnerships

- A partnership agreement can be altered by the express or implied consent of all of the partners.

- Subject to the partners agreeing otherwise, the Partnership Act 1890 lays down the following rules about the management of a partnership:

- Capital and profits are to be shared equally. Partners must contribute equally to losses of capital.

- Partners are not entitled to any interest on the capital which they contribute. Interest on loans should be paid at a rate of 5% per annum.

- All partners have the right to take part in the management of the firm.

- No partner is entitled to a salary.

- Disputes about ordinary matters are to be settled by a simple majority vote.

- The nature of the partnership cannot be changed without the consent of all of the partners.

- Partners owe each other a duty of good faith. This involves, among other things, the three following duties: the duty to render full accounts and full information to the other partners; the duty not to make a secret profit; and the duty not to compete with the firm without the other partners' permission.

Winding up of companies

- When a company is wound up (or liquidated) it will cease to exist.

- If a company cannot pay its debts (which has a technical meaning) the court may order that it be compulsorily wound up.

- The company members may themselves wind the company up. A special resolution will be needed to do this if the directors can file a declaration of solvency. An extraordinary resolution will be needed if the directors cannot file a declaration of solvency.

- When a company is wound up the assets of the company are gathered in and then distributed in the following order. First, the costs of winding up are paid, then the debts of preferential creditors, then the debts of those who have taken a floating charge as security for a loan to the company, then the debts of unsecured creditors, then debts owing to company members. Any surplus is divided amongst the members according to their rights in the articles.

Winding up of partnerships

- The court will order a partnership to be wound up if it can only be carried on at a loss.

- The partners themselves may wind up a partnership. Any partner can dissolve the partnership by giving notice unless the partnership was for a fixed time.

- A partnership for a fixed time will be dissolved when the time has expired, or if all the partners agree to terminate it before the time has expired.

- When a partnership is wound up its assets are gathered in. Then these assets are distributed in the following order. First, outsiders are paid what they are owed, second, loans made by the partners are repaid, then capital is repaid to partners. Any surplus is divided amongst the partners in the ratio in which they were to share profits.

- If there are not enough assets to pay the outside creditors then all the partners become personally liable to pay these debts.

- Partnership property belongs to all of the partners who hold it on trust for each other. When a firm is wound up the partnership property will be used to pay the debts and liabilities of the firm.

Relative advantages and disadvantages of trading as a company or a partnership

- Members of a limited company have limited liability for the debts of the company. Partners have unlimited liability for the debts of the partnership.

- All partners have the right to manage the firm and are agents of it. The power to manage a company is vested in the board of directors, who are the agents of the company.

- Partners can withdraw from the firm by giving notice or after a fixed term has expired. The articles of a private company may allow shareholders to sell their shares to any person at any time, but might restrict their ability to do this.

- Companies may give security for a loan by granting a floating charge over their assets. Partnerships cannot do this.

- Companies can raise capital by selling shares.

- A partnership can be formed without any formalities. Companies are formed by registration with the Registrar of Companies.

End of chapter questions

Question 1

Ace Ltd has three shareholders; Arthur, Cherie and Edward. Each of the shareholder holds 100 ordinary shares. For the past 5 years Arthur and Cherie have been elected as the company directors. Arthur has been the company secretary for 6 years. Edward considers that the affairs of the company are not being run as well as they might be. Edward thinks that the company should pass a special resolution to alter the articles to make each of the three shareholders company directors for life. Arthur and Cherie have not commented on this suggestion. Advise Edward of the following matters:

a) The steps he should take to ensure that his resolution is proposed at the next AGM of the company.

b) Any way in which he could ensure that a special resolution is proposed before the next AGM is held.

c) The support he would need in order for the resolution to be passed.

d) The extent to which he can influence the way in which the company is run.

Question 2

Alan, Bernie and Charles are in partnership as landscape gardeners. They do not have formal partnership agreement and have not fixed a definite period for which they should be in partnership. Alan frequently disagrees with Bernie and Charles as to how the firm should be run. In particular, Alan is concerned that Bernie and Charles want to expand the business to start acting as interior designers. Advise Alan of the following matters.

a) Whether Bernie and Charles can outvote him as to the ordinary way in which the business is run.

b) Whether he could prevent the firm from working as interior designers.

c) Whether he could terminate the partnership.

Question 3

Three years ago Sarah finished a college course in Health and Beauty Therapy. After a year working in a salon she spent three months in the United States. On a trip to California Sarah was extremely impressed by some of the alternative beauty treatments available there.

Sarah now wants to market some of the Californian ideas in England, and is worried that if she waits too long others will beat her to it.

Sarah's grandfather, Stanley, has recently retired from the board of a multinational company. He has a variety of interests but, seeing Sarah as a 'chip off the old block,' he is prepared to invest in her proposed business and help her in the running of it.

Sarah is very fond of her grandfather but thinks that he is too cautious, not realising that in the modern age opportunities must be seized immediately, before it becomes too late. Stanley is very proud of Sarah but feels that, expert though she might be in the field of beauty therapy, she has a great deal to learn as far as business goes.

Stanley has agreed to invest £25,000 in the business and put in three or four hours work a week. Sarah is putting in her savings of £5,000 and will devote all of her time to the business.

a) Do you think that Stanley would prefer that the business was a company or a partnership?

b) Which do you think Sarah would prefer?

c) As an objective outsider, which type of business organisation do you think they should become?

(It should be pointed out that there are no absolutely right or wrong answers to questions such as these. Both types of business organisation have considerable advantages and disadvantages. However, at least five of the matters considered in the chapter will have a bearing on the decisions. Try and identify these five and then decide how important each one is.)

Task 8

Five friends of yours are considering going into business together as painters and decorators. Your friends have asked you to draw up a report, dealing briefly with the following matters.

a) How limited companies and partnerships are controlled and managed.

b) How companies and partnerships are wound up, and the order in which the business assets are distributed when they are wound up.

c) The relative advantages and disadvantages of trading as a company or as a partnership.

9 Resolution of business disputes

Throughout this book we have studied rights and obligations. Ultimately, these rights and obligations can only be enforced by taking a case to court. For all business organisations this is a last resort. The process is lengthy and expensive, and it is also likely to cause ill will. If a business sues a customer then, win or lose, the customer is unlikely to deal with the business again.

The vast majority of legal disputes do not go to court. They are settled between the parties themselves. This saves time and money and perhaps keeps a business relationship alive. If a civil dispute does reach the stage of going to court then it will begin either in the county court or in the High Court. Both courts can award the same remedies.

Jurisdiction of the county court

There are 230 county courts in England and Wales. Each county court has one circuit judge and one district judge. These judges hear civil disputes. The county court can hear any contract or tort cases, and 90% of civil cases are heard in the county court. However, some 10% of civil cases are heard in the High Court. There are three main reasons why a case would be heard in the High Court rather than in the county court. First, the case may be very complex. Second, the amount of damages claimed might be so large that the High Court is more appropriate. Third, the case might be likely to set an important precedent. This last reason reflects the fact that High Court decisions have force as legal precedents, whereas county court decisions do not. (The system of precedent is explained in the Introduction to this book, which can be downloaded from the book's Website: www.porchesterpublishing.com.)

Appeals from the county court go to the Court of Appeal and possibly from there to the House of Lords.

County court judgements are registered with the Registry of County Court Judgements and can remain on the register for six years. However, if the judgement is satisfied within one month then the judgement debtor's name is altogether removed from the register. Unsatisfied judgements remain on the register. If the judgement is satisfied more than one month after the judgement is given, the judgement debtor's name remains on the register, along with a note stating that the judgement has been satisfied. Those who have judgements registered against them are unlikely to be granted credit by a commercial lender. The county court does not directly enforce its judgements, although it does provide the machinery by which judgements can be enforced.

Jurisdiction of the High Court

The High Court sits in London and several provincial towns. The High Court will not hea
a case which does not include a claim for personal injuries unless the amount claimed is
more than £15,000. If the case does involve a claim for personal injuries the claim mus
be for more than £50,000 if the High Court is to hear the case. It would be most unusua
for a claim for slightly more than £15,000 to be heard by the High Court. However, as
we have seen, this might happen if the claim is very complex or likely to set an impor
tant precedent.

The High Court is divided into three divisions. The largest of these is the Queen's Bencl
Division and it is in this division that contract and tort cases are heard. Currently there
are 101 High Court judges, 68 of whom sit in the Queen's Bench Division. These judge
are assisted by Masters, who hear cases which are slightly less complex. Dispute
concerning companies and partnerships are generally heard in the Chancery Division
which currently has 17 judges.

Appeals from the High Court are normally made to the Court of Appeal and from there
to the House of Lords. It is however possible to appeal straight from the High Court to the
House of Lords, under the 'leapfrog' procedure. This is most unusual, only being possible
if the case involves a point of law of public importance, and if the House of Lords give
permission for the appeal. The following figure shows the civil court structure.

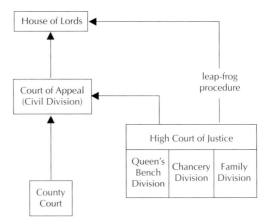

Figure 9.1 The civil court structure

Any court can refer a dispute to the European Court of Justice to get an authoritive
opinion on a matter of European Union law. The court then waits for the European Cou
of Justice to give the ruling. When this has been done the court then applies the ruling
The House of Lords must refer a question of EU law to the European Court of Justic
where a relevant point of EU law is at issue and where the European Court of Justice ha
not previously ruled on the matter.

Civil procedure

It is not appropriate for this book to consider civil court procedure in any degree of detail. However, three matters are dealt with in outline. These matters are: how a claim is made; the possible responses to a claim; and the track to which the case will be allocated if the case proceeds to court.

Making a claim

A legal claim is formally commenced by filling in a claim form and serving this upon the defendant. However, it is very important to realise that this should be a last resort. First, the claimant should make a genuine attempt to settle the claim. If no satisfactory response is received, the claimant should send a final letter to the other party, explaining that if a satisfactory response is not received within a certain time then a claim will be made and formal legal proceedings will be started. This letter should not be too unreasonable or hostile. The time limit should be definite but should give the defendant a reasonable time in which to reply. Copies of all correspondence should be kept. If no satisfactory response is received then it will be necessary to fill in and serve a claim form.

Claim forms, which are called Form N1, can be collected free from any local county court. A copy of such a form is included in the Appendix at the back of this book. As can be seen, the form is relatively easy to complete. County court staff or Citizens Advice Bureaux staff will give advice on completion of the form if this is needed. Interest on money owed by the defendant can be claimed at the rate of 8% per annum from the date on which the money became owed.

In order to bring a case in the county court the claimant must pay a fee to the court. The amount of the fee depends upon the size of the claim. At the moment the fees are as follows:

Claim of under £200	£27
Between £200 and £300	£38
Between £300 and £400	£50
Between £400 and £500	£60
Between £500 and £1,000	£80
Between £1,000 and £5,000	£115
Between £5,000 and £15,000	£230
Between £15,000 and £50,000	£350
Over £50,000	£500

If the claim includes a claim for personal injuries the claimant will have to state whether the amount which he or she expects to recover in respect of the personal injuries is more or less than £1,000. If the amount of the claim is not for personal injuries, but the exact amount of the claim is not known, the claimant will have to state whether he or she expects to recover either more than £5,000, or between £5,000 and £15,000, or over £15,000. As we shall see, these figures are the ones which determine the track to which the case will be allocated.

Once the claim form has been completed the claimant should photocopy it twice. The form and a copy of it are given to the court. The court will keep the form and send the copy to the defendant along with a 'response pack' which outlines the various responses which the defendant might make. The claimant should keep one copy of the claim. As an alternative to getting the court to serve the documents on the defendant the claimant may serve them personally. This involves giving the documents to the defendant and explaining what they are. If the defendant refuses to take the documents the claimant serves them by dropping them at the defendant's feet. If the defendant is a partnership the documents may be personally served upon any partner. If the defendant is a company the documents may be personally served upon any director of the company or upon the company secretary.

The claimant will need to indicate on the claim form the full name and address of the defendant. If the defendant is in trade as a sole trader the claimant should give the defendant's name and add any name under which the defendant is trading. For example, 'Jane Smith trading as Smith's Florists'. If a partnership is sued the claimant should give the firm name and add the words 'a firm'. For example, 'Smith & Co, Florists -a firm'. When either an individual or a firm is sued the claimant should give as the address for service of the documents either the individual's residential address or the principal place of business conducted by the individual or the firm. When a company is sued the claimant should give the full name of the company and the address given should be either the company's registered office or any other place where the company carries on business if this has real connection with the case. For example, in a case in which the claimant claims to have been injured by faulty goods sold by Acme Ltd, a retailer, the address might either be Acme Ltd's registered office or the address of the shop where faulty goods were bought.

Responses to a claim

The defendant must respond to the claim form within 14 days of receiving it. If the defendant offers no response then judgement can be entered against him or her. This means that the claimant will have won the case. The various responses which the defendant can make are illustrated by Figure 9.2.

In order to make a counterclaim against the claimant, the defendant will need to pay court fee. This fee will be calculated according to the size of the counterclaim. The fee payable is the same amount as if the defendant was making an original claim. If an acknowledgment of service is made, this is done on a form which is sent to the defendant in the response pack.

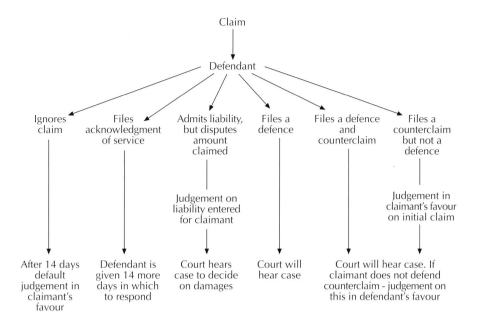

Figure 9.2 The possible responses to a claim which has been served

Allocation to a track

Once the defendant has responded to the claim (other than to admit all of the claim) then the case will be allocated to one of three tracks.

If a claim is made for an amount of money over £1,000 the claimant must pay an allocation fee when the claim is allocated to one of the three tracks. At the moment this fee is £80. If a case is allocated to the multi-track the claimant must pay a trial fee, which is currently £300. The trial fee is currently £200 if the case is allocated to the fast track. No trial fee is payable where a case is allocated to the small claims track.

Small claims track

Claims for £5,000 or less, which are straightforward will be allocated to the small claims track. However, if the claim includes a claim of £1,000 or more for personal injuries then it is not allocated to the small claims track. If both parties agree, cases which are outside these financial limits can be heard on the small claims track. One obvious advantage of this would be that the costs would be reduced.

Small claims track cases are heard by a district judge. Although the proceedings are conducted informally, a small claims track case will generally be open to the public. Documents to be used during the case must be deposited with the court 14 days before the case is heard. Expert witnesses can be allowed only if the district judge agrees that they should be. A claimant who wins the case will be able to recover the court fees paid to start the case, as well as up to £50 per day expenses for attending the court, travelling and accommodation. Apart from these matters, the parties generally pay their own costs and so a claim for the costs of legal representation cannot be made. This is because the system is designed to be usable without legal representation. When the case is heard the parties explain their positions and the judge applies the law on their behalf. However, the court can allow up to £200 costs for an expert witness whom the court has allowed to give evidence. The hearing of the case will be relatively informal and an appeal can only be made with the judge's permission. In order to apply for permission to appeal the claimant must pay a fee of £100. If the application is refused £50 of this fee is refundable to the claimant.

Fast track

Claims which are outside the financial limits for the small claims track will be allocated to the fast track if the claim is for not more than £15,000. Fast track cases will be heard by a circuit judge. It is anticipated that judgement will be given within 30 weeks of allocation to the fast track. The parties to a fast track will almost always be legally represented by a barrister or a solicitor. The winner of the case will almost always be able to claim the cost of legal representation from the other party. This means that the loser will have to pay both side's costs, including the cost of expert witnesses used by both sides and the court fees. The actual hearing of a fast track case will usually take five hours and be conducted on one day.

Multi-track

Cases are allocated to the multi-track if they are not suitable for the small claims track or the fast track.

The three main reasons for an allocation to the multi-track are that the amount claimed is over £15,000, or that there is likely to be considerable expert evidence, or that the hearing of the case is likely to take more than one day in court. There is no standard procedure for a multi-track case. The judge actively manages the case and sets the most appropriate procedure. The judge may hold case management conferences in advance of the trial. These meetings resemble business meetings and are designed both to make the parties co-operate on certain issues and to identify precisely what issues are in dispute. In a particularly complex case the judge might order a pre-trial review to consider both preliminary issues and the way in which the trial should be run. At the end of the case the loser will generally be ordered to pay the costs of both parties. As the parties will generally be represented by barristers, these costs are likely to be very considerable. The legal costs will include all the pre-trial work done by the parties' solicitors and might include very considerable costs of expert witnesses.

Payment into court and offers to settle

When a big civil case is looming the costs of the litigation are likely to be very large. It is in everybody's interests that a settlement is made before the trial, as the costs of the trial may be very substantial. A defendant faced with a claim for a debt or damages might pay a sum of money into court in settlement of the dispute. This can be an important tactic. If the claimant is not awarded more than the sum which the defendant paid into court, then the claimant will normally have to pay all costs incurred 21 days after the money was paid into court. (This is because the claimant has 21 days in which to take the money paid into court in settlement of the dispute.) If the claimant is awarded more than the sum paid into court then costs will be calculated in the usual way.

Similarly, the claimant might make a written offer, stating the sum of money which he or she would take in order to settle the dispute. If the defendant does not accept this, and if the claimant is awarded more than the amount he or she offered to accept, then the defendant will (as the loser of the case) have to pay all the costs of both parties. In addition, the defendant will normally be penalised in that the court will order him or her to pay interest on the sum for which the claimant offered to settle at a rate of interest which can be as high as 10% above the base rate. The judge who tries the case must not be told that a payment into court or an offer to settle has been made until he or she has decided on liability and awarded a sum as damages.

Example

> John has been badly injured by David's negligence. The amount of damages are likely to be high and the case is allocated to the multi-track. After a few months of negotiations both John and David have each incurred legal costs of £5,000. David then pays the sum of £100,000 into court. John responds immediately by offering to settle the matter for a payment of £160,000. The parties do not settle the case, which goes to court. John's legal fees incurred after the offer to settle amount to £43,000. David's legal fees after the payment into court was made amount to £46,000.
>
> a) At the trial John is awarded damages of £100,000 or less. John must pay all of his own costs of £48,000 (£5,000 + £43,000) and David's costs incurred after David's payment into court (£46,000). If John was awarded damages of less than £94,000 he would therefore be out of pocket.
>
> b) John is awarded damages of more than £100,000 but less than £160,000. David, as the loser of the case, will have to pay the costs of both sides.
>
> c) John is awarded damages of more than £160,000. David, as the loser of the case, will have to pay the costs of both sides. In addition the court can order that David pays interest on the £160,000 for which John offered to settle, at a rate which must not be more than 10% above the base rate.

Alternative dispute resolution

As mentioned earlier, litigation should always be a last resort. We have seen that if a ca does reach the stage of going to court then the loser will generally have to pay the co of both sides. We have also seen that these costs can be very substantial. In many cas the costs are greater than the amount being claimed. As well as the costs which a claimable by the winner, other hidden costs (such as the cost of time spent instructi solicitors) are likely to be incurred. The winner of the case will not be able to cla anything in respect of these hidden costs. Furthermore, there is the risk that the otl party will become insolvent if he or she loses the case. If this happens then the winner the case is likely to have to pay all the legal costs which he or she has incurred, ev though the winner does not normally have to pay costs.

A further disadvantage of litigation is that it is a very stressful experience. The wo involved can take a toll on health. One factor which makes this particularly true is tl litigation takes time, particularly when a case is allocated to the multi-track. Anotl disadvantage is that a court case is heard in public and this publicity can be very harm if the other side makes allegations about the business. Furthermore, litigation is alm certain to mean that the parties do not deal with each other again.

In the light of all these disadvantages, many legal disputes are settle by alternative disp resolution. That is to say, they are settled without a court case. The simplest way in whi this can happen is that the parties, usually through their lawyers, voluntarily agree to settlement. As we saw in Chapter 1, if the parties agree to settle out of court this agr ment is a binding contract. There are various other methods of alternative dispute re lution, which are considered below.

Arbitration

Business disputes are often settled by arbitration. If a dispute is settled in this way ther is resolved by an impartial referee, an arbitrator, who takes over the role of the co Once the parties have agreed to arbitration they will not be able to change their min and take the dispute to court. If one party does try to take the dispute to court the ot party will be able to get any court proceedings stayed (discontinued).

Advantages of arbitration

The main advantage of arbitration is that the proceedings are conducted privat whereas court proceedings are held in public. Privacy can be a very important facto business disputes. Let us assume, for example, that a dispute has arisen between Ac Ltd and Bill's Bakery Co. Acme Ltd supplied a new boiler to Bill's Bakery Co and are su for the price. Bill's Bakery Co are refusing to pay the price because they say that the bo supplied was not of satisfactory quality. Neither of the parties would want the publi which might arise if this dispute were to be heard in open court. Acme Ltd would want it to be publicly claimed that their boilers were not of satisfactory quality. B

Bakery Co would not want it to be publicly claimed that the business does not pay its debts. If the dispute is referred to arbitration this adverse publicity will be avoided.

A second advantage of arbitration is that an arbitrator with specialist knowledge can be chosen. Eventually the dispute between Acme Ltd and Bill's Bakery Co would depend upon whether or not the boiler supplied was of satisfactory quality. If the case went to court the judge would make this decision, probably after listening to expert witnesses from both sides. It is highly unlikely that the judge would know much about boilers. The side which loses the case would be likely to feel that the judge got it wrong. Both Acme and Bill's Bakery Co might have more faith in the decision if it was taken by an expert in the field, perhaps by the chairman of the local Boiler Maker's Federation.

Arbitration might also be cheaper than going to court. However, this is by no means certain. Arbitrators can demand good money for their skills and the lawyers arguing the case in front of an arbitrator will often charge the client the same rate as they would for going to court. It is also the case that in large commercial disputes the arbitrators are often High Court judges or Masters. Often the procedures followed by such arbitrators are very similar to High Court procedures. The advantage of privacy is retained, but the proceedings are unlikely to be substantially cheaper than High Court proceedings. Of course, the parties have the choice of arbitrator and might choose less formal and cheaper proceedings if they were satisfied that these would not prejudice their interests.

A dispute sent to arbitration is likely to be resolved relatively quickly. It takes a long time for a case to get to court, whereas arbitration can be quickly arranged. Delays in arbitration are usually caused because the parties cannot agree who the arbitrator should be. The Arbitration Act 1996 has considerably reduced the delays which used to arise.

A final advantage of arbitration is that the right to appeal is severely restricted. The parties know that once the arbitrator has made the award that is the end of the dispute. If a dispute is taken to court an appeal, or the threat of one, can hang over the winner for some considerable time.

erence to arbitration

A dispute can only be referred to arbitration if both sides agree that it should be. If the dispute is a contractual one then a term of the contract may provide for arbitration. Such terms are common in contracts made in the context of certain industries, including the insurance industry and the building industry. But arbitration clauses are by no means restricted to contracts made in those industries. It is quite possible that a contract between a boilermaker and a business customer, such as the example used in relation to Acme Ltd and Bill's Bakery Co, might have contained a clause stating that any dispute arising under the contract should be resolved by arbitration.

Alternatively the parties might agree to arbitration once the dispute has arisen and both sides have made their positions clear. Perhaps the arrival of Acme Ltd's claim form would be enough to convince Bill's Bakery Co that the dispute was serious, and lead them to suggest arbitration.

Whether the agreement is made in the contract itself or later, the important thing is th
once the parties have agreed to arbitration neither of the sides will be able to unilatera
change their minds. If a party who has agreed to an arbitration clause tries to take t
dispute to a court instead of to the arbitrator the court will stay (discontinue) the procee
ings.

It is a principle of contract law that no clause in a contract may oust the jurisdiction
the courts (prevent matters of law from being decided by the ordinary courts of the lan
Arbitration is the only exception to this principle.

In addition to the parties in dispute agreeing to arbitration, many trade associatio
provide that particular types of disputes should be referred to arbitration. These schem
do not take away a customer's rights or prevent a customer from taking a dispute to cou
but do provide a cheap way of resolving a dispute without going to court. These arbitr
tion schemes try to ensure that members of the particular trade association stick to
association's Codes of Practice. These Codes of Practice are generally agreed to volu
tarily as a condition of membership of the trade association. Generally the Codes
Practice will set out the standards which customers are entitled to expect. Perhaps
best known of these arbitration schemes is the scheme run by the Association of Brit
Travel Agents which attempts to resolve disputes arising in connection with the tra
industry. Other schemes apply to very many trades, including double glazing, laun
services, electrical repairs and the processing of photographs. These schemes may v
give a remedy to a customer where the law would not do so. They also have the adv
tage that the arbitrators will be closely connected with the trade in question and will
able to apply this knowledge in settlement of any dispute. Disadvantages are that
Codes of Practice are not always enthusiastically enforced and that customers might
that the arbitrator is not truly independent. It is also the case that those who do not bel
to the trade association in question are outside the Codes of Practice altogether.

The Arbitration Act 1996 has introduced important new rules about arbitration. It sta
that the purpose of arbitration is to obtain a fair resolution of disputes by an impa
tribunal without unnecessary delay or expense. The Act also requires the arbitrato
deal fairly with the parties and to allow them to present their case and deal with t
opponent's case. Under the Act the parties to the arbitration must do everything ne
sary to allow the arbitration to proceed properly and quickly. Before the Act came
force it was common for some parties to arbitration to delay matters by every poss
means in the hope that this would force the other side to either give up or settle the c

Mediation

When a dispute is referred to mediation, a mediator tries to help the parties to settle t
dispute. There are no set rules about how this should be done. The most common met
would probably be that the mediator asks the parties to put their case to each other i
or her presence. The mediator might then get the parties to agree what the esse
matters in dispute were. Then the parties in dispute might go to different rooms an
visited in turn by the mediator. The mediator would put forward the points of view of
party to the other and suggest various compromises. Eventually the parties might mar

to reach agreement with each other and settle the dispute. Many disputes which are not settled during the mediation are settled soon afterwards.

In the United States of America mediators have worked through the Internet. They ask the parties to give three figures on which they would be prepared to settle. One figure is the very least which they would settle for, the next figure is somewhat higher and the third figure higher still. The mediator sees if there is any common ground and if so passes on the relevant figures to the parties.

Often solicitors act as mediators. When this is the case they are bound by a Law Society Code of Conduct and a high standard of service is therefore ensured. One disadvantage of mediation is that the parties might enter into it without any intention of settling the case, merely to find out more about the other party's case.

onciliation

Conciliation involves a conciliator bringing the parties together and suggesting a compromise which they might agree to. It is therefore similar to mediation, except that the conciliator takes a more active approach, not merely passing on the other side's point of view but also actively suggesting the basis on which the dispute might be settled. In employment cases conciliation has been around for a long time. An official from ACAS attempts to conciliate before an employment dispute is taken to an employment tribunal. Mediation and conciliation are not strictly defined, and not everyone agrees that mediators do not suggest the basis of agreement whereas conciliators do.

mbudsmen

Ombudsman is the Swedish word for a representative. As regards certain types of disputes ombudsmen exist to investigate complaints which arise within a certain trade or industry. The British and Irish Ombudsman Association will approve Ombudsmen only if it is satisfied that they are independent, effective, fair and accountable.

Generally an ombudsman will not investigate a complaint if the complaint is currently the subject of legal proceedings. Nor will the ombudsman investigate a complaint until the complainant has completely exhausted any internal complaints procedure which might exist.

Ombudsmen may be limited in the amount which they can award, but generally this amount is fairly generous. As well as investigating a particular complaint, an ombudsman might make recommendations to improve matters generally within the area concerned. It is often the case that the awards of ombudsmen cannot be legally enforced. However, most traders will comply with any award because the publicity attached to not doing so would be very undesirable. In England and Wales the following ombudsmen operate in the private sector: the Legal Services Ombudsman, the Independent Housing Ombudsman, the Banking Ombudsman, the Building Societies Ombudsman, the Broadcasting Standards Ombudsman, the Estate Agents Ombudsman, the Funeral Ombudsman, the Insurance Ombudsman Bureau, the Investment Ombudsman, the Pensions Ombudsman, and the Personal Investment Authority Ombudsman Bureau.

There are also ombudsmen operating in the public sector, including: the Parliamenta[ry] Ombudsman, the Health Service Ombudsman, the Local Government Ombudsman a[nd] the Police Complaints Authority.

Complaint-handling bodies which do not involve an ombudsman exist in relation [to] complaints about the Inland Revenue, Customs and Excise, Social Security, the Ch[ild] Support Agency, barristers, prisons, subsidence and waterways.

Although Ombudsmen schemes differ, most are essentially the same. By considering [an] outline of the Insurance Ombudsman Bureau we can get an idea of how ombudsm[en] operate. The I.O.B. exists to resolve disputes between its members and consumers in [an] independent, impartial, cost-effective, efficient, informal and fair way. Over 220 insur[ers] are members of the scheme. The Bureau employs over 50 full-time staff who deal w[ith] 200 calls a day and it replies to over 300 written enquiries a week. Complaints are inve[s]tigated by a written procedure. The complainant and the insurer never meet as t[he] Bureau takes an inquisitorial approach. Any conclusion reached takes into account t[he] relevant Code of Practice and is designed to reach a fair and reasonable conclusi[on] which reflects good insurance practice. Decisions are communicated in plain writt[en] English, and reasons for the decision are given. Complaints must relate to t[he] complainant personally and must not relate to the complainant's trade or business.

When a complaint is made to the I.O.B. the details are put on the I.O.B.'s computer a[nd] then sent back to the complainant to be checked and signed. If the complainant agre[es] a copy will be sent to the insurer against whom the complaint is made. The insurer v[ill] then attempt to settle the matter directly with the complaint. If the insurer does not al[ter] his position, or if the dispute continues for more than 8 weeks, the I.O.B. calls for [the] insurer's file. As a member of the association, an insurer is obliged to send this file. On[ce] received, the file is allocated to an Executive Officer for investigation. The investigat[ing] officer will write to the insurer and to the complainant, asking for answers to questio[ns] At the end of the process the conclusion of the officer will be communicated. Th[ere] would generally be no hearings in person or interviews.

The I.O.B. can award up to £100,000 to the complaint. If the complainant accepts t[he] award the insurer is bound by it. (The insurer is not strictly legally bound, but there [has] never been a case where an insurer did not pay the amount recommended.) T[he] complainant is not bound by the recommendation and if he or she chooses not to acc[ept] it then the recommendation will have no effect. An appeal against the decision can[not] be made. The scheme is free to complainants.

Essential points

The civil courts

- Civil disputes are first heard in either the county court or the High Court.

- Any UK court can refer a matter of EU law to the European Court of Justice to [get] an authoritative opinion on the matter.

Civil procedure

- A civil claim is commenced by completing a claim form and serving this upon the defendant. If a claim form is handed in to the county court, along with two copies of it, the court will serve the form upon the defendant.

- If the defendant makes no response to a claim form which has been served, within 14 days, the court will enter judgement for the claimant.

- A defendant who completes an acknowledgment of service form, within 14 days, will be given a further 14 days in which to respond to a claim.

- If the defendant files a defence or a counterclaim then the case will be heard by a court (unless the parties settle the case before the case is due to be heard).

- If the defendant responds to the claim, and does not admit full liability, then the case will be allocated to one of three tracks.

- Straightforward claims for no more than £5,000, which do not include a claim for personal injuries amounting to more than £1,000, will be allocated to the small claims track.

- A case on the small claims track will be heard by a district judge. The parties do not need to be legally represented.

- The loser of a case heard on the small claims track will have to pay any court fees which the other party had paid and perhaps also up to £50 per day costs for attending the court, accommodation and travel. Apart from these matters both sides usually pay their own costs.

- Generally, claims which are not within the small claims track financial limits will be heard on the fast track if the amount claimed is not more than £15,000.

- It will usually be the case that a fast track case will be heard within 30 weeks of allocation and that the case will actually last for one day.

- Cases which are not suitable for the small claims track or the fast track are allocated to the multi-track. The judge actively manages a multi-track case, trying to identify the issues in dispute and to encourage the parties to settle some or all of the case.

- If a claimant fails to accept a sum of money which the defendant has paid into court in settlement of the case, the claimant will usually have to pay all costs subsequently incurred if the court does not award him or her more than the sum paid into court.

- If the claimant makes a written offer to settle the case for a certain amount, the defendant will generally have to pay a punitive rate of interest on this amount (as well as the costs of both sides) if the claimant is awarded more than the amount which he or she offered to accept.

Alternative dispute resolution

- Litigation in court has many disadvantages: the costs of litigation can be very high; litigation is very stressful; it can take a long time; it can destroy business relationships, and the public nature of hearings can lead to bad publicity.

- Alternative dispute resolution can avoid some or all of the disadvantages of litigation.

- The simplest form of alternative dispute resolution occurs when the parties agree to settle their case out of court.

- Arbitration involves an impartial third party, an arbitrator, making a binding resolution of a dispute.

- The parties in dispute may themselves agree to refer the dispute to arbitration, in which case a court will not hear the case. The agreement to refer to arbitration might be a term of a contract or might be made after the dispute has arisen.

- Arbitration has several advantages over litigation: the proceedings are conducted privately; the arbitrator may have specialist knowledge of the type of matter in dispute; arbitration may be cheaper and quicker than litigation; and the decision of the arbitrator will usually be the end of the dispute, as no appeal will be allowed.

- Some trade associations provide that disputes concerning their members should go to arbitration. Such schemes do not prevent the claimant from going to court. They may provide the customer with a remedy in circumstances in which the law would not.

- A mediator tries to help the parties settle a dispute by seeking agreement on certain matters and by communicating to the parties the position of the other party.

- A conciliator attempts to resolve a dispute by suggesting a compromise to which both parties might agree.

- Ombudsmen investigate complaints arising within certain trades or industries. Ombudsmen will generally not hear complaints which are being pursued through the courts. Nor will they pursue complaints until all internal complaint procedures have been exhausted.

- Although ombudsmen cannot enforce their recommendations, traders generally comply with them to avoid bad publicity.

- Many ombudsmen use an inquisitorial written approach to resolving disputes.

- Generally ombudsmen schemes are free to complainants and generally appeal from the recommendation can be made.

End of chapter question

For many years a wholesaler has supplied a garden centre with flower seeds. The wholesaler and supplier have always enjoyed good relations, but a serious dispute has now arisen over the quality of seeds delivered last year. The garden centre say that many of the seeds did not produce flowers and that customers have been complaining. The wholesaler has not received any similar complaints from other retailers supplied from the same batch of seeds.

a) List, in order of importance, the reasons why the parties might prefer to resolve this dispute through arbitration rather than through the courts.

b) Explain how the dispute might be settled by mediation or conciliation.

c) If the dispute eventually did lead to a court case, on which track would the case be likely to be heard if the damages claimed were;

  i) £800?

  ii) £12,000?

  iii) £63,000?

c) To which court could the loser appeal if the case was first heard in:

  i) the county court?

  ii) the High Court?

ask 9

Mrs Macleod bought some flower seeds from Greenco Garden Centre. Mrs Macleod is claiming that the seeds did not produce flowers and that this entitles her to damages of £900. Greenco Garden Centre do not believe Mrs Macleod's story, as they have had no other complaints.

a) As Mrs Macleod, fill in a summons (Form N1) claiming the £900.

b) As Greenco Garden Centre, fill in a Defence and Counterclaim form, disputing the whole claim.

Appendix —
Forms and specimen contract

Companies House
— for the record —

Please complete in typescript,
or in bold black capitals.
CHWP000

Notes on completion appear on final page

10

First directors and secretary and intended situation of registered office

Company Name in full

Proposed Registered Office

(PO Box numbers only, are not acceptable)

Post town

County / Region

Postcode

If the memorandum is delivered by an agent for the subscriber(s) of the memorandum mark the box opposite and give the agent's name and address.

Agent's Name

Address

Post town

County / Region

Postcode

Number of continuation sheets attached

Please give the name, address, telephone number and, if available, a DX number and Exchange of the person Companies House should contact if there is any query.

Tel

DX number   DX exchange

Companies House receipt date barcode

This form has been provided free of charge by Companies House.

Form revised July 1998

When you have completed and signed the form please send it to the Registrar of Companies at:

Companies House, Crown Way, Cardiff, CF14 3UZ   DX 33050 Cardiff
for companies registered in England and Wales
or
Companies House, 37 Castle Terrace, Edinburgh, EH1 2EB
for companies registered in Scotland   **DX 235 Edinburgh**

Form 10   First directors and secretary and intended situation of registered office — page 1

Company Secretary (see notes 1-5)

Company name		

| NAME | *Style / Title | | *Honours etc | |

* Voluntary details

Forename(s)

Surname

Previous forename(s)

Previous surname(s)

Address

Usual residential address
For a corporation, give the registered or principal office address.

Post town

County / Region   Postcode

Country

I consent to act as secretary of the company named on page 1

Consent signature   **Date**

Directors (see notes 1-5)

Please list directors in alphabetical order

NAME   *Style / Title   *Honours etc

Forename(s)

Surname

Previous forename(s)

Previous surname(s)

Address

Usual residential address
For a corporation, give the registered or principal office address.

Post town

County / Region   Postcode

Country

Day   Month   Year

Date of birth   **Nationality**

Business occupation

Other directorships

I consent to act as director of the company named on page 1

Consent signature   **Date**

Form 10   *First directors and secretary and intended situation of registered office — page 2*

Directors (continued)   (see notes 1-5)

NAME   *Style / Title _____   *Honours etc _____

* Voluntary details   Forename(s) _____

Surname _____

Previous forename(s) _____

Previous surname(s) _____

Address _____

Usual residential address
For a corporation, give the
registered or principal office
address.   _____

Post town _____

County / Region _____   Postcode _____

Country _____

	Day	Month	Year		
Date of birth				Nationality	

Business occupation _____

Other directorships _____

_____

I consent to act as director of the company named on page 1

Consent signature _____   **Date** _____

This section must be signed by
Either

**an agent on behalf
of all subscribers**   **Signed** _____   **Date** _____

Or the subscribers   **Signed** _____   **Date** _____

(*i.e those who signed
as members on the
memorandum of
association).*   **Signed** _____   **Date** _____

Signed _____   **Date** _____

Signed _____   **Date** _____

Signed _____   **Date** _____

Signed _____   **Date** _____

Form 10   First directors and secretary and intended situation of registered office — page 3

Notes

1. Show for an individual the full forename(s) NOT INITIALS and surname together with any previous forename(s) or surname(s).

   If the director or secretary is a corporation or Scottish firm - show the corporate or firm name on the surname line.

   Give previous forename(s) or surname(s) except that:

   - for a married woman, the name by which she was known before marriage need not be given,

   - names not used since the age of 18 or for at least 20 years need not be given.

   A peer, or an individual known by a title, may state the title instead of or in addition to the forename(s) and surname and need not give the name by which that person was known before he or she adopted the title or succeeded to it.

   Address:

   Give the usual residential address.

   In the case of a corporation or Scottish firm give the registered or principal office.

   Subscribers:

   The form must be signed personally either by the subscriber(s) or by a person or persons authorised to sign on behalf of the subscriber(s).

2. Directors known by another description:

   - A director includes any person who occupies that position even if called by a different name, for example, governor, member of council.

3. Directors details:

   - Show for each individual director the director's date of birth, business occupation and nationality. **The date of birth must be given for every individual director.**

4. Other directorships:

   - Give the name of every company of which the person concerned is a director or has been a director at any time in the past 5 years. You may exclude a company which either **is** or at **all times during the past 5 years,** when the person was a director, **was**:

   - dormant,

   - a parent company which wholly owned the company making the return,

   - a wholly owned subsidiary of the company making the return, or

   - another wholly owned subsidiary of the same parent company.

   If there is insufficient space on the form for other directorships you may use a separate sheet of paper, which should include the company's number and the full name of the director.

5. Use Form 10 continuation sheets or photocopies of page 2 to provide details of joint secretaries or additional directors.

orm 10   First directors and secretary and intended situation of registered office — page 4

Companies House
······ *for the record* ······

**Please complete in typescript,
or in bold black capitals.**

CHWP000

12

Declaration on application for registration

Company Name in full

I,

† Please delete as appropriate

do solemnly and sincerely declare that I am a † [Solicitor engaged in the
formation of the company][person named as director or secretary of the
company in the statement delivered to the Registrar under section 10 of the
Companies Act 1985] and that all the requirements of the Companies Act
1985 in respect of the registration of the above company and of matters
precedent and incidental to it have been complied with.

And I make this solemn Declaration conscientiously believing the same to
be true and by virtue of the Statutory Declarations Act 1835.

Declarant's signature

Declared at

Day	Month	Year

On

❶ Please print name.

before me ❶

Signed | **Date**

† A Commissioner for Oaths or Notary Public or Justice of the Peace or Solicitor

Please give the name, address,
telephone number and, if available,
a DX number and Exchange of
the person Companies House should
contact if there is any query.

Tel

DX number | DX exchange

Companies House receipt date barcode

*This form has been provided free of charge
by Companies House.*

Form revised June 1998

When you have completed and signed the form please send it to the
Registrar of Companies at:
Companies House, Crown Way, Cardiff, CF14 3UZ   DX 33050 Cardiff
for companies registered in England and Wales
or
Companies House, 37 Castle Terrace, Edinburgh, EH1 2EB
for companies registered in Scotland   **DX 235 Edinburgh**

Form 12   Declaration on application for registration

Claim Form

In the

Claim No.

Claimant

SEAL

Defendant(s)

Brief details of claim

Value

Defendant's name and address

	£
Amount claimed	
Court fee	
Solicitor's costs	
Total amount	
Issue date	

The court office at

is open between 10 am and 4 pm Monday to Friday. When corresponding with the court, please address forms or letters to the Court Manager and quote the claim number.

N1 Claim form (CPR Part 7) (10.00)

Printed on behalf of The Court Service

orm N1   Claim form — page 1

	Claim No.	

Does, or will, your claim include any issues under the Human Rights Act 1998? ☐ Yes ☐ No

Particulars of Claim (attached)(to follow)

Statement of Truth
*(I believe)(The Claimant believes) that the facts stated in these particulars of claim are true.
* I am duly authorised by the claimant to sign this statement

Full name _____

Name of claimant's solicitor's firm _____

signed _____ position or office held _____
*(Claimant)(Litigation friend)(Claimant's solicitor)   (if signing on behalf of firm or company)
*delete as appropriate

Claimant's or claimant's solicitor's address to which documents or payments should be sent if different from overleaf including (if appropriate) details of DX, fax or e-mail.

Form N1   Claim form — page 2

Notes for claimant on completing a claim form
Further information may be obtained from the court in a series of free leaflets.

- Please read all of these guidance notes before you begin completing the claim form. The notes follow the order in which information is required on the form.
- Court staff can help you fill in the claim form and give information about procedure once it has been issued. But they cannot give legal advice. If you need legal advice, for example, about the likely success of your claim or the evidence you need to prove it, you should contact a solicitor or a Citizens Advice Bureau.
- If you are filling in the claim form by hand, please use black ink and write in block capitals.
- Copy the completed claim form and the defendant's notes for guidance so that you have one copy for yourself, one copy for the court and one copy for each defendant. Send or take the forms to the court office with the appropriate fee. The court will tell you how much this is.

Notes on completing the claim form

Heading

You must fill in the heading of the form to indicate whether you want the claim to be issued in a county court or in the High Court (The High Court means either a District Registry (attached to a county court) or the Royal Courts of Justice in London). There are restrictions on claims which may be issued in the High Court (see 'Value' overleaf).

Use whichever of the following is appropriate:

'In the ....County Court'
(inserting the name of the court)

or

'In the High Court of Justice........................Division'
(inserting eg. 'Queen's Bench' or 'Chancery' as appropriate)
'.............................District Registry'
(inserting the name of the District Registry)

or

'In the High Court of Justice........................Division,
(inserting eg. 'Queen's Bench' or 'Chancery' as appropriate)
Royal Courts of Justice'

Claimant and defendant details

As the person issuing the claim, you are called the 'claimant'; the person you are suing is called the 'defendant'. Claimants who are under 18 years old (unless otherwise permitted by the court) and patients within the meaning of the Mental Health Act 1983, must have a litigation friend to issue and conduct court proceedings on their behalf. Court staff will tell you more about what you need to do if this applies to you.

You must provide the following information about yourself **and** the defendant according to the capacity in which you are suing and in which the defendant is being sued. When suing or being sued as:-

an individual:

All known forenames and surname, whether Mr, Mrs, Miss, Ms or Other (e.g. Dr) and residential address (**including** postcode and telephone number) in England and Wales. Where the defendant is a proprietor of a business, a partner in a firm or an individual sued in the name of a club or other unincorporated association, the address for service should be the usual or last known place of residence **or** principal place of business of the company, firm or club or other unincorporated association.

Where the individual is:

under 18 write '(a child by Mr Joe Bloggs his litigation friend)' after the name. If the child is conducting proceedings on their own behalf write '(a child)' after the child's name.

a patient within the meaning of the Mental Health Act 1983 write '(by Mr Joe Bloggs his litigation friend)' after the patient's name.

trading under another name

you must add the words 'trading as' and the trading name e.g. 'Mr John Smith trading as Smith's Groceries'.

suing or being sued in a representative capacity

you must say what that capacity is e.g. 'Mr Joe Bloggs as the representative of Mrs Sharon Bloggs (deceased)'.

suing or being sued in the name of a club or other unincorporated association

add the words 'suing/sued on behalf of' followed by the name of the club or other unincorporated association.

a firm

enter the name of the firm followed by the words 'a firm' e.g. 'Bandbox - a firm' and an address for service which is either a partner's residential address or the principal or last known place of business.

a corporation (other than a company)

enter the full name of the corporation and the address which is either its principal office **or** any other place where the corporation carries on activities and which has a real connection with the claim.

a company registered in England and Wales

enter the name of the company and an address which is either the company's registered office **or** any place of business that has a real, or the most, connection with the claim e.g. the shop where the goods were bought.

an overseas company (defined by s744 of the Companies Act 1985)

enter the name of the company and either the address registered under s691 of the Act **or** the address of the place of business having a real, or the most, connection with the claim.

N1A - w3 Notes for claimant (4.99)　　　　　　　　　　　*Printed on behalf of The Court Service*

rm N1a Notes for claimant — page 1

Brief details of claim

Note: The facts and full details about your claim and whether or not you are claiming interest, should be set out in the 'particulars of claim' *(see note under 'Particulars of Claim').*

You must set out under **this** heading:

- a concise statement of the nature of your claim
- the remedy you are seeking e.g. payment of money; an order for return of goods or their value; an order to prevent a person doing an act; damages for personal injuries.

Value

If you are claiming a **fixed amount of money** (a 'specified amount') write the amount in the box at the bottom right-hand corner of the claim form against 'amount claimed'.

If you are not claiming a fixed amount of money (an 'unspecified amount') under 'Value' write "I expect to recover" followed by whichever of the following applies to your claim:

- "not more than £5,000" **or**
- "more than £5,000 but not more than £15,000"**or**
- "more than £15,000"

If you are **not able** to put a value on your claim, write "I cannot say how much I expect to recover".

Personal injuries

If your claim is for 'not more than £5,000' and includes a claim for personal injuries, you must also write "My claim includes a claim for personal injuries and the amount I expect to recover as damages for pain, suffering and loss of amenity is" followed by either:

- "not more than £1,000" **or**
- "more than £1,000"

Housing disrepair

If your claim is for 'not more than £5,000' and includes a claim for housing disrepair relating to residential premises, you must also write "My claim includes a claim against my landlord for housing disrepair relating to residential premises. The cost of the repairs or other work is estimated to be" followed by either:

- "not more than £1,000" **or**
- "more than £1,000"

If within this claim, you are making a claim for other damages, you must also write:

"I expect to recover as damages" followed by either:

- "not more than £1,000" **or**
- "more than £1,000"

Issuing in the High Court

You may only issue in the High Court if one of the following statements applies to your claim:-

"By law, my claim must be issued in the High Court. The Act which provides this is ....(specify Act)"

or

"I expect to recover more than £15,000"

or

"My claim includes a claim for personal injuries and the value of the claim is £50,000 or more"

or

"My claim needs to be in a specialist High Court list, namely..................................(state which list)".

If one of the statements does apply and you wish to, or must by law, issue your claim in the High Court, write the words "I wish my claim to issue in the High Court because" followed by the relevant statement e.g. "I wish my claim to issue in the High Court because my claim includes a claim for personal injuries and the value of my claim is £50,000 or more."

Defendant's name and address

Enter in this box the full names and address of the defendant receiving the claim form (ie. one claim form for each defendant). If the defendant is to be served outside England and Wales, you may need to obtain the court's permission.

Particulars of claim

You may include your particulars of claim on the claim form in the space provided or in a separate document which you should head 'Particulars of Claim'. It should include the names of the parties, the court, the claim number and your address for service and also contain a statement of truth. You should keep a copy for yourself, provide one for the court and one for each defendant. Separate particulars of claim can either be served

- with the claim form **or**
- within 14 days after the date on which the claim form was served.

If your particulars of claim are served separately from the claim form, they must be served with the forms on which the defendant may reply to your claim.

Your particulars of claim must include

- a concise statement of the facts on which you rely
- a statement (if applicable) to the effect that you are seeking aggravated damages or exemplary damages
- details of any interest which you are claiming
- any other matters required for your type of claim as set out in the relevant practice direction

Address for documents

Insert in this box the address at which you wish to receive documents and/or payments, if different from the address you have already given under the heading 'Claimant'. The address must be in England or Wales. If you are willing to accept service by DX, fax or e-mail, add details.

Statement of truth

This must be signed by you, by your solicitor or your litigation friend, as appropriate.

Where the claimant is a registered company or a corporation the claim must be signed by either the director, treasurer, secretary, chief executive, manager or other officer of the company or (in the case of a corporation) the mayor, chairman, president or town clerk.

Form N1a   Notes for claimant — page 2

Response Pack

You should read the 'notes for defendant' attached to the claim form which will tell you when and where to send the forms

Included in this pack are:

- either **Admission Form N9A** (if the claim is for a specified amount) or **Admission Form N9C** (if the claim is for an unspecified amount or is not a claim for money)
- either **Defence and Counterclaim Form N9B** (if the claim is for a specified amount) or **Defence and Counterclaim Form N9D** (if the claim is for an unspecified amount or is not a claim for money)
- **Acknowledgment of service** (see below)

Complete

If you admit the claim or the amount claimed and/or you want time to pay	▶ the admission form
If you admit part of the claim	▶ the admission form and the defence form
If you dispute the whole claim or wish to make a claim (a counterclaim) against the claimant	▶ the defence form
If you need 28 days (rather than 14) from the date of service to prepare your defence, or wish to contest the court's jurisdiction	▶ the acknowledgment of service
If you do nothing, judgment may be entered against you	

Acknowledgment of Service

Defendant's full name if different from the name given on the claim form

In the	
Claim No.	
Claimant (including ref.)	
Defendant	

Address to which documents about this claim should be sent (including reference if appropriate)

	if applicable
	fax no.
	DX no.
	e-mail

Tel. no.   Postcode

Tick the appropriate box

1. I intend to defend all of this claim ☐
2. I intend to defend part of this claim ☐
3. I intend to contest jurisdiction ☐

If you file an acknowledgment of service but do not file a defence within 28 days of the date of service of the claim form, or particulars of claim if served separately, judgment may be entered against you.

If you do not file an application within 28 days of the date of service of the claim form, or particulars of claim if served separately, it will be assumed that you accept the court's jurisdiction and judgment may be entered against you.

Signed

(Defendant)(Defendant's solicitor) (Litigation friend)

Position or office held (if signing on behalf of firm or company)

Date

The court office at

is open between 10 am and 4 pm Monday to Friday. When corresponding with the court, please address forms or letters to the Court Manager and quote the claim number.

N9 -w3- Response Pack (4.99)   *Produced on behalf of The Court Service*

orm N9   *Response pack*

Defence and Counterclaim
(unspecified amount, non-money and return of goods claims)

In the	
Claim No.	
Claimant (including ref.)	
Defendant	

- Fill in this form if you wish to dispute all or part of the claim and/or make a claim against the claimant (a counterclaim)
- You have a limited number of days to complete and return this form to the court.
- Before completing this form, please read the notes for guidance attached to the claim form.
- Please ensure that all the boxes at the top right of this form are completed. You can obtain the correct names and number from the claim form. The court cannot trace your case without this information.

How to fill in this form
- Set out your defence in section 1. If necessary continue on a separate piece of paper making sure that the claim number is clearly shown on it. In your defence you must state which allegations in the particulars of claim you deny and your reasons for doing so. **If you fail to deny an allegation it may be taken that you admit it.**
- If you dispute only some of the allegations you must
  - specify which you admit and which you deny; and
  - give your own version of events if different from the claimant's.

- If the claim is for money and you dispute the claimant's statement of value, you must say why and if possible give your own statement of value.
- If you wish to make a claim against the claimant (a counterclaim) complete section 2.
- Complete and sign section 3 before returning this form.

Where to send this form
- send or take this form immediately to the court at the address given on the claim form.
- Keep a copy of the claim form and the defence form.

Community Legal Service Fund (CLSF)

You may qualify for assistance from the CLSF (this used to be called 'legal aid') to meet some or all of your legal costs. Ask about the CLSF at any county court office or any information or help point which displays this logo.

Community Legal Service

1. Defence

N9D Defence and Counterclaim (unspecified amount) (9.00)　　　　　　　　　　　　　　*Printed on behalf of The Court Service*

Form N9D   Defence and counterclaim (unspecified amount) — page 1

Defence (continued)

Claim No.

2. If you wish to make a claim against the claimant (a counterclaim)

If your claim is for a specific sum of money, how much are you claiming? £

- To start your counterclaim, you will have to pay a fee. Court staff will tell you how much you have to pay.

My claim is for *(please specify)*

- You may not be able to make a counterclaim where the claimant is the Crown (e.g. a Government Department). Ask at your local county court office for further information.

What are your reasons for making the counterclaim?
If you need to continue on a separate sheet put the claim number in the top right hand corner

3. Signed

(To be signed by you or by your solicitor or litigation friend)

*(I believe)(The defendant believes) that the facts stated in this form are true. *I am duly authorised by the defendant to sign this statement

*delete as appropriate

Position or office held
(if signing on behalf of firm or company)

Date

Give an address to which notices about this case can be sent to you

Postcode

Tel. no.

if applicable

fax no.

DX no.

e-mail

® Crown copyright

HIRE ASSOCIATION EUROPE — CONDITIONS FOR HIRE AND SALE OF PRODUCTS IN ENGLAND AND WALES

1 INTERPRETATION

1.1 In these conditions the following words have the following meanings: "Contract" means a contract which incorporates these conditions and made between the Customer and the Supplier for the hire of Hire Goods and/or the sale of Products;

"Customer" means the person, firm, company or other organisation hiring Hire Goods;

"Deposit" means any advance payment required by the Supplier in relation to the Hire Goods which is to be held as security by the Supplier;

"Hire Goods" means any machine, article, tool, and/or device together with any accessories specified in a Contract which are hired to the Customer;

"Hire Period" means the period commencing when the Customer holds the Hire Goods on hire (including Saturdays Sundays and Bank Holidays) and ending upon the happening of any of the following events: (i) the physical return of the Hire Goods by the Customer into the Supplier's possession; or (ii) the physical repossession or collection of Hire Goods by the Supplier;

"Liability" means liability for any and all damages, claims, proceedings, actions, awards, expenses, costs and any other losses and/or liabilities;

"Products" means the products sold to the Customer by the Supplier;

"Rental" means the Supplier's charging rate for the hire of the Hire Goods which is current from time to time during the Hire Period;

"Supplier" means [NAME OF HAE MEMBER] and will include its employees, servants, agents and/or duly authorised representatives;

"Services" means the services and/or work (if any) to be performed by the Supplier for the Customer in conjunction with the hire of the Hire Goods including any delivery and/or collection service for the Hire Goods.

2 BASIS OF CONTRACT

2.1 Hire Goods are hired subject to them being available for hire to the Customer at the time required by the Customer.

2.2 Where hire of the Hire Goods is to a customer who is an individual and the hire would be covered by the Consumer Credit Act 1974 the duration of the hire shall not exceed three months. Accordingly the hire of any Hire Goods is not covered by the Consumer Credit Act 1974.

2.3 Nothing in this Contract shall exclude or limit any statutory rights of the Customer which may not be excluded or limited due to the Customer acting as a consumer. Any provision which would be void under any consumer protection legislation or other legislation shall, to that extent, have no force or effect.

3 PAYMENT

3.1 The amount of any Deposit, Rental and/or charges for any Services shall be as quoted to the Customer or otherwise as shown in the Supplier's current price list from time to time. When a Deposit is required for the Hire Goods it must be paid in advance of the Customer hiring the Hire Goods. The Hirer may also require an initial payment on account of the Rental in advance of the Customer hiring the Hire Goods.

3.2 The Customer shall pay the Rental, charges for any Services, monies for any Products and/or any other sums payable under the contract to the Supplier at the time and in the manner agreed. The Supplier's prices are exclusive of any applicable VAT for which the Customer shall additionally be liable.

3.3 The time for any payments by the Customer under a Contract shall be of the essence. Payment shall not be deemed to be made until the Supplier has received either cash or cleared funds in respect of the full amount outstanding.

3.4 If the Customer fails to make any payment in full on the due date the Supplier may charge the Customer interest (both before and after judgment) on the amount unpaid at the rate of 4% above the base rate from time to time of the Supplier's bank. Such interest shall be compounded with quarterly rests.

3.5 The Customer shall pay all sums due to the Supplier under this contract without any set-off, deduction, counterclaim and/or any other withholding of monies.

3.6 The Supplier may set a reasonable credit limit for the Customer. The Supplier reserves the right to terminate or suspend the Contract for hire of the Hire Goods and/or the provision of Services if allowing it to continue would result in the Customer exceeding its credit limit or the credit limit is already exceeded.

4 RISK TITLE AND INSURANCE

4.1 Risk in the Hire Goods and any Products will pass immediately to the Customer when they leave the physical possession or control of the Supplier.

4.2 Risk in the Hire Goods will not pass back to the Supplier from the Customer until the Hire Goods are back in the physical possession of the Supplier. This shall apply even if the Supplier has agreed to cease charging the Rental.

4.3 Title in the Hire Goods remains at all times with the Supplier. The Customer has no right, title or interest in the Hire Goods except that they are hired to the Customer. Title in any Products remains with the Supplier until all monies payable to the Supplier by the Customer for the Products have been paid in full.

4.4 The Customer must not deal with the title or any interest in the Hire Goods. This includes but is not limited to selling, assigning, mortgaging, pledging, charging, securing, hiring, exerting a lien and/or lending. However the `Customer may re-hire the Hire Goods to a third party with the prior written consent of the Supplier.

4.5 The Supplier may provide insurance in respect of the Hire Goods at additional cost to the Rental. Alternatively the Supplier may require the Customer to insure the Hire Goods on such reasonable terms and for such reasonable risks as the Supplier may specify. The proceeds of any such insurance shall be held by the Customer in trust for the Supplier and be paid to the Supplier on demand. The Customer must not compromise any claim in respect of the Hire Goods and/or any associated insurance without the Supplier's written consent.

5 DELIVERY COLLECTION AND SERVICE

5.1 It is the responsibility of the Customer to collect the Hire Goods from the Supplier. If the Supplier agrees to deliver the Hire Goods to the Customer it will do so at its standard delivery cost and such delivery will form part of any Services.

5.2 Where the Supplier provides Services the persons performing the Services are servants of the Customer and are under the direction and control of the Customer. The Customer shall be solely responsible for any instruction, guidance and/or advice given by the Customer to any such person and for any damage which occurs as a result of such persons following the Customer's instructions, guidance and/or advice.

5.3 The Customer will allow and/or procure sufficient access to and from the relevant site and secure sufficient unloading space, facilities, equipment and access to power supplies for the Supplier's employees, sub-contractors and/or agents to allow them to carry out the Service. The Customer will ensure that the site where the Services are to be performed is, where necessary, cleared and prepared before the Services are due to commence.

5.4 If any Services are delayed, postponed and/or cancelled due to the Customer failing to comply with its obligations the Customer will be liable to pay the Supplier's additional standard charges from time to time for such delay, postponement and/or cancellation.

6 CARE OF THE GOODS

6.1 The Customer shall:

6.1.1 not interfere with the Hire Goods, their working mechanisms or any other parts of them and take reasonable care of the Hire Goods and only use them for their proper purpose in a safe and correct manner in accordance with any operating and/or safety instructions provided or supplied to the Customer and notify the Supplier immediately after any breakdown, loss and/or damage to the Hire Goods;

6.1.2 take adequate and proper measures to protect the Hire Goods from theft, damage and/or other risks

6.1.3 notify the Supplier of any change of its address and upon the Supplier's request provide details of the location of the Hire Goods and permit the Supplier at all reasonable times to inspect the Hire Goods including procuring access to any property where the hire goods are situated;

6.1.4 keep the Hire Goods at all times in its possession and control and not to remove the Hire Goods from the United Kingdom without the prior written consent of the Supplier;

6.1.5 be responsible for the conduct and cost of any testing, examination and/or check in relation to the Hire Goods required by any legislation, best practice and/or operating instructions except to the extent that the Supplier has agreed to provide them as part of any Services;

6.1.6 not to omit to do any thing which will or may be deemed to invalidate any policy of insurance related to the Hire Goods;

6.1.7 not continue to use Hire Goods when they have been damaged and will notify the Supplier immediately if the Hire Goods are involved in an accident resulting in damage to the Hire Goods, other property and/or any person;

6.1.8 where the Hire Goods require fuel, oil and/or electricity ensure that the proper type is used and that, where appropriate, the Hire Goods are properly fitted by a qualified and competent person.

6.2 The Hire Goods must be returned by the Customer in good working order and condition (fair wear and tear excepted) and in a clean condition (everyday grime excepted) together with all insurance policies, licences, registration and other documents relating to the Hire Goods.

7 BREAKDOWN

7.1 Allowance will be made in relation to the Rental for the Customer for any non-use of the Hire Goods due to breakdown caused by the development of an inherent fault and/or fair wear and tear on condition that the Customer informs the Supplier immediately of the breakdown.

7.2 The Customer shall be responsible for all expenses, loss (including loss of Rental) and/or damage suffered by the Supplier arising from any breakdown of the Hire Goods due to the Customer's negligence, misdirection and/or misuse of the Hire Goods.

7.3 The Supplier will at its own cost carry out all routine maintenance and repairs to the Hire Goods during the Hire Period and all repairs which are required due to fair wear and tear and/or an inherent fault in the Hire Goods. The Customer will be responsible for all repairs necessary to Hire Goods during the Hire Period which arise otherwise than as a result of fair wear and tear and/or an inherent fault.

Hire Association Europe — Conditions for hire — page 1

7.4 The Customer must not repair or attempt to repair the Hire Goods unless authorised to do so in writing by the Sup[plier.

8 LOSS OR DAMAGE TO THE HIRE GOODS

8.1 If the Hire Goods are returned in damaged, unclean and/or defective state except where due to fair wear and tear the Customer shall be liable to pay the Supplier for the cost of any repair and/or cleaning required to return the Hire Goods to a condition fit for re-hire and the Rental until such repairs and/or cleaning have been completed.

8.2 The Customer will pay to the Supplier the replacement cost on a new for old basis of Hire Goods which are lost, stolen and/or damaged beyond economic repair during the Hire Period less the amount paid to the Supplier under any policy of insurance taken out in accordance with these conditions.

8.3 The Customer shall also pay the Supplier the Rental until the supplier has been paid the amount representing the replacement cost of such Hire Goods.

9 TERMINATION BY NOTICE

9.1 If the Hire Period has a fixed duration neither the Customer nor the Supplier shall be entitled to terminate the Contract before the expiry of that fixed period unless agreed with the other party.

9.2 If the Hire Period does not have a fixed duration either of the Customer or the Supplier is entitled to terminate the Contract upon giving to the other party any agreed period of notice.

9.3 If no period of notice has been agreed or specified the Customer may terminate the Hire Period by the physical return of the Hire Goods to the Supplier and the Supplier shall be entitled to terminate the hire of the Hire Goods by giving not less than 14 days' notice to the Customer.

10 DEFAULT

10.1 If the Customer:-

10.1.1 fails to make any payment to the Supplier when due;

10.1.2 breaches the terms of the Contract and, where the breach is capable of remedy, has not remedied the breach within 14 days of receiving notice requiring the breach to be remedied;

10.1.3 persistently breaches the terms of the Contract;

10.1.4 provides incomplete, materially inaccurate or misleading facts and/or information in connection with the Contract;

10.1.5 pledges, charges, or creates any form of security over any Hire Goods, or ceases or threatens to cease to carry on business, or proposes to compound with its creditors, applies for an interim moratorium in respect of claims and/or proceedings or has a Bankrupt Petition presented against it, or being a company, enters into voluntary or compulsory liquidation, has a receiver, administrator or administrative receiver appointed over all or any of its assets, any attachment order is made against the Customer or any distress, execution or other legal process is levied on any property of the Customer or the Customer takes or suffers any similar action in any jurisdiction;

10.1.6 appears to the Supplier due to the Customer's credit rating to be financially inadequate to meet its obligations under the Contract and/or

10.1.7 appears reasonably to the Supplier to be about to suffer any of the above events;
then the Supplier shall have the right, without prejudice to any other remedies, to exercise any or all of the rights set out in clause 10.2 below.

10.2 If any of the events set out in 10.1 above occurs in relation to the Customer then:-

10.2.1 the Supplier may enter, without prior notice, any premises of the Customer (or premises of third parties with their consent) where Hire Goods owned by the Supplier may be and repossess any Hire Goods;

10.2.2 the Supplier may withhold the performance of any Services and cease any Services in progress;

10.2.3 the Supplier may cancel, terminate and/or suspend without Liability to the Customer the Contract and/or any other contract with the Customer and/or

10.2.4 all monies owed by the Customer to the Supplier shall immediately become due and payable.

10.3 Any repossession of the Hire Goods shall not affect the Supplier's right to recover from the Customer any monies due under the Contract and/or damages in respect of any antecedent breach.

10.4 Upon termination of a Contract the Customer shall immediately:

10.4.1 return the Hire Goods to the Supplier or make the Hire Goods available for collection by the Supplier as requested by the Supplier; and

10.4.2 pay to the Supplier all arrears for Rentals, Charges for any Services, moneys for any products and/or other sums payable under the Contract.

11 LIMITATIONS OF LIABILITY

11.1 All warranties, representations, terms, conditions and duties implied by law relating to fitness, quality and/or adequacy are excluded to the fullest extent permitted by law.

11.2 If the Supplier is found to be liable in respect of any loss or damage to the Customer's property the extent of the Supplier's Liability will be limited to the retail cost of replacement of the damaged property.

11.3 Any defective Hire Goods must be returned to the Supplier for inspection if requested by the Supplier before the Supplier will have any Liability for defective Hire Goods.

11.4 The Supplier shall have no liability to the Customer if any monies due in respect of the Hire Goods and/or the Services has not been paid in full by the due date for payment.

11.5 The Supplier shall have no Liability for additional damage, loss, liability, claims, costs or expenses caused or contributed to by the Customer's continued use of defective Hire Goods and/or Services after a defect has become apparent or suspected or should reasonably have become apparent to the Customer.

11.6 The Customer shall give the Supplier a reasonable opportunity to remedy any matter for which the Supplier is liable before the Customer incurs any costs and/or expenses in remedying the matter itself. If the Customer dies not do so the Supplier shall have no Liability to the Customer.

11.7 The Supplier shall have no liability to the Customer to the extent that the Customer is covered by any policy of insurance arranged as a result of the Contract and the Customer shall ensure that the Customer's insurer waives any and all rights of subrogation they may have against the Supplier.

11.8 The Supplier shall have no liability to the Customer for any:-

11.8.1 consequential losses (Including loss of profits and/or damage to goodwill);

11.8.2 economic and/or other similar losses;

11.8.3 special damages and indirect losses; and/or

11.8.4 business interruption, loss of business, contracts and/or opportunity.

11.9 The Supplier's total liability to the Customer under and/or arising in relation to any Contract shall not exceed five times the amount of the Rental and charges for the Services (if any) under that Contract or the sum of £1,000 whichever is the higher. To the extent that any Liability of the Supplier to the Customer would be met by any insurance of the Supplier then the Liability of the Supplier shall be extended to the extent that such Liability is met by insurance.

11.10 Each of the Limitations and/or exclusions in this Contract shall be deemed to be repeated and apply as a separate provision for each of:

11.10.1 liability for breach of contract;

11.10.2 liability in tort (including negligence); and

11.10.3 liability for breach of statutory duty;
except clause 11.9 above which shall apply once only in respect of all the said types of Liability.

11.11 Nothing in this Contract shall exclude or limit the Liability of the Supplier for death or personal injury due to its negligence or any other Liability which it is not permitted to exclude or limit as a matter of law.

12 GENERAL

12.1 Each hire of an item of Hire Goods shall form a distinct Contract which shall be separate to any other Contract relating to other Hire Goods.

12.2 The Customer shall be liable for the acts and/or omissions of its employees, agents, servants and/or other subcontractors as though they were its own acts and/or omissions under this Contract.

12.3 The Customer agrees to indemnify and keep indemnified the Supplier against any and all losses, lost profits, damages, claims, costs (including legal costs on a full indemnity basis), actions and any other losses and/or liabilities suffered by the Supplier and arising from or due to any breach of contract, any tortious act and/or omission and/or any breach of statutory duty by the Customer.

12.4 No waiver by the Supplier of any breach of this Contract shall be considered as a waiver of any subsequent breach of the same provision or any other provision. If any provision is held by any competent authority to be unenforceable in whole or in part the validity of the other provisions of this Contract and the remainder of the affected provision shall be unaffected and shall remain in full force and effect.

12.5 The Supplier shall have no Liability to the Customer for any delay and/or non performance of a Contract to the extent that such delay is due to any events outside the Supplier's reasonable control including but not limited to act of God, war, flood, fire, labour disputes, strikes, sub-contractors, lock-outs,riots, civil commotion, malicious damage, explosion, governmental actions and any other similar events. If the Supplier is affected by any such event then time for performance shall be extended for a period equal to the period that such event or events delayed such performance.

12.6 All third party rights are excluded and no third parties shall have any rights to enforce the Contract. This Contract is governed by and interpreted in accordance with English law and the parties agree to submit to the non-exclusive jurisdiction of the English courts.

Index